REVOLUTIONS

Introduction ©2020 Peter Furtado
Text edited by Peter Furtado
Typeset by Mark Bracey

First published in 2020 in the United States of America by
Thames & Hudson Inc., 500 Fifth Avenue, New York, New York 10110

www.thamesandhudsonusa.com

Library of Congress Control Number 2020932213

ISBN 978-0-500-02241-2

Printed and bound in Singapore by 1010 Printing International Ltd

Edited by

PETER FURTADO

REVOLUTIONS

HOW THEY CHANGED HISTORY AND
WHAT THEY MEAN TODAY

CONTENTS

INTRODUCTION
Peter Furtado 7

THE ENGLISH REVOLUTION 1642–1689
Simon Jenkins 15

THE AMERICAN REVOLUTION 1776–1788
Ray Raphael 28

THE FRENCH REVOLUTION 1789–1799
Sophie Wahnich 41

THE HAITIAN REVOLUTION 1791–1804
Bayyinah Bello 55

THE YEAR OF REVOLUTIONS 1848
Axel Körner 70

JAPAN: THE MEIJI RESTORATION 1868
Shin Kawashima 85

THE YOUNG TURK REVOLUTION 1908
Mehmed Şükrü Hanioğlu 96

THE MEXICAN REVOLUTION 1910–1917
Javier Garciadiego 109

THE IRISH REVOLUTION 1913–1923
Diarmaid Ferriter 123

THE RUSSIAN REVOLUTION 1917
Dina Khapaeva 136

THE INDIAN REVOLUTION 1947
Mihir Bose 151

VIETNAM: THE AUGUST REVOLUTION 1945
Stein Tønnesson 166

CHINA: THE COMMUNIST REVOLUTION 1949–1976
Mobo Gao 178

THE CUBAN REVOLUTION 1959–2006
Luis Martínez-Fernández 193

THE STUDENT REVOLUTION 1968
Stephen Barnes 213

PORTUGAL: THE CARNATION REVOLUTION 1974
Filipe Ribeiro de Meneses 227

CAMBODIA: THE KHMER ROUGE REVOLUTION 1975–1979
Sorpong Peou 238

THE IRANIAN REVOLUTION 1979
Homa Katouzian 252

NICARAGUA: THE SANDINISTA REVOLUTION 1979
Mateo Cayetano Jarquín 264

POLAND: SOLIDARITY 1980
Anita Prażmowska 280

EASTERN EUROPE 1989
Vladimir Tismaneanu and Andres Garcia 291

SOUTH AFRICA: THE END OF APARTHEID 1990–1994
Thula Simpson 304

UKRAINE: THE ORANGE REVOLUTION 2004–2014
Yaroslav Hrytsak 319

THE ARAB SPRING: EGYPT 2011
Yasser Thabet 333

FURTHER READING 343

CONTRIBUTORS 345

SOURCES OF ILLUSTRATIONS 346

INDEX 347

INTRODUCTION

On the evening of 14 July 1789, King Louis XVI of France heard the news of the storming of the Bastille on his return from hunting. Notoriously he asked, 'Is this a revolt?', to which the Duc de La Rochefoucauld replied, 'No, Sire – it is a revolution.'

Less than a week later, the Duke was serving as president of the National Constituent Assembly, the body set up by the Third Estate (commoners) as an authority to challenge that of the king, and which thereby embodied the revolution he had predicted.

La Rochefoucauld's quote is famous for his perspicacity and for Louis's myopia; but what exactly did he mean? At the time, there were just two precedents considered worthy of the name 'revolution'. One was the ousting of James II of England in 1688, and his replacement on the throne by his daughter Mary and her Dutch husband, William of Orange – this was the so-called Glorious Revolution that created Britain's constitutional monarchy, which in turn became the envy of the enlightened 18th century. The other was the overthrow of British rule in North America, establishing the republic of the United States in the 1770s–80s. Both events certainly offered alarming precedents for Louis: ruling monarchs lost their crown or their claim to rule, in the face of widespread opposition reinforced by military muscle. Both were justified by a libertarian ideology that offered an alternative legitimacy to divinely inspired monarchy, and both became enshrined in institutions – in England, the Bill of Rights; in America, the Constitution of the United States – that changed the direction of their country's history. These events were still resonating round the globe decades later.

This was what revolution meant on the day the Bastille fell. But during the next dozen years, the word acquired many other layers of meaning: the assertion of popular sovereignty and social justice, the sweeping away of oppressive institutions and corrupt privilege, a root-and-branch change in institutions and ways of thinking, the release of creative energy and imagination to escape the cruel stasis of a failed system; and also chaos, mob rule, the adoption of terror as a tactic to enforce the new order, and increasingly authoritarian government prepared to enforce social and political change at all costs.

In the following century, after Karl Marx and Friedrich Engels published the *Communist Manifesto* in 1848, revolution came to mean the overthrow of one class by another, the creation of a new society in which the workers own the means of production. This definition held sway throughout much of the 20th century with Marxist, Marxist–Leninist or Maoist revolutionary movements in many countries across the world (and the sympathy of many intellectuals analysing their successes and failures).

The word revolution has also been applied, though usually in retrospect by historians or other commentators, to amorphous social, cultural or technological changes: the Industrial Revolution, the sexual revolution, the digital revolution. These are among the largest, most powerful drivers of all human history, with profound long-term consequences, but tend to result in less dramatic outcomes in the political arena, if no other.

Political revolutions have a similar reputation as events that inexorably force change within a particular country, though many revolutionaries seek to spread their message beyond geographical borders. The word, though, is too large, too capacious, to be owned by any particular ideology. Since the late 19th century there have been not just communist or socialist revolutions, but nationalist revolutions, democratic revolutions and constitutional revolutions too. There have been revolutions that have brought violence to millions of people, and others that were entirely bloodless; revolutions led by men and women with a lifelong commitment to bringing them about, and revolutions with no leaders at all, or with accidental or reluctant figureheads. Revolutions that made genuine, extended and sometimes successful efforts to improve the lot of the people, and revolutions that brought nothing but heartache and hardship.

The late 20th century saw one major popular revolution in favour of conservative theocracy (in Iran in 1979), and the popular revolutions in eastern Europe against the very workers' states that Marxist regimes had themselves established. Since the late 1980s, the term revolution has more often been applied not to root-and-branch attacks on established values or the capitalist system, but to sudden popular surges to sweep aside dictatorships in the name of democracy – to establish human rights and personal freedoms. Unlike Leninist or Maoist revolutions, these have been welcomed by the people with their hands on the world's levers of power – at least so long as they pose little threat to established commercial or geopolitical interests. Yet even when modern revolutions have succeeded in their original aims of ousting tyranny, their longer-term outcomes – like those of many earlier revolutions – may still prove ambiguous, or worse.

The word itself was first applied to radical political change within a polity only in the 17th century, though it did not yet carry the meaning that La Rochefoucauld understood. Although the execution of King Charles I and establishment of an English republic in 1649 may look revolution-ary to us, contemporaries preferred to call this the 'Great Rebellion' and ascribed the name revolution only to its aftermath: the restoration of Charles II in 1660 – and then to the expulsion of his unpopular brother James in 1688. It is with those events that this book begins.

Revolution may be hard to define in the abstract; yet people gen-erally believe they can recognize one when they see it. A revolution is often contrasted with a rebellion – not only in that a revolution suc-ceeds in its immediate aims, whereas a rebellion probably fails, but in its choice of aims as well. The rebel typically seeks autonomy from the tyrant, whereas the revolutionary seeks to overthrow him. The revolution releases a heady sense of liberation, an urgent and sudden change like the opening of a dam (most revolutions are preceded by a long period of political stasis, usually combined with a building sense of injustice based on structural imbalances such as an increase in population or economic downturn, exacerbated by anger at the corruption of those in power). And this intoxicating liberation can be powerfully felt across time and space: the extraordinary creativity of the early Bolshevik Revolution – the art of Vladimir Tatlin and Kazimir Malevich, the films of Sergei Eisenstein, the music of Dmitri Shostakovich – was echoed in the creative hothouses of the Mexican revolution, the Cuban and others.

Another aspect of revolutions that holds a lasting fascination is their moral dimension. They involve revolutionaries in making dramatic decisions in circumstances that are usually unprecedented, and their rhetoric – 'from each according to his ability, to each according to his need' – rings out over the centuries, while their socio-political analysis (the collapse of capitalism through its internal contradictions, for example) continues to engage our imaginations. This is equally true whether or not we sympathize fully with their aims or their actions. There is an irresistible lure in those moments when there seems to be everything to play for, with all their mesmerizing counter-factual 'what-ifs'. We may be both fascinated and horrified by the destructive forces unleashed – the guillotine, the Gulag, the killing fields of Cambodia – and what these reveal about how humans behave at times when conventional moral, legal and social restrictions on behaviour have broken down.

Ever since the early 1790s when Edmund Burke and Thomas Paine debated the morality of the French Revolution, philosophers and politicians, historians and the general public have argued about the choices made by Louis XIV and Maximilien Robespierre, Georges Danton and Napoleon Bonaparte, taking sides and, implicitly or explicitly, supporting or recoiling from their actions. It is not just liberals and radicals who use the revolutions of the past as models to learn from and emulate; conservatives find much to deplore in these events, and by maintaining a vivid focus on the chaos and rough justice that so often feature, they can claim the moral high ground for their own worldview.

Revolutions also throw into high relief some other key questions of historical causality. Some make universal claims: by justifying the overthrow of what the revolutionaries saw as the tyrannical rule of the British king George III for his failure to preserve the citizens' inalienable 'rights...[to] life, liberty and the pursuit of happiness', the events in America in the 1770s–80s opened the door to would-be revolutionaries across the globe to challenge their own rulers in similar terms. Marx's argument that revolution was the inevitable result of inexorable contradictions within capitalism between the working classes and the bourgeoisie meant that it would be a universal experience of humanity, restricted only by the evolution of each state's economy to reach the tipping point (or, as Lenin saw it, by the emergence of a revolutionary vanguard to precipitate that tipping point). Not all observers have accepted these universalist arguments, but see each revolutionary situation as unique; even historians who agree that long-term structural factors are as important in explaining a revolutionary outbreak as the more immediate choices of key actors may still focus on the particularity of a revolution, analysing it in its own terms rather than placing it within a grander, more general framework of history.

Whether one is conservative or liberal, universalist or particularist, a believer in the inexorability of historical laws of class conflict or in accident and human agency as the main driver of revolutionary change, revolutions can serve as major signposts in the often confusingly inchoate terrains of history and politics. This is even more true when the revolutions form a major part of the narrative that a society tells itself about who it is and where it has come from. The revolutionary ambitions of 'liberty, fraternity and equality' are foundational to the sense of what France is; the American Constitution is endlessly debated and reinterpreted in the ever-changing present; Mexico was ruled by the PRI (Partido Revolucionario Institucional), a party with revolution enshrined in its name, for more than seventy years from 1929; Nelson Mandela and the African National Congress are intrinsic to any sense of the modern South Africa. What people in these countries learn and understand about their revolutions is absolutely core to their identity.

But circumstances may change, and as they do the meaning of the revolution changes with them. Russia's October Revolution was foundational to the Soviet Union, its official narratives and interpretations drummed into every Soviet citizen. But since the collapse of the USSR in 1991, things have changed, and in 2017, the centenary of that same revolution proved awkward for the government of Vladimir Putin. Putin has involved himself in the commemoration of several of the tsars, but he had nothing at all to say about the event that changed Russia utterly, shaped its history and society for seven decades and defined Russia's reputation, of good or ill, across the world. Where once the image of Lenin, standing resolute in swirling overcoat and urging the Russian people on to forge a new socialist world, had been projected via statues, posters and prints until it became the virtual embodiment of the idea of revolution itself on every continent, now he and his revolution were such an embarrassment that his successor in the Kremlin ignored them. The marginalized Russian Communist Party held a colourful parade, and Russian television broadcast a costume drama on the life of Leon Trotsky – but Putin stayed out of sight. He remained equally silent nine months later, when hundreds of thousands of people flocked to Ekaterinburg to commemorate the murder there of the former Tsar Nicholas II and his family by Bolsheviks.

The legacy of the events of 1917–18 had proved too complex, too contested, too uncomfortable for the authoritarian, cynical leader of 21st-century capitalist, nationalistic Russia. The memory of Mao Zedong is proving similarly uncomfortable to an increasingly capitalist China – despite the fact that the Communist Party he once dominated remains firmly entrenched in power. And even in more democratic regimes, the memory of revolution may be obliterated: in several countries that were freed from Soviet control by popular pressure in 1989, the men and women who were at the forefront of that pressure have already been forgotten or actively suppressed. Perhaps, in all these cases, the legacy of the revolutions is just too dangerous to those in power today.

With this in mind, the aim of this book is to look at revolutions around the world and through history: not only at their causes, crises and outcomes, but also, for the more distant events, at their long-term legacies and their changing, sometimes contested meanings today. Historians, mostly native of or active within those societies, have been asked to reflect on the following questions: What were the essential causes of the revolution? What narrative of events, protagonists and ideologies is most commonly accepted? What impact is it believed to have had? What legacy does it have today in national self-perception and values? Has this changed significantly over past decades? This approach, combined with the insights that can be gleaned from comparisons between countries (and, indeed, from the interactions between revolutions), throws a very different light on the revolutions, and their relevance today, from the old ideological arguments.

We have, of course, had to be selective: not least because some countries have had several revolutions. In addition to 1789, a comprehensive study of the legacy of revolution in France should consider, at the least, the events of 1830, 1848, 1870–71 and 1968. And just as the study of revolution encourages an approach that is, in Baudelaire's words, 'partial, passionate and political', so consideration of its legacy is interpretative rather than analytical when written at the length of an essay rather than a monograph. Nonetheless, this way of looking can be revealing about the history and political life of each country; about the range and variety of what we perceive to be revolutions; about the diversity of the revolutionary experience through time and place; about how revolutions evolve after their protagonists have achieved power; about the interactions, practical and ideological, between revolutions; and much more.

Additionally, the essays offer insight into 'public history', the uses that history is put to in different places, the changing relevance of the past, the disputes over historical memory and who controls it. We cannot properly consider the meaning of a revolution without looking at this afterlife. How a country sees its revolutionary past throws a light not only on that past itself, but on the inner dynamics and mentality of the contemporary society. Invitably, this means the book reflects the time in which it was compiled. As the Chinese revolutionary and premier Zhou Enlai said in 1972, when asked what he thought about the French Revolution, 'it's too soon to tell'. The fact that it transpired, much later, that Zhou thought the question referred to '*les événements*' of May 1968 rather than the crisis of 1789 detracts little from the wisdom of his reply. It will always be too soon to define definitively the meaning of an event such as a revolution – but never too soon to ask how that meaning may be being interpreted, disputed, distorted and used. For good or ill, the legacy lives on.

THE ENGLISH REVOLUTION, 1642–1689

Simon Jenkins

The overthrow of James II of England and VII of Scotland by William of Orange and Mary Stuart in 1688 was given the name 'the Glorious Revolution' by one of its participants, John Hampden (1653–96). In retrospect, it became a major landmark in British history: the moment when the monarchy finally accepted its place within the parliamentary system and subject to the laws of the land, and – according to its chief ideologist, John Locke – to an unspoken 'social contract' with its subjects. As such, a hundred years later it became a beacon for radicals seeking to overthrow what was perceived as tyrannical rule in France and in Britain's American colonies.

It was not the first such sudden change of regime to be described as a revolution: that honour appears to belong to the restoration of James's elder brother Charles II in 1660 following England's republican experiment – and it has little in common with most of the other revolutions in this volume. Edmund Burke, writing in 1790, described it as 'made to preserve our ancient indisputable laws and liberties', in contrast with what he saw as the disastrous innovations of the French Revolution. In contrast with the views of the time, the overthrow of James's father Charles I by Parliament in the civil wars of 1642–8, and his subsequent trial and genuinely shocking execution have been described by historians as the English Revolution – a kind of proto-Marxist overthrow of the aristocratic and monarchical system by the middle classes supported by the common people. On this view, the events of 1688–9 were little more than a demonstration of the shift in power that had happened forty years previously.

Neither the traditional 'Whig' view nor this quasi-Marxist one is seen as quite correct by most scholars today. On this view, the entire period from 1640 to 1688 was a slow, interrupted revolution of a kind: but the revolutionary aspects of the accession of William and Mary came from the developments that stemmed from William's involvement in the great European wars against Louis XIV over the succeeding decades.

Even if 1688 was limited in scope and by no means a conventional revolution, its legacy was immense – ironically, far more so than the legacy of Oliver Cromwell's republican experiment. By cementing the supremacy of Parliament, it initiated 200 years of unchallenged conviction of progress and trust in a particular English and then British liberty based on constitutionalism, which, in combination with Britain's emerging naval supremacy, fuelled the self-belief behind the British Empire. Meanwhile, in Ireland, William's victory over James at the Boyne made him the hero of the Ulster Protestants, and thereby contributed to the divisions in that island that continued into the late 20th century.

The settlement of 1688–9, with its balanced constitutional monarchy subject to the rule of law, continue to reverberate even in the 21st century: as Britain's government, faced with a divided Parliament where no party or faction was able to maintain a majority, struggled to honour the result of the 2016 referendum to leave the European Union, the crown was drawn into the fray when Prime Minister Boris Johnson sought to prorogue Parliament at a crucial time in the autumn of 2019 for more than a month. The prorogation, though agreed and signed by the Queen, was later ruled unlawful by the Supreme Court and overturned. Both government and monarch were seen to be subject to the rule of law.   PF

The Glorious Revolution of 1688, whereby the Catholic Stuart king James II (r. 1685–8) was driven from the throne and forced into exile, to be replaced by the joint monarchy of Mary II (r. 1689–94) and her Dutch husband William III (r. 1689–1702), is the most entrenched myth in England's political history. It is presented as the birth of constitutional liberty after the turmoil of the Civil War in mid-century. It merits pride of place in the story of spin. The event itself was straightforward, involving the ousting of a legitimate king not by a Parliament or even an insurrection, but by a foreign military and naval power with main force, which occupied the capital and demanded the throne.

The invasion was then politically hijacked by one faction, the aristocratic, Protestant and constitutionalist Whigs, in their struggle with pro-Stuart Tories (who became known as Jacobites for their support for the exiled James). The Whigs deftly rewrote history as if the entire affair were their own doing. The work of so-called Whig historians of the 18th and 19th centuries, culminating with Thomas Babington Macaulay's influential *History of England* (1848–55), presented the events of 1688 as a triumphal turning point on England's long path to parliamentary ascendancy. This 'Whig theory of history' was challenged as partisan and teleological from the 1930s by historians including Herbert Butterfield, but its potency lives on, still dominating Parliament's image of itself. The question is, does the theory hold even a grain of truth?

According to the Whig theory, the origins of 1688 date back to the principle that the king was subject to the law, enshrined in Magna Carta (1215), and England's consequent divergence from the norm of European autocracy. Subsequent clashes between monarch and Parliament were usually over the issue of taxation, leading, in the late 14th century, to Edward I's barter of war revenue in return for 'redress of grievances'.

In the 16th century the balance between monarch and Parliament shifted in favour of the monarchy, largely because Henry VIII's dissolution of the monasteries (1536–40) brought vast wealth to the royal coffers. The monarch's status was further enhanced by the English Reformation, whereby England was detached from its subordination to Rome and the monarch became head of the English church. Many of the troubles that were later to afflict the Stuart crown in the 17th century were due to its wearers taking Henry's religious ascendancy too seriously.

Yet Henry's monastic dissolution also enriched a new mercantile and landowning class, strengthening Parliament with men of Protestant faith and with pecuniary interests to defend. While James I (r. 1603–25) was a Protestant, his concept of the 'divine right of kings' – which he saw as the right to personal extravagance – clashed with Parliament's control of his purse strings. The chief justice Sir Edward Coke, saying 'Magna Carta is such a fellow he will have no sovereign', would have none of this, seeing the rule of law as absolute with Parliament as its interpreter. The conflict culminated in the 1628 Petition of Right, asserting Parliament's supremacy in everything from justice and taxation to war and peace. Charles I (r. 1625–49) might rebut it, on the grounds that kings 'are not bound to give account of their actions but to God alone', but that would never be acceptable to Parliament. After Charles tried to rule as an autocrat for eleven years, the outcome was civil war and his defeat and execution in 1649.

To us, that execution ranks as the truly revolutionary event of English history. But to see revolutions as incidents rather than processes is misleading. Charles's execution was not seen at the time as a revolutionary triumph, whether for democracy or for Parliament. It was rather, as its instigator Oliver Cromwell (1599–1658) put it, a 'cruel necessity' to secure the sanctity of the Petition of Right. If that required violence, so be it.

Yet Cromwell was prepared to rebut that Petition in his treatment of Parliament on his path to dictatorship. By 1653 Cromwell was dismissing its members as 'sordid prostitutes…grown intolerably odious to the whole nation. The Lord hath done with you, go.' It was this retreat to autocracy that led Parliament to acquiesce in the restoration of the Stuart monarchy in 1660. But the Restoration was not a counter-revolution: its essence was Charles II (r. 1660–85) returning at Parliament's request, and accepting the letter and spirit of the Petition of Right in his Declaration of Breda (April 1660). He was to be a constitutional monarch under the thumb of Parliament.

That, of course, was not how his reign turned out. To Charles, autocracy was as genetic as extravagance. He was soon playing cat and mouse with his parliamentary benefactors, notably in matters of money. In 1670 he reached a secret treaty with the Catholic Louis XIV (r. 1643–1715) of France, committing himself to aid Louis against the Protestant Dutch and also to bring England back to the Roman church 'as soon as the welfare of his kingdom would permit'. In return, Louis would give Charles regular subsidies. As the details of the treaty leaked, only Parliament's abrogation of it and Charles's popularity and genial nature prevented the events of 1688 from erupting ten years earlier.

In 1677 Charles's Protestant niece Mary, second in line to the throne as daughter of his brother James, married the Dutch hero of the wars against Louis, William of Orange (1650–1702). Despite England's three conflicts with the Dutch over trade since 1652, the prospect of a Protestant queen with a Protestant consort was seen as the 'saving grace' of the Stuart dynasty. An attempt in 1679 by the Whigs to exclude any Catholic from the succession – which included the overtly Catholic James – failed only when Charles flagrantly dissolved successive Parliaments that were elected to oppose him.

As Charles defaulted to his father's autocratic habits, his throne returned to the vulnerability of the 1640s. On his deathbed in 1685, he showed more concern for his mistresses than his monarchy, and predicted his brother's reign would be short. So it proved. Louis's revocation the same year of the Edict of Nantes (which had guaranteed freedom of worship for Protestants) flooded England with Protestant refugees, and every pulpit resounded to tales of Catholic atrocities. James II's Catholicism was toxic. He had to suppress a rebellion by the Protestant Duke of Monmouth, and began appointing Catholics to senior positions in the army, the church and Oxford University. He used his patronage to pack Parliament with loyal Tories.

Even so, with the succession securely Protestant, all might have survived but for a final crisis. In June 1688, James's wife gave birth to a son, thus removing Mary and William from the succession and substituting a Catholic infant. The battered Restoration compromise was in tatters.

The question of what initiated subsequent events remains moot. Many Whigs were sufficiently opposed to James to have engaged in treasonable correspondence for some months with William in The Hague. In this they were ardently encouraged by William's London agent, Hans Willem Bentinck. It is also important that, despite the Dutch wars, England was in constant intercourse with the Low Countries. Dutch taste dominated English art, fashion, architecture and horticulture – not least in tulips. William himself was half-Stuart, son of Charles's sister, and was James's nephew as well as his son-in-law. Usurper he might be, but he was not entirely 'foreign'.

However, William at the time had more pressing worries about James. As stadtholder, William was head of the Dutch state, then under perpetual threat from France; a Catholic alliance between James and France would be devastating. In April 1688 James had signed a naval treaty with Louis, and some drastic adjustment in relations with England was essential. Indeed, an alliance of the Dutch and English monarchies would secure a useful bulwark against France.

That summer William acted with astonishing speed. In June, shortly after the birth of James's son, a letter was procured by Bentinck from a group of mostly Whig aristocrats who became known as 'the immortal seven'. They wrote that 'the people are so generally dissatisfied with the present conduct of the government in relation to their religion, liberties and properties...that Your Highness may be assured there are nineteen parts of twenty of the people throughout the kingdom who are desirous of a change'. Only a token force, they said, would be needed to stir an uprising against James. The letter was replicated in a declaration in William's name, dispersed secretly to printers throughout England, to be released to local churches on the moment of an invasion.

The venture was brazen. Like his Norman namesake, William had at best an equivocal claim to the English throne. The Dutch States General initially declared that he and his wife 'have decided to start on the said matter...in their own names'. William could argue that he was being strategic, since James's attachment to France was a clear threat to the Netherlands, but that was an argument for diplomacy rather than a full-frontal assault. Besides, taking troops to England would denude the Netherlands and embolden Louis. William had to promise that his intention was not to dethrone James, but rather to shift the balance of advantage his way. Only at the last minute did he gain support from his assembly.

William was able in a matter of weeks to amass a small fortune, partly from a Jewish banker, Francisco Suasso. This was to be no token force. The invasion was to be on a colossal scale, comprising 463 fighting ships and transports, and 40,000 soldiers equipped from Protestant allies across northern Europe. This was three times the size of Philip of Spain's Armada of exactly a century before, in what was essentially a private venture.

The Dutch invasion force took no chances. Setting sail in November, William bypassed Dover with a salvo of cannon and sailed on west to Devon, blown by a 'Protestant wind' from the east. Landing in Torbay, he avoided early combat with James's army, hoping that his landing and accompanying propaganda would spark the promised insurrection. He met little resistance beyond a skirmish with royalist troops in Reading, but there was no uprising. England was nervous. An older generation had lived through the Civil War. Despite James's unpopularity, many Britons were averse to toppling a crowned monarch. The issue of succession should be determined by Parliament, not overseas invasion.

The Dutch arrival caused panic in London, where substantial elements were loyal to James. But a critical event was the defection to William of Lord Churchill, one of James's most senior commanders, with 400 of his fellow officers. He wrote the King a cringing note, excusing his treachery as 'actuated by a higher principle'. Negotiations ensued between William and emissaries from the King, but these proved fruitless. Eventually James lost heart and fled, William allowing him to escape and seek refuge in France. But London was by no means secure. William expelled all English soldiers from the capital, replacing them with his own troops. Not since the Norman conquest had London been occupied by an enemy army.

Whether James could have defeated the Dutch, many of them professional mercenaries, is questionable. His army was substantial and its Catholic commanders were loyal. So too was the navy, of which he had been admiral as Duke of York in the Dutch wars (New York, captured from the Dutch in 1664, was named after him). But resistance was never put to the test. Churchill's mutiny and James's own loss of nerve led to his capitulation. There was, however, to be a decidedly violent reaction in both Ireland and Scotland, where the toppling of James was anything but bloodless.

At no point in this saga did Parliament request William's invasion, let alone usurpation of the throne. The invitation from the 'immortal seven' was clearly treasonable, though as the saying goes, 'If treason prospers, none dare call it treason.' James did not even abdicate, merely tossing the Great Seal into the Thames estuary, never to be retrieved. Even William's in-house spin doctor, the philosopher John Locke (1632–1704), explained it in pragmatic terms. It was justified by 'the miscarriages of the former reigns...and to recover our oppressed and sinking laws'. Locke personally accompanied Mary to London in the new year.

The public response to the coup was chiefly one of relief that the danger of civil war had been averted. As William began negotiations with Parliament, on one matter he was adamant. He would be king on equal terms with Mary, who had promised 'to be no more than his wife' and obey him as in her marriage vow. In the event of her predeceasing him (as she did) he would remain king. To emphasize the point, two separate ceremonial stairs had to be constructed at Kensington Palace and Hampton Court by architect Christopher Wren (1632–1723). As a Calvinist, William mocked 'the comedy of the coronation'. But he and Mary were not averse to Stuart expense and ostentation. James Thornhill's painted ceiling in the Royal Hospital at Greenwich depicted him as none other than Alexander the Great, crushing underfoot not James II but Louis XIV. At least he was mortal: on the ceiling of Whitehall's Banqueting House, James I had been depicted in his apotheosis, ascending to sit with God.

In February 1689, Parliament formally read the King its Declaration of Right, listing thirteen curbs on the monarch. These were hardly new. They re-stated Parliament's sovereignty in taxation, legislation and the raising of armies. Parliament could sit without the summons of the monarch, and its membership and freedom of speech were to be absolute. The Declaration was then enshrined in a Bill of Rights, largely a reassertion of the Petition of Right and of the Declaration of Breda. Though many Tories fought for a less restrictive concept of monarchy, the Whigs were in control. There was to be no more Stuart backsliding.

Nor was England to be in any way subordinate to the Netherlands. The monarch could not travel to the Continent without Parliament's permission. As for the future, an Act of Settlement stated that 'it hath been found by experience that it is inconsistent with the safety and welfare of the Protestant kingdom to be governed by a popish prince'. William accepted these terms, agreeing to submit himself to the 'statutes of Parliament'. His wife concurred.

William's dour manner and Dutch accent – said to 'sound like a bad cough' – did not win public affection, but his was a popular and productive reign. Parliament baulked at expending English money on Dutch wars, but William was able to lay the foundation for a Protestant coalition against Louis XIV, culminating in England's commitment to the War of Spanish Succession (1701–14). What 1688 did not do was halt Jacobite revanchism. Sympathy for James lingered on in Tory backrooms, and when James died in exile in 1701, his son James and his grandson, Bonnie Prince Charlie, received French support for their restoration. Armed invasions of Ireland in 1691 and Scotland in 1715 and 1745 all failed.

If 1688 was the culmination of a revolution, final confirmation came only when Queen Anne, William's successor and the last Stuart monarch, approached death in 1714. Tories led by Robert Harley and Lord Bolingbroke wrote pleading with James's son in Paris to convert to

Protestantism to bid for the throne. Only when he refused was the matter closed. Prince George of Hanover (1660–1727), the first Protestant of fifty-six descendants of James I in line to the throne, was summoned to become George I, and the Hanoverian era began. England, which had united with Scotland in 1707 as Great Britain, was now blessed with a constitutional monarchy under a parliamentary regime, whose stability was the envy of Europe for two centuries to come.

Revolutions customarily involve armed conflict and seismic upheaval. As such, 1688 was a disappointment. At the time little blood was spilled, and the event has always lacked classroom appeal. 'Glory' was ascribed to it at the time by a Whig MP, John Hampden, and was taken up delightedly by liberal historians to imply Whig credit for it, and for all that followed. It would not do to have the subsequent Whig ascendancy credited to a foreign invasion.

But if 1688 was not strictly a revolution, in its outcome it brought finality to a revolutionary process. It showed that reforms sought and hesitantly achieved over the sixty years since the Petition of Right were robust. They were given the stamp of permanence. That this stamp required the intervention of a foreign power may well have saved England from another civil war, which Parliament would probably but not certainly have won. But English history has always been opportunist. What happened was for the best.

The true hero of the 'long' revolution was neither William nor the Whigs; it was the institution of Parliament itself. Throughout the 17th century, Parliament never quite lost its nerve – except perhaps under Cromwell. Sitting at Westminster, it was the unchallenged forum of the nation. Through each crisis, it gave monarchy every chance to save itself. Its membership may have been undemocratic, but its dross of bishops and aristocrats was leavened by new men and new interests. Neither mobs in the street nor rebellions in the provinces ever seize the initiative.

The British people were not revolutionized. The events of 1688 did not widen the parliamentary franchise or extend constituency representation. But they were a step on the long road to democracy. As such, they were, as Cromwell would have said, a cruel necessity.

William of Orange

William of Orange (1650–1702), grandson of Charles II, became stadtholder of the Netherlands in 1672. He spent much of his reign engaged in wars with Louis XIV of France and seeking to build a Protestant alliance against him. In 1677 he married his first cousin Mary Stuart, daughter of James II. After arriving in England in November 1688 and advancing unopposed to London, he and Mary were offered the crown jointly. Having secured his throne with a victory over James at the Boyne in 1690, William resumed his conflict with Louis, which continued until 1697, then resumed in 1700. A reserved man who spent most of his energies on military matters, he made little effort to seek popular favour and was not greatly mourned at his death.

John Locke

John Locke (1632–1704), English philosopher, argued in his *Two Treatises of Government* (1689) that the source of authority was not divine or unquestionable. Instead he proposed that in a hypothetical 'state of nature', a 'social contract' had been made whereby people delegated certain rights to their chosen governors for their mutual protection (through force or law). This voluntary acceptance of the state's authority means that if the government fails to secure those natural rights or fulfil what citizens perceive as the best interests of society, the citizens can withdraw from their obligation to obey – or they can change the leadership. As well as justifying the Glorious Revolution, this argument greatly influenced the American revolutionaries of the 1770s.

TIMELINE

1628   Parliament issues its Petition of Right, restricting the use of the royal prerogative

1642   Civil war breaks out between Charles I and Parliament

1645   Parliamentary army led by Thomas Fairfax and Oliver Cromwell achieves decisive victory at Naseby

1646   Charles I surrenders to the Scots

1648   Charles I is imprisoned in Windsor Castle

1649   Charles I is convicted of treason and executed; the monarchy is replaced by a commonwealth

1653   Cromwell becomes Lord Protector of England, Wales, Scotland and Ireland

1658   Cromwell dies and is succeeded by his son Richard

1660   Parliament restores Charles II to the throne

1670   Charles makes a secret treaty with Louis XIV of France, promising to convert to Catholicism

1673   Test Act bans Catholics from public office; Charles's brother James, Duke of York is forced to resign from the office of Lord High Admiral

1677   Mary Stuart, daughter of James, Duke of York, marries William of Orange, grandson of Charles I

1685   Charles II dies; his brother James succeeds as James II

1685   James II defeats a rising by the Protestant Duke of Monmouth, illegitimate son of Charles II

1687   James II issues Declaration of Indulgence, promising religious toleration

1688

June   Seven English aristocrats write to William of Orange, inviting him
            to take the throne

November   William invades with a large army and lands at Torbay in Devon

December   James II flees from England

1689

April   William and Mary are crowned

December   John Locke publishes *Two Treatises of Government*

December   Bill of Rights is passed, asserting sovereignty of Parliament and
            promising toleration

1690   William defeats James at the Boyne in Ireland

THE AMERICAN REVOLUTION, 1776–1788

Ray Raphael

In the first of the 'classic' revolutions of the 18th century, the way in which Britain's American colonists conceived their opposition to rule from across the Atlantic, and then resisted the government's attempts to force them to back down, became a template for anti-colonial revolutions across the globe. But it has been far more. The terms in which Thomas Jefferson drafted the Declaration of Independence are not only a statement of values whereby social justice can be asserted, but a clarion call, in the language of the Enlightenment, to revolution to end oppression wherever it is found:

> When in the Course of human events it becomes necessary for one people to dissolve the political bands which have connected them with another and to assume among the powers of the earth, the separate and equal station to which the Laws of Nature and of Nature's God entitle them, a decent respect to the opinions of mankind requires that they should declare the causes which impel them to the separation.
>
> We hold these truths to be self-evident, that all men are created equal, that they are endowed by their

Creator with certain unalienable Rights, that among these are Life, Liberty and the pursuit of Happiness. – That to secure these rights, Governments are instituted among Men, deriving their just powers from the consent of the governed, –That whenever any Form of Government becomes destructive of these ends, it is the Right of the People to alter or to abolish it, and to institute new Government, laying its foundation on such principles and organizing its powers in such form, as to them shall seem most likely to effect their Safety and Happiness.

By stating its case in such universal terms, before detailing the many offences of the British crown and government against the life, liberty and pursuit of happiness of the American people, Jefferson's text has inspired revolutionaries not only in the immediately succeeding decades in France and Haiti, but for more than two centuries.

Despite such apparent clarity of language and lofty aims, and despite (or perhaps in part because of) the speedy raising of the American Founding Fathers to a kind of secular Pantheon, the revolution was in fact a complex event, and conflict about its meaning has shaped American social and political life ever since.

Despite this, its status as a revolution at all is in some doubt – partly due to the self-imposed limits on the aspirations of the Founding Fathers that meant they left slavery in place within the society they designed expressly for the safety and happiness of its people. The gap between rhetoric and reality has led some later revolutionaries to question whether this was more than a transfer of power between elites. Whatever its legacy for the people of the United States, it has a separate legacy for the rest of the world. PF

All nations like to celebrate their origins, but the storyline generated in the United States is fortuitously cohesive, commemorating the exertions of a single generation. Across the globe, by contrast, other realms have sprawling narratives. China's, an astounding four millennia in length, embraces a series of ancient dynasties, the Nationalist Revolution in 1911, and the Communist Revolution in 1949. Britain's covers the Norman invasion (1066), the Magna Carta (1215), the Glorious Revolution (1688) and the Act of Union (1707). Mexico's two founding moments, independence in 1821 and a revolution in the 1910s, are separated by a gap of ninety years, a wide disconnect in the plotline. Canada eased into nationhood so gracefully that it hardly has a story to tell.

The American story starts in 1763 with the end of the French and Indian War, known elsewhere as the Seven Years War. France ceded its vast claims in North America to Britain, but to pay the added expense of administering its new holdings, Parliament levied a series of taxes on the American colonies. Many colonists complained that they could not be taxed without representation in Parliament – these protesters called themselves 'Whigs' after the political party in Britain, and they labelled those who supported the parliamentary measures 'Tories'. When colonial Whigs refused to purchase British goods, Parliament repealed some, but not all, of the taxes. In 1773, responding to an Act of Parliament that granted special favours to the East India Company, a band of protestors dumped three shiploads of tea into the Boston harbour. To punish the perpetrators of the 'Boston Tea Party', Parliament closed the port of Boston and, worse yet, revoked the 1691 Massachusetts Charter, which had granted colonials the right of self-government in most matters. Citizens of Massachusetts reacted by shutting down imperial government everywhere outside of Boston and preparing for armed resistance. In April 1775, when British soldiers tried to seize a rebel storehouse, local militiamen resisted and blood was shed. Twelve other colonies joined the Massachusetts rebellion in what Americans call the Revolutionary War.

Militarily outmatched by the strongest army in the world, rebels appealed for aid to France, Britain's perennial rival. France, however, would not intervene in a British civil war, so in 1776 colonials declared themselves to be an independent nation: the United States of America. For the next several years, Britain, supported by colonial 'Loyalists', tried to defeat the Continental Army and local 'Patriot' militias. Overwhelming superiority at sea enabled Britain to seize and control several crucial ports, but forays beyond the coastline met stiff resistance; on the other hand, Americans could not dislodge the British from their coastal strongholds. The stalemate was finally broken in 1781, when a combined French and American force trapped 8,000 British soldiers on a peninsula in Virginia called Yorktown, and a French fleet prevented British ships from resupplying the besieged encampment. The war had expanded internationally since its inception, so Britain withdrew from the contest in the Americas in order to focus on its other enemies – France, Spain, the Netherlands and colonials in India – in military theatres across the globe. Americans rarely acknowledge Britain's embroilment elsewhere as a factor in the outcome; they prefer a simple David and Goliath version, with outmanned colonies besting the mightiest empire in the world.

After the war, the United States struggled. Thirteen former colonies were now states, each with its own constitution and governing body. They had joined in a confederation, but the only collective body, 'The United States in Congress Assembled', lacked the power to levy taxes or pass laws. In 1787, facing internal rebellions by indebted farmers, prominent landowners and merchants drafted a new plan that featured a strong central government while leaving some authority with the states. Their constitution, ratified by the states in 1788, completed the sweep of the American Revolution. This story, told and retold, defined the nation from the outset and continues to do so today.

A twenty-year-old who protested 'taxation without representation' in 1768 and fought in the army a decade later would be only forty when he voted on ratification of the constitution in 1788. If the birth of United States was relatively brief, however, it was more complex than appears in the common telling. America's Revolutionary War was in fact a gangly affair that featured diverse players and a convoluted plotline. Loyalists included not only well-heeled merchants but also tenant farmers who pitted themselves against their Whig landlords. In the Southern backcountry, neighbours fought neighbours in brutal internecine warfare. Native American nations, carefully calculating how their actions might best curb Euro-American expansion, chose to support one side or the other. Enslaved African Americans also tried to play the war to their best advantage – some fled to the British, hoping to be freed, while others served with the rebelling colonists, enticed by promises of freedom which might or might not be honoured at war's end.

The war was bloody. Some 7,000 American revolutionaries perished on the battlefield, another 8,500 in prisons, and an estimated 10,000 from war-related diseases endemic to military camps. Per capita, that would amount to three million Americans today. In addition, a comparable number of British soldiers and Loyalist militiamen died on American battlefields. (British mortality from disease and imprisonment was less, but their battle casualties were much greater worldwide, once the war had spread to global theatres.) This revolution, the total war of its day, impacted civilian populations on every level. In the South, reported General Nathanael Greene (1742–86), 'the whole country' was being 'laid waste by the Whigs and Tories who pursue each other with as much relentless Fury as Beasts of Prey'. Another American general, William Moultrie (1730–1805), wrote after one campaign that a countryside once rich with livestock and wild fowl was 'destitute of all....Not the vestiges of horses, cattle, hogs, or deer, &c. was to be found. The squirrels and deer of every kind were totally destroyed.' After the war, survivors did not wish to dwell on the myriad human tragedies that clouded victory. In the words of historian John Shy, 'Much about the event called the Revolutionary War had been very painful and was unpleasant to remember; only the outcome was pleasant, so memory, as ever, began to play tricks with the event.'

To serve the interest of national unification, the story of the American Revolution had to be simplified, sanitized, romanticized and, in the end, mythologized. Consciously, not haphazardly, notable Americans took on the task. Noah Webster (1758–1843), who would later declare linguistic independence from Great Britain with his groundbreaking *American Dictionary of the English Language*, wrote in 1790, less than a decade following the Revolutionary War: 'Every child in America should be acquainted with his own country....As soon as he opens his lips, he should lisp the praise of liberty, and of those illustrious heroes and statesmen, who have wrought a revolution in her favor.' And so it would be. With the advent of public education in the early 19th century, young Americans were presented with a steady diet of patriotic tales, suitably whitewashed and carefully crafted to produce sound morals and national pride. Children learned that George Washington (1732–99), the commander-in-chief of the Continental Army and 'the father of our country', had been scrupulously honest. Once, when a boy, his father had accused him of cutting down the family's cherry tree. He responded: 'I cannot tell a lie. I did it with my little hatchet.'

In gentrifying their revolution, Americans in the young republic drew a contrast with revolutions elsewhere. Following the French Revolution, with its guillotines, and the Black Haitian Revolution, so terrifying to American slaveholders, the word 'revolution' took on new and dangerous connotations. Americans would have none of this; theirs had been a simple family affair, a child casting off parental control. It ended peacefully, with no tumultuous aftershocks. It created a nation based on the treasured ideal of freedom and ruled by the people themselves.

But political discord, perhaps inevitably, hampered attempts at unification. While all could agree that their revolution was a noble endeavour, Americans from the outset have sharply contested its meaning. On 5 September 1787, while delegates from the states were busily drafting a new constitution that would bind these separate bodies together under a 'vigorous' and 'energetic' government, a writer for the *Pennsylvania Gazette* reported: 'The Year 1776 is celebrated for a revolution in favor of *Liberty*. The year 1787, it is expected, will be celebrated with equal joy, for a revolution in favor of *Government*.' Yet if some favoured the new scheme, others did not. Americans calling themselves Federalists focused on the need for an operational government, while opponents believed that the proposed constitution sacrificed the liberties promulgated in the Declaration of Independence and fought for during the war. Here, in the debates over ratification, was an initial fault line: 'liberty' versus 'government'.

Each side got something from this opening round: Federalists secured ratification, but the constitution's opponents pushed for, and soon enshrined, ten amendments now known as the Bill of Rights. As complex and divisive questions emerged in the 1790s, however, the fissure grew. Were federal powers expressly limited to those laid out in the constitution, or did they include *implied* powers, without which the government would flounder once again? And if the federal government appeared to overreach, could the constituent states rein it in? The body politic bifurcated, each side convinced that the other was hell-bent on undermining the revolution's gains.

Emblematic of that bifurcation was the changing nature of Fourth of July celebrations, which marked the nation's declaration of independence in 1776. By the end of the war, these had become ritualized affairs. Early in the morning, bells or cannon announced the beginning of commemorative festivities. Militia or volunteer units marched in parade, followed by a procession of the people. A prominent citizen then preached a secular gospel, and people responded by singing hymns. With all the proper trappings, here was a civic *holy day* – the first national *holiday*, 'the Sabbath of our Freedom'. By the late 1790s, however, patriotic Americans of opposing persuasions were celebrating the Fourth of July with parallel parades and competitive street theatre, burning effigies of political opponents and even fighting in the streets.

In the mid-19th century, a second fault line literally split the nation in two – slavery. The hypocrisy of fighting a war for liberty while enslaving other humans had been apparent from the outset, but the price of unity at the close of the revolution was allowing chattel slavery to persist. If that was a pragmatic necessity, it was also, as many have noted, the nation's 'original sin'. In 1852 Frederick Douglass (1818–95), an escaped slave and ardent abolitionist, delivered a Fourth of July oration lambasting the duplicity of the revolution. He opened with traditional tribute:

Fellow Citizens, I am not wanting in respect for the fathers of this republic. The signers of the Declaration of Independence were brave men....The point from which I am compelled to view them is not, certainly, the most favorable; and yet I cannot contemplate their great deeds with less than admiration. They were statesmen, patriots and heroes, and for the good they did, and the principles they contended for, I will unite with you to honor their memory.

But he closed with hellfire damnation:

What, to the American slave, is your 4th of July? I answer; a day that reveals to him, more than all other days in the year, the gross injustice and cruelty to which he is the constant victim. To him, your celebration is a sham; your boasted liberty, an unholy license; your national greatness, swelling vanity; your sound of rejoicing are empty and heartless; your denunciation of tyrants brass fronted impudence; your shout of liberty and equality, hollow mockery; your prayers and hymns, your sermons and thanks-givings, with all your religious parade and solemnity, are to him, mere bombast, fraud, deception, impiety, and hypocrisy....This Fourth July is yours, not mine. You may rejoice, I must mourn.

Polemicists for the slave-owning South, on the other hand, mimicked revolutionary cries of 'tyranny'. By limiting slavery's expansion, the North was acting like Parliament, imposing its will on others.

At Gettysburg in 1863, during the Civil War, with men dying by the hundreds of thousands, President Abraham Lincoln (1809–65) paid tribute to the nation's beginning: 'Four score and seven years ago, our fathers brought forth upon this continent a new nation, conceived in liberty, and dedicated to the proposition that all men are created equal' – for Lincoln, who had issued his Emancipation Proclamation a few months earlier, *all men* included those held in bondage. Jefferson

Davis (1808–89), president of the Southern Confederacy, held that the 'people' in 1776 were only 'men of the political community'. He chose to emphasize a different passage in the Declaration of Independence: 'Whenever any form of government' failed to protect people's rights, 'it is the right of the people to alter or to abolish it.' The South could legitimately secede from the Union. When Northern soldiers invaded, they were 'reenacting the blunders that statesmen in Great Britain committed'. The revolutionary response, Davis proclaimed, was the same: 'Southern valor still shines as brightly as in the days of '76.'

Polarized camps ever since have laid claim to the revolution's heritage. One has viewed it as a golden age, subsequently undermined by degenerative influences; the other as an inspirational beginning, but only that. Its promise would unfold. While Jefferson Davis was historically correct when he said that the 'people' in 1776 referred exclusively to free white men, that needed correction. African Americans, women and diverse minorities had to be included if the promise of the revolution was to be realized.

Inclusionary moves inevitably triggered reactionary responses. After the Civil War, when former slaves were granted citizenship and immigrants flooded into the United States from southern and eastern Europe, lineage societies such as the Sons of the American Revolution and Daughters of the American Revolution set a standard for the *true* American: revolution pedigree and white. In the mid-20th century, when African Americans tried to cash in on promises of equality that remained unfulfilled, they met a fierce backlash that evolved, with time, into 'Make America Great Again' as proclaimed by Donald Trump (b. 1946).

At each and every juncture, both progressives and conservatives call upon America's founding moment to bolster their cause. The culture wars of today are fought, in part, by contesting the legacy of the American Revolution. Interpreters at George Washington's home Mount Vernon and Thomas Jefferson's Monticello have resurrected slave quarters, highlighting the core contradiction of the revolution but angering those who prefer an uplifting message. Exhibits at Philadelphia's Museum of the American Revolution vividly depict the roles that African

Americans, Native Americans and women played in the revolution – but this 'inclusiveness', said the *Wall Street Journal* in 2017, creates 'strange proportions' that 'de-sacralize the Revolution' and 'weaken the event's symbolic power'. They have 'less to do with the war's significance than with today's preoccupations with identity-based tensions'.

Historians join the fray. While academics probe once-forgotten constituencies, popular authors produce a never-ending stream of bestselling biographies of iconic 'Founders' – capitalizing the F is the norm. There is a new and humanizing twist, however. Joseph Ellis, in his Pulitzer Prize-winning *Founding Brothers: The Revolutionary Generation* (2000), views the traditional 'Founding Fathers' more like brothers. They squabbled and sometimes misbehaved, and evidenced 'their mutual imperfections and fallibilities, as well as their eccentricities and excesses', yet Ellis still concludes that 'they comprised, by any informed and fair-minded standard, the greatest generation of political talent in American history. They created the American republic.' Ironically, despite the subtitle, his narrative entirely omits the Revolutionary *War*.

Reverence for the Founders spills over to the Supreme Court. For the last quarter-century, conservative justices have espoused a judicial doctrine they call 'originalism': the constitution must be interpreted according to the intent of its framers or the meaning of the text in the late 18th century. This produces strange and inconsistent results. Despite the constitutional proscription of 'cruel and unusual punishments', capital punishment is deemed permissible because hanging was a common practice back then – but so were branding of hands and public lashing for minor offences, punishments that no judge, even an originalist, would sanction today. Opponents of originalism uphold what they call a 'living constitution', in which meanings can adapt with the times. Again, one school looks backward, the other forward – but even those who favour a more flexible constitution freely weaponize quotations from the Founders to buttress their arguments.

Out of court as well as within, Americans argue contemporary issues in constitutional terms. The Bill of Rights, ten amendments quickly added to the constitution, is widely regarded as the final act of the Founding Era, the last word of the esteemed 'Revolutionary Generation'. The second of these reads: 'A well regulated militia being necessary to the security of a free state, the right of the people to keep and bear arms shall not be infringed.' Separating the two components of this amendment is a disputed comma. For gun-safety advocates, that comma links the dependent and independent clauses of the sentence, the first providing the reason for the second – the entire text refers to militias, they maintain. Gun-rights advocates argue that the comma is essentially a semi-colon – the amendment makes two distinct statements, the first about militias and the second about (private) gun ownership. The actual issue for our times, triggered by gun violence and mass shootings, is the regulation of gun ownership, but arguments centre on a controversial punctuation mark penned at a time when single-shot muskets were the norm, not automatic rifles firing hundreds of rounds per minute.

Yet, importantly, both sides are scrutinizing the same bedrock document. Since the revered Founders produced a constitution that is universally honoured, that document provides a playing field for contesting any issue. Trust in 'government' might be at an all-time low, but faith in the constitution endures. Following the election of Barack Obama (b. 1961) in 2008, right-wing activists, assuming the label 'Tea Party' from the event that sparked the Revolutionary War, waved pocket-sized copies of the constitution at their street demonstrations. They might not grasp its pro-tax and pro-government historical purpose, but they felt in a general way that the federal government taxed too heavily and violated their 'constitutional rights'. Eight years later, in reaction to the election of Donald Trump, liberals called upon the same constitution, interpreted differently. Fearful of Trump's dictatorial manner and ambition, they saw in it an antidote that provided for the separation of powers, a circumscribed executive and periodic elections. The myriad, incessant references from all sides are like applause, and, like applause, reassuring.

George Washington

George Washington (1732–99), wealthy Virginian landowner and slave-owner of the estate of Mount Vernon, began his military career fighting the French in 1754. By the late 1760s he anticipated the possibility of taking up arms to defend the colony's rights against the British, although he still remained opposed to the idea of independence. Elected to the second Continental Congress in 1775, he was appointed commander-in-chief of the colonies' Continental Army. Despite early setbacks, he achieved the surrender of the British forces in 1781. He was president of the Constitutional Convention held in Philadelphia in 1787, and reluctantly elected the first president of the United States in 1789, a post he held for eight years. He was described after his death in 1799 as 'First in war – first in peace – and first in the hearts of his countrymen.'

Thomas Jefferson

Thomas Jefferson (1743–1826), lawyer and landowner, was a Virginian representative to the second Constitutional Congress in 1775 and the main drafter of the Declaration of Independence in 1776. He was appointed governor of Virginia in 1779, and later American minister to France (1785–9), where he sympathetically observed the revolution at first hand. He was appointed the first American secretary of state in 1790, vice president in 1796 and Republican president of the United States (1801–9); during this period he built up the country's military capacity, and was responsible for the westward expansion of the United States with the Louisiana Purchase of 1803. His reputation as a progressive Enlightenment figure and the inspiration for a new, free society has been seriously affected by revelations of his treatment of his slaves.

TIMELINE

1607   First successful English colony in North America founded at
            Jamestown, Virginia

1754–63 French and Indian War fought in North America, leading to French
            ceding all possessions east of the Mississippi

1756   Parliament passes the Stamp Act, imposing direct taxation on
            North American transactions

1770   Boston Massacre: British troops kill five protestors

1773   Boston Tea Party: Massachusetts protestors against taxes throw
            tea into Boston harbour

1774   First Continental Congress meets with delegates from all colonies
            except Georgia

1775   War breaks out with battle of Lexington (Massachusetts)

1776
July   Declaration of Independence is written and adopted

December   George Washington achieves decisive victory at Trenton, having
            crossed the Delaware River at night

1777–8 Washington's Continental Army winters at Valley Forge, emerging
            as a disciplined force

1778   France allies with the United States

1781   British commander Lord Cornwallis surrenders at Yorktown, ending
            the war

1783   Treaty of Paris confirms the independence of the United States

1787   Constitutional Convention meets in Philadelphia; constitution is
            signed in September

1789   Washington is elected first president of the United States

THE FRENCH REVOLUTION, 1789–1799

Sophie Wahnich

The fall of the Bastille on 14 July 1789 led, a few years later, to the declaration of a republic and the execution of King Louis XVI, a state-imposed programme of terror against all those perceived to be enemies of the revolution, and numerous constitutional experiments including a French empire under Napoleon Bonaparte. This complex chain was understood by contemporaries everywhere as unprecedented and truly revolutionary. The revolutionaries took up the universalist themes they found in the American Revolution, and carried them further with their slogan '*liberté, egalité, fraternité*', and their proclamation of the rights of man and the triumph of reason. Conservatives, however, saw all this as proof that the old order should be shored up at all costs, while radicals hailed the dawn of liberty – 'Bliss was it in that dawn to be alive', as the poet William Wordsworth wrote, even though what many onlookers saw in that dawn was the long shadow of the guillotine.

Ever since, the chain of events that began in 1789 has been debated endlessly, both in France and across the world, and politicians of every hue have drawn lessons from it. Consensus will never be achievable – and may not be desirable. As the poet, art critic and active 1848 revolutionary Charles Baudelaire wrote, 'criticism must be partial, passionate, political, that is to say it must adopt an exclusive point of view, provided always the one adopted opens up the widest horizons'.

The revolution is traditionally considered to have ended with the coup that brought Napoleon to power in 1799, although in some respects his rule saw a working through of the revolutionary vision. His ultimate defeat in 1814–15 may have brought the return of the traditional monarchy to France, but it did little to resolve the many issues raised in the revolution; and over the following century and a half the country underwent a series of aftershocks – 1830, 1848, 1870, 1944, 1968 – on each of which occasions the people, notably but not exclusively in Paris, took what direct action they could to drive through changes that had been left unfinished after 1789.   PF

The French Revolution was a complex event, its roots deep in the history of the preceding 150 years. Throughout the long reign of Louis XIV (r. 1643–1715), the monarch had sought to assert his 'divine right' to rule, developed new centralized institutions to govern France and limited the political power of the aristocracy. In his determination to rule with absolute and untrammelled power, he had allowed the ancient legislative and consultative assembly known as the Estates General to fall into disuse. This comprised three groups or Estates of the realm: the First Estate, or clergy; the Second Estate, or the wealthiest nobility; and the Third Estate, known as the commoners, but including the bourgeoisie as well as many intellectuals and professionals. The Third Estate, though most numerous in terms of delegates, could be outvoted by the others.

Under Louis XIV and his successors, the Estates never met to resolve or discuss issues of the day, but the financial problems of the country grew under the heavy burden of wars from the 1740s onward – particularly from French support for the American War of Independence (1776–83) and the national debt that resulted from a series of loans.

The aristocracy was traditionally exempt from taxation, and two other aristocratically controlled bodies, the consultative Assembly of Notables and the judicial *parlement* of Paris, refused to bail out the coffers of the state. New taxes were necessary, and only the Estates General had the legitimacy to introduce them. The nobility, however, refused any reforms that would threaten their traditional right to exemption from taxation. They wanted to make the bourgeoisie pay, considering this reasonable since the bourgeoisie wanted its share of power.

The start of the French Revolution can be traced to three key moments in the summer of 1789. First, on 5 May, the Estates General met for the first time in 160 years; this meeting ignited the revolutionary impulse and allowed it to spread. Second, on 9 July, the Third Estate (commoners) met without the aristocracy or clergy and against the expressed wishes of King Louis XVI (r. 1774–92), in a separate body known as the National Constituent Assembly. This aimed to bring the three orders of the kingdom together on the same footing, effectively opening the future to a liberal society that would give each individual an equal voice. It constituted a challenge to the authority both of the monarchy and of the First and Second Estates, and therefore a new order in French political life. Finally, on 14 July, the people of Paris defended this new order against government forces when they took matters into their own hands and stormed the royal fortress of the Bastille to release the political prisoners held there.

The revolution began, therefore, with the most privileged orders refusing to pay taxes and questioning the king's authority to levy them. In addition, the most ancient families (the so-called 'Nobility of the Sword') demanded their right to give counsel to the king, while the *noblesse de robe* (aristocratic office-holders) aspired to the British parliamentary model that would, in the last resort, give them the power to make laws. The *parlements* of 1787 to 1789 were to be given the title 'the voice of the nation'. Thus both aristocratic reaction and revolt played decisive roles in what was to occur.

Although the later history of the revolution – notably the Terror of 1793–4, which asserted the absolute authority of the state – brought other ideologies to the fore, what triumphed in 1789 might be called the liberal vision. There were three related reasons for this success: the values of the Enlightenment; the social cohesion of the Third Estate; and the radicalization of its deputies.

The Enlightenment – with its rationalistic challenge to traditional knowledge and religious authority – had already ushered in a deep cultural change. Literacy rates had risen steadily throughout the 18th century. Reading habits changed, too. At the start of the century, half of all titles published in France had been on religious topics, but by 1789 this figure was only one in ten. Even in the countryside, where books were distributed by hawkers, a new universe of knowledge allowed people to shift their attention from heaven back down to earth. In the towns, libraries and reading rooms opened, where for a small fee people could obtain access to the *Encyclopédie* of Diderot and d'Alembert, or the highly popular editions of publisher Charles-Joseph Panckoucke. Demand was so high that readers sometimes had to pay for access by the hour. Even the illiterate could hear readings of these texts, which were given to a roomful gathered together to discuss the news.

As a result, the old ties of faith loosened their grip over people, and were replaced by a radical new idea: that happiness could be found here on earth. The church's teachings on marriage had devalued love, even within marriage, and reinforced the repression of extramarital sexual relations. But the cult of abstinence was swept away by the assertion of joyful sexuality. By 1750 there was a rise in illegitimate births, conception outside marriage and the use of contraception, allowing people to introduce a new tenderness into everyday life and into relations between parents and children.

The old concept of the divine right of kings seemed outdated in the face of these ideas, and as a result censorship and repression abounded. It became dangerous to write, edit or publish any opinions critical of the established order; there was an ever-present threat of confiscation of property or being thrown in the Bastille, which only served to demonstrate how much those in power believed that the written word fed into the desire for radical change. Such arbitrary and reactionary justice came to be seen as unacceptable as novels and the theatre impressed people with ideas that would assure the eventual victory of the discourse about human rights.

The second factor in the liberal triumph of 1789 was the social cohesion of the Third Estate. The previous year, the nobility – which claimed to represent the voice of the nation – had sought its support against the King. But when a poor harvest brought widespread unrest in the summer of 1788, this unstable alliance broke down over issues of indirect taxation and feudal rights – for instance, the nobility claimed the right to hunt freely, but in doing so they could devastate a farmer's crops. A feeling arose that it was time to call an end to a society that failed to respect the humanity and dignity of all its members in the name of iniquitous privilege. It made no sense for privilege to be based on the traditional orders when few of the nobility were soldiers and the clergy had lost interest in saving souls. In the face of huge social and economic problems and falling rents, a climate of latent or actual revolt took hold, and clashes with the forces of law and order took place across the kingdom. Yet the regional *parlements* did not support the suffering people, but the nobility – particularly so in Brittany in January 1789, where a full-scale armed rising broke out in Rennes. The very poorest, the penny-scrapers, the servants, the porters, demanded respect for the Breton constitution: that is to say, demanded respect for the people.

The worst violence occurred in Paris in April 1789, when workers began to riot in response to a wallpaper manufacturer lowering wages. The French Guard, the mounted police and the cavalry used live ammunition against the rioters, resulting in 300 deaths and 1,000 wounded. In response, on 27 April, the elected representatives of the sixty districts who were assembled to draft the Parisian *Cahiers de doléances* (petitions that set out the sufferings of the people) decided to begin with a declaration of the rights of man – the ultimate Enlightenment challenge to the traditional social order.

The third factor in the rise of liberal values was political. Up to this point, the riots had been, initially, against taxation and against the monarch, then against the aristocracy. Now a party of patriots emerged who demanded the admission of commoners to all responsibilities and the doubling in size of the representation for the Third Estate; voting by head count; and a written constitution to outlaw abuses of power and justice. This was the context within which the famous *Cahiers* from across the nation were presented to the King. Even in the aristocratic assembly, a lively debate took place between liberals (who were, unsurprisingly, in a minority there) and the majority who were more protective of their privileges. The assembly of the clergy also split between the high clergy and the rest. Meanwhile, in the Third Estate, model *Cahiers* were distributed by the patriots. Even if village communities did not always comply, these discussions helped unite the Third Estate and its deputies.

It was after the inaugural meeting of the Estates General in May 1789 proved fruitless that the bourgeois deputies of the Third Estate refused to return, and instead set up the National Constituent Assembly. They gave an ultimatum to the other two Orders: join us, or stop pretending to represent the nation. This was a radical challenge to the King and a moment of crisis, represented by the so-called Tennis Court Oath ('not to disperse until the constitution of the kingdom is established') of 20 June. By revealing their unity and seeing themselves visibly supported by the people, who applauded them as they left each session (in stark contrast to the deathly silence that greeted the aristocrats), the representatives of the Third Estate found the courage to stand firm. They drafted their own constitution in the National Assembly.

When this assembly, though long anticipated and much welcomed, found itself in danger of being dismissed by Finance Minister Necker, the people of Paris took it upon themselves to organize – and they soon took the Bastille, symbol of monarchical power. The crisis had tipped over into revolution.

Since the bicentenary of the French Revolution in 1989, the most common narrative of events describes this legal revolution of May–July 1789, which took place with little effort or risk. It had been made upstream, through an alliance of the bourgeois elites and the liberal nobility. However, after the legal revolution had taken place, a genuinely popular uprising brought the surge of violence and radicalization that saw the monarchy replaced by a republic, brought the King to the scaffold (21 January 1793) and led to the Terror of 1793–4, which saw many others lose their lives on the flimsiest of evidence. The Terror is often presented as a prototype of totalitarian government – even a template for totalitarianism. On this reading, the liberal elites initially tried to restrain the excesses of the intemperate populace, but the mob was led by idealistic Jacobin ideologues such as Maximilien Robespierre (1758–94) and Louis-Antoine de Saint-Just (1767–94), tyrants who invoked state terror as a matter of policy and used violence without respect for the founding principles of liberty.

But this is not the only story in circulation. A more traditional account sees the revolution itself as the foundation of French republicanism, and presents Robespierre less as a tyrant and more as a founder of the most innovative strand of republicanism. Supporters of this view argue that he not only asserted the right to education and social security, but also, with Henri Grégoire (1750–1831), the emancipation of the Jews and the abolition of slavery. By this account, the Terror represented a wound that the revolution received only when it was facing the threat of being overthrown by counter-revolutionary armies. Reactionary émigrés from revolutionary France, many of them based on the Rhine in Coblenz, had raised a European coalition against this process of emancipation; while internally a quasi-civil war, both religious and political, took place with recalcitrant priests and federalist secessions. The Jacobin use of state terror was a response to this existential threat.

Two other traditional accounts of the revolution are also in existence. The classic Marxist version sees it as the result of a socio-economic crisis whose contradictions pointed the way towards a bourgeois future whose political model was parliamentary; while the conservative, nationalist vision (championed above all by Charles Maurras in the mid-20th century) saw it as a catastrophe, as evidenced by the death of the King and the demise of the values of the *ancien régime*.

There is, however, a new narrative: one which sees revolutionary radicalism from the outset in the project that produced the Declaration of the Rights of Man and the Citizen on 26 August 1789. All the major actors of the revolution took a position on this Declaration, and their conflicts created the political spectrum of the left and right wings. The counter-revolutionaries hated it, foreseeing, even in 1789, not only the end of the *ancien régime* itself but of colonial slavery as well. The liberals effectively betrayed the Declaration when they refused to grant the political equality it promised, established a form of suffrage that excluded women, the poor and foreigners, and maintained slavery; they believed that only property owners were capable of political activity. On the other hand, the Declaration was defended and then deepened by those who argued for a universal, cosmopolitan civic engagement – men such as Condorcet, Danton, Robespierre, Saint-Just, Billaud-Varenne and Grégoire. These men made resistance to oppression the duty of every citizen, and by doing so their permanent legacy was a republic based on equality and fraternity. Admittedly, this project remained unfinished, as true equality was not granted to women or foreigners; nevertheless, it acknowledged the dignity of the thoughtful, opinionated populace, and paved the way for universal male suffrage. The horrors of the Terror were deployed to defend just these cosmopolitan rights. As Saint-Just, chief theoretician of the Terror, said, 'What do those desire who neither virtue nor terror want?' The words of Blaise Pascal (1623–62) continually resonated within the head of Robespierre: 'Justice without force is powerless. Force without justice is tyranny.' Robespierre was devoted to not appearing to be a tyrant of this sort, while still accepting the necessity of violence to protect the revolution. This narrative restores the uncertainties of the historical moment: we must not judge the revolution so much as understand its ambitions, its achievements and its limitations.

These various accounts correspond to different social, political and cultural groups in French society. But today there is something paradoxical in the way that French people see the revolution. On the one hand, they are proud that the Declaration of the Rights of Man and the Citizen remains a sacred object and a building block of the constitution; on the other, they are ashamed, because the Terror seems impossible to understand and the revolution has become a blueprint that leads to totalitarianism – and they are disgusted that 20th-century Nazism and Stalinism soil the image of the revolution. The French are not easily able to reconcile the optimism of the Rights of Man with the horrors of the Terror, and as a result the revolution has become a kind of buried treasure for them.

In 1945, reference to the revolution was powerfully and naturally used to counter the collaborationist ideology of Marshal Philippe Pétain (1856–1951), whose 'National Revolution' at the heart of his pro-Nazi Vichy state was based on the absolute reversal of revolutionary values: 'liberty, equality and fraternity' being replaced by 'work, family, fatherland'. The memory of Saint-Just was mobilized by the communist-inspired Resistance in 1943 to convince young people to join them rather than the STO (*service du travail obligatoire*, whereby French workers were sent to labour camps in the east). In 1942, lawyer René Cassin (1887–1976) began to adapt the 1789 Declaration of the Rights of Man and the Citizen, and his drafting was key to the final text of the Universal Declaration of Human Rights that was agreed by the United Nations in 1948.

The intellectual context of the 1950s and 1960s, when many intellectuals were fellow-travellers with the French Communist Party, meant that the revolutionary period became a major arena of debate for Marxists. The entry of Soviet tanks into Budapest in 1956 dealt the first blow to this Marxist hegemony. Nevertheless, Jean-Paul Sartre's *Critique of Dialectical Reason* (1960) and Claude Lévi-Strauss's response in *The Noble Savage* (1962) made the revolutionary period an essential laboratory for thought, not only in relation to its politics but its very definition. The position of the revolution in the collective imagination of much of the French left was challenged by Michel Foucault (1926–84), who saw traditional accounts of the revolution as too Western-centric, and by historian François Furet (1927–97), who took an essentially historical approach, challenging the ideological assumptions of many previous thinkers. As a result, the revolution, originally seen as a political revolt that had 'slipped away' when the populace became involved, and then as a template for totalitarianism, now became a purely historical event without direct relevance to the present – there has been a long path of denial of the revolutionary moment. The civic vision, utopian and monumental, seems irretrievable.

Yet the anti-totalitarian movement divides into two streams. On the libertarian left are those who wish to be both anti-totalitarian and anti-capitalist, and to build a utopian mode of thought that can prevent the repetition of the horrors of the 20th century. To these, the revolution is one of those incomplete utopias that can restore faith in the impossible. On the other hand, the centrist tendency of the liberal left, which accepts adaptation to capitalism and claims to defend a supposedly peaceful democracy that is entirely enmeshed in the development of the free market, denies the value of any such utopian vision and accepts the world as it is. This group sees any thought of revolutionary or radical transformation as potentially totalitarian.

The most interesting developments in this debate are those that see that the world must keep changing, and wish to revisit the ambition of the revolutionaries – but to do so with clarity, seeking to learn not just from their unfulfilled ambitions but also from their failures, in order to avoid repeating past mistakes.

Honoré Gabriel Riqueti

Honoré Gabriel Riqueti, comte de Mirabeau (1749–91), was an early leader of the revolution. After a scandalous youth and life as a secret agent, he was elected to the Estates General in 1789, arguing for a constitutional monarchy and strong executive with representative government on the English model. He became spokesman for the nation in the summer of 1789. Seeing himself as the voice of moderation and a link between the King and the nation, he sought the trust of both sides and rejected the Declaration of the Rights of Man. He became secret counsellor to Louis XVI in 1790 and, although a member of the Jacobins, he opposed their republican ambitions while arguing for the abolition of slavery and the sale of church lands to pay the national debt. Accused of treason, he died in April 1791.

Maximilien Robespierre

Maximilien Robespierre (1758–94), a lawyer from Artois, attended the Estates General in 1789 and joined the National Assembly. He supported the Declaration of the Rights of Man and the constitution of 1791, and in December 1790 he was the first to use the phrase '*liberté, égalité, fraternité*'. He was involved with the Jacobin Club, where radical republicans organized. In the summer of 1793, Robespierre and the Jacobins were in the ascendancy and set up the Committee for Public Safety; Robespierre argued for the use of state terror to protect the revolution against internal and external enemies. By July 1794, this policy had resulted in more than 17,000 deaths, and Robespierre, though known as 'the Incorruptible' for his personal austerity, was described as a dictator by his opponents. In July he was arrested, and guillotined the following day.

TIMELINE

1774   Louis XVI comes to the throne

1774-83   France supports American states in War of Independence
                  against Britain

1787   First Assembly of Notables convened; conflict between the
                  King and the *parlement* of Paris

1788   Insurrection at Grenoble; King and his minister, Brienne,
                  convoke Estates General for May 1789; Paris *parlement*
                  presents the *Cahiers de doléances*

1789
5 May   Estates General assemble at Versailles

20 June   Members of the Third Estate take the Tennis Court Oath

9 July   Third Estate proclaims the National Constituent Assembly

14 July   Fall of the Bastille

5-11 August   National Assembly decrees the abolition of feudalism, equality
                  of taxation and the sale of offices

26 August   National Assembly approves the text of the Declaration of the
                  Rights of Man and the Citizen

5-6 October   Women's march to Versailles; return of the King to Paris

1790
13 February   Suppression of religious orders and monastic vows

19 June   Abolition of nobility and titles by Constituent Assembly

1791
20 June   Louis XVI flees Paris for Varennes, is captured and taken back
                  to Paris

13-14 September   Louis XVI formally accepts constitution

28 September	Slavery is abolished in France, but not in colonies
1 October	First meeting of Legislative Assembly
9 November	Assembly orders *émigrés* to return under pain of death; civil marriage and divorce are instituted

1792

20 April	'War of the First Coalition' begins – France declares war on Austria
10–13 August	Storming of the Tuileries; Louis XVI and his family are imprisoned
2–6 September	'September Massacres': Paris crowd murders 1,200
20 September	French revolutionary army defeats Prussians at Valmy
20–21 September	First session of the Convention; unanimous vote to abolish monarchy
19 November	Edict of Fraternity offers aid to people everywhere 'struggling to be free'
11 December	Trial of the King begins

1793

21 January	Louis XVI executed
1 February	France declares war on Britain and Holland
6 April	Committee of Public Safety established
27 July	Robespierre and Saint-Just appointed to Committee of Public Safety
17 September	Law of Suspects and beginning of the Terror
10 October	Decree suspending constitution and sanctioning revolutionary government for the 'duration of the war'

1794

4 February   Abolition of slavery in all French colonies

28 July   Robespierre arrested and guillotined without trial

1795

22 August   Convention approves 'Constitution of Year III' to establish
               Directory

1796

2–23 February Napoleon is given command of French army in Italy

1799

12 March   France declares war on Austria

9–10 November Napoleon's coup d'état of 18–19 Brumaire; he is proclaimed
               First Consul

1804

2 December   Napoleon crowns himself emperor

THE HAITIAN REVOLUTION, 1791-1804

Bayyinah Bello

The revolution that broke out in the French slave colony of Saint-Domingue, on the western third of the Caribbean island of Ayiti (later named Hispaniola, and ironically the place where Columbus first made landfall in the New World in December 1492), is the world's only example of a successful slave revolt leading to the creation of a new state, free from slavery and ruled by those formerly held captives as slaves themselves. This island bore the Arawak name Ayiti for over 4,000 years; after independence in 1804–6 it became Hayti, Empire of Freedom; also the Kingdom of Hayti in the north until 1820; then in 1807, the west and south became known as the Republic of Haiti. After 1820, the entire island became Hayti or Haiti. All three forms are used here, according to the moment being spoken about.

Although the example of the revolutionaries in France, and their abolition of slavery, is often presented as inspiring and providing a context for events in Saint-Domingue, the revolt was essentially homegrown, and stemmed both from the knowledge and qualities of the people themselves, and the unique conditions on the island – a place that arguably suffered the most severe regime of slavery and racism to be found anywhere in the Americas.

The Haytian Revolution had huge global impact. The success of the former captives in throwing off the shackles was both threatening to the European slaving nations (in particular France, where Napoleon sought to overthrow the revolution), and inspiring to others in the European colonies of the so-called New World, who sought to emulate their example. Over the coming decades, many peoples – both black and white – fought for their independence, and gradually the crime of slavery was abolished across the Americas. Napoleon's failure to reconquer Hayti ended his ambition for building a French empire in the Americas and paved the way for the western expansion of the United States. Meanwhile the revolutionary leader Toussaint Louverture, though left to rot in prison by Napoleon, has been, after his death, widely feted as 'the black Jacobin', an inspiration for radicals and liberals in Europe, into the late 20th century.

Yet the revolution was made by, and its legacy belongs to, the Haytians; and its narrative can only be properly understood in its own terms – in terms of the indigenous peoples, the Africans themselves, their belief systems and values.

As a state founded in a revolution, Haiti's history sported a healthy mistrust of slavers in the first half of the 19th century, confirmed thereafter by ever-growing interference and pillage from the US and others. (The US Marines landed in Haiti in December 1914 and took the country's gold reserve to Fort Knox, Kentucky; it is still there.) As a result, prosperity and stability have proved elusive, and by the later 20th century it remained very poor, while also suffering international and national human right abuses. A devastating earthquake in 2010 exacerbated its problems. Professor Bello sees a recovery of Haitian selfhood and identity, by recovering its history and pride – with the revolutionary era of 1791–1820 at the heart of this – as a crucial step to taking the country forward with confidence.   PF

I n the name of all founders of Ayiti/Hayti/Haiti, females and males, I greet you: invisible ones, powerful children yet to be conceived: Alafia, Sannu! Onè/Respè! In our tradition, writing is a photo of talking, therefore the two should be quite similar.

In our tradition, when communicating about ourstory, we must present ourselves. I am the daughter of Marie Christine Domerson (secretary/nurse) with Yves Auguste, lawyer, diplomat, professor; granddaughter of Julienne Dronette, homemaker, and Joseph Domerson, lawyer, on the mother's side and Sylvie Prunier and Louis Auguste, land- and store-owners, on the father's side. I've been blessed to climb the family tree up to the African, from the Yoruba ethnic group, Messan Kwachi, who experienced more than twenty-eight years in slavery; he is the father of Faustin Soulouque, who was born in slavery in 1782, freed by the revolution in 1793, then as a soldier rose to become the seventh president (1847–9) and second emperor (1849–59) of Haiti.

The primary purpose of ourstory ('our history') is to empower a people. Every writer writes from his or her own worldview; no knowledge is neutral. That is why victors so often impose their views on others. But in the case of Haiti, the vanquished armies of Spain, Britain and France still wrote their own template of 'his story' and gave it back to us as 'ours' via schools implanted by the church. When a people receive a version of history written by yesterday's enemies, then that history can only handicap them and thwart their progress.

To properly appreciate this revolution and its legacies, we must understand that this traditional 'world history' is generally written from a cyclopean point of view. Acting in the name of God (or so they claimed), the Eurochristians slaughtered a large portion of the population of Africa, sold Africans across the planet, mass produced opium in an attempt to disable the Asians and committed genocide on the original peoples of the so-called Americas; after all this, they set themselves up as the exclusive authority on the history of what happened everywhere in the world! Unless we understand that this has happened and is still going on, we are not yet ready to appreciate ourstorical truth about the peoples of our planet.

All Haitians embrace Vodou philosophy, but our schools were created by the Eurochristian slavers' church. The 'historical' narrative fabricated by this church created a fundamental schism separating schooled Haitians from those who have not attended school; those who practise Vodou and those who don't; those who speak French and those who don't. The traditional narrative of Haitian history as taught in our schools is that the good Christians landed on the island in 1492; but while the savage Arawak were in the process of being civilized by the Spaniards, these weak folks died. So, by 1503, the Europeans were obliged to send for Africans to do the necessary work. And in barely eleven years, Eurochristians practically wiped out the original peoples of the island. According to the French botanist Michel Descourtilz (1775–1835), colonization also destroyed more than 90 per cent of the vegetation of the island. Even though the historical protagonists of the revolution may be similar in the two traditions, African and Arawak, the Eurochristian narrative divides them into 'good' and 'bad'. Thus General Toussaint Louverture (1743–1803), one leader of the 1791 rebellion who was then kidnapped by the French in 1802, sent to France and died in prison, is projected as the good revolutionary, the saint; whereas his lieutenant General Jean-Jacques Dessalines (1758–1806), who eventually brought us to independence and caused the Eurochristians to lose the source of their most abundant profits, is seen as bad.

This Eurochristian narrative has caused Haitians to lose the essence of their true ourstory. Most of us schooled ones have lost any understanding of the duration of the fight, the collaboration between the Arawak and African peoples, the continuity and accumulation of African knowledge and strength; and there has been insufficient appreciation of natural ancestral powers.

True revolution involves not just political change, but a complete change of perception and conception. It brings about drastically different ways of thinking, speaking and acting. True revolution begins in the mind. When a people who have been conditioned to perceive themselves as 'slaves' – as things, possessions of others, incapable of thinking or acting by or for themselves – manage to turn their mental structures around and begin to establish their own goals and rediscover their ability to will: at this point, an invisible revolution occurs.

Many such revolutions took place among the enslaved Africans around the Americas and Caribbean. In Saint-Croix (now part of the US Virgin Islands) in 1878, three women – Mary Thomas, Rebecca Frederik and Axelline Salomon – decided to liberate the island from the claws of Danish slavers, and took action. They executed a brilliant strategy by setting fire to the barrels of rum that stood on the quay, waiting to be embarked for Europe. That was a revolution; it took the Danish colonial government nearly a year to regain control of the island.

By contrast, what is called the American Revolution was not a true revolution. This battle between Eurochristian cousins in Britain and on the eastern seaboard of North America to determine who would get a greater percentage of the wealth generated by the abuse and humiliation imposed upon enslaved non-whites was no revolution, but a family feud that paid little heed to questions of justice, human rights or freedom. Before, during and after this family feud, Eurochristians in the Americas and Europe stuck to the same mentality: *I must have it all; any inhumane behaviour is justifiable; non-white peoples are sub-human.*

The Arawak or Taino people who were the original inhabitants of the island of Ayiti (its original name, meaning 'land of high mountains') led a life very close to nature, holding few private possessions; each thing belonged to the one who needed it at a particular time. Together they produced what they needed, built homes to protect themselves, built boats to travel from island to island and to the mainland; but vital to them was their role as co-creators, helping Sun to bring out her light every morning through songs and dances. They played sports, meditated a great deal, ate mostly raw fruits and vegetables. They believed that everything, including animals, plants, people, astral and spiritual bodies, deserves respect and kindness. Contentment and happiness were vital to their culture. The island was governed by a crown of five *kasiks*, which must be constituted of both female and male energies.

Kasikess Anakaona of Ayiti, member of the crown in the 1490s at the time of the invasion of her island by Eurochristians, put up a fight for over a decade. Ultimately she was subdued and put on trial by Spanish greed. Her execution in 1503 by hanging and fire dealt a major blow to the fight to retain freedom. Africans were then forcibly brought to the island by Eurochristians, but they continued spiritual, geographical, ourstorical and botanical studies and training while carrying on the struggle. Both the Arawaks and Africans carried out a 312-year war in Ayiti – more actively at some times than others, but always the fight went on.

The Spanish quickly created a slave colony on the island of Ayiti, which they named Hispaniola. Many colonists fought over this island, including the French and British, but in the mid-17th century the French took over the western third of the island and made their own colony, called Saint-Domingue. They made huge profits from the sugar, cotton and coffee grown on the plantations here. Millions of Africans found themselves subjugated to the harshest tasks. The typical working day began before sunrise and continued in certain seasons until midnight. Punishment ranged from cutting off limbs or tongues to castration, to burying people alive up to the neck and pouring honey over them while betting on how long ants would take to kill them. The Catholic religion was imposed, but the captive Africans feigned conversion while creating their own belief system and language. It is said that fewer than 50,000 colonists ran this murderous show against millions of Africans. Eventually, the people rose up, producing many incredible fighters, both female and male – until the revolution crushed Saint-Domingue out of existence and gave birth to Hayti, Empire of Freedom.

The revolution reached a new height on 14 August 1791, when a group of enslaved Africans met at Bois Caiman (Alligator Wood), where they secretly held an assembly to agree on how to stop slavery. It concluded with a Vodou ritual under a full moon, to bestow blessings and power to participants. On 22 August, the revolt began. Boukman Dutty, the first leader, was soon killed, but other leaders continued the fight. Then Toussaint Louverture built an army with his own people.

He sometimes joined the Spanish army in fighting against the French, and other times vice versa, while always seeking advantages for his people. Eventually he became the head of the French army in Saint-Domingue as well as head of the colonial government. He won many victories against both the British and Spaniards, conquered Spanish Santo Domingo and freed the slaves there, unifying the island as a French colony – before being kidnapped by French officers and sent to France, where this child of the sun was placed in the coldest jail on a mountaintop with no firewood. Here he died. Ultimately, his general Jean-Jacques Dessalines, his back scarred from more than thirty years of living under a barbarous slavery system, rose up and won the war against the French, declaring independence on 1 January 1804, in the city of Gonaïves. He was crowned Jacques, first emperor of Hayti, Empire of Freedom, with Empress Félicité by his side. When Dessalines was assassinated in 1806, another general, Christophe Henry (1767–1820), was elected president, then in 1811 proclaimed King Henry I with Queen Marie-Louise of Hayti.

One key to success was for the rebels to enter all armies present on the island – French, Spanish, British – to gain knowledge of the enemy's fighting skills, then integrate them with our own. As a result, even though a large French force was sent by Napoleon to restore French rule and force the Ayitians back into slavery, in March 1802 after fierce fighting over three weeks at Crête-à-Pierrot, a mere 1,000 Ayitian soldiers held their own and inflicted heavy losses on the more than 12,000 troops of the French army. In May the following year, the high command of the Ayitian army held a congress at Arcahaie to sketch out the creation of the nation and choose the colours of its black and red flag. Six months later, on 18 November 1803, a final battle took place at Vertières: the Ayitians drove back the might of France and the French general Donatien Rochambeau surrendered to Dessalines, who provided boats, weapons and munitions to the vanquished French army so that they might find their way back to France. Only one request was made to them: 'Tell your government to never set foot on this island again!'

The revolution not only established a free and independent Hayti (the empire and the kingdom) but contributed to the liberation struggle across Latin America. In 1806, Francisco de Miranda (1750–1816), revolutionary from Venezuela, arrived and received help from Dessalines to carry out his liberation war against Spain. In 1816, Simón Bolívar (1783–1830) – liberator of Venezuela, Colombia, Ecuador, Peru, Panama and Bolivia – came to the republic of Hayti when wounded, and was helped; likewise he received support from President Pétion, including Haytian soldiers who fought with him in Venezuela.

Not a single country recognized Hayti's independence for decades after it was a reality, and the US president Thomas Jefferson tried hard to break Hayti's economy. The biggest blow came from the Vatican, which imposed a concordat in 1860 as a condition to recognizing independence; its Article 12 gave the church a monopoly of the educational system. So how did Hayti manage to achieve all this, even while the world turned its back on her and continually attacked her? The invisible revolution had already taken place when Ayitians maintained their African soul, while forging their Ayitian hearts and minds. Whether dressed in colonial uniform, slave garb or naked, they were able to establish goals in their collective best interests. In that position, they mustered the necessary strength and determination. As they worked to become themselves more each day, they registered the process in songs, illustrations, prayers and occasionally texts on paper.

Even today, our children all grow up singing this song:

Zonbi mannmannan, wi wa; you must catch the chicken, yes king; it ran away, yes king; catch it on this side, yes king; catch it on the other side, yes king; the queen must have it, yes king; to make a potage, yes king. What sort of potage? Chicken doudou potage, king.

As a researcher, I came to understand that the chicken refers to us in captivity and the last line is our answer to the slavers: 'If the queen had to have this chicken, it could only be its shit, because we are not catching today's runaway.'

And when the French elaborated the Code Noir (1685) to define the conditions of slavery, they dehumanized the children of Africa within their colonies and declared that we were no more than furniture. In response, we began to sing this song:

Nou tout se Zanj o, Zanj anba a se mwen. We are all angels, the Angel below is me (2), Danbala Wedo, Ayida Wedo, we're all angels, the Angel below is us.

This meant that, whatever slavers declared on paper, within our souls we perceived ourselves as angels on Earth, awaiting the right moment to make our reality evident in the material world.

The primary cause of revolutions lies in the fact that freedom is the natural state of all life forms, including human beings. Whenever a life form finds itself in a situation that imposes a level of constraint rejected by its nature, it will move into a revolutionary functioning mode.

In the case of Ayiti/Hayti, some unique secondary causes made a successful revolution possible. Most important was the way in which the enslaved people built their own knowledge and understanding of the world. The Africans had acquired a high level of knowledge of the environment of Ayiti, and integrated it into their own perception. They built some vital skills that proved invaluable during the conflict, such as combat tactics and strategies that had been learned in Dahomey and Ayiti, tactics in which military women were trained; botanical healing knowledge from the homeland and competence in reading the night sky – as well as transmission of knowledge from the indigenous Arawak peoples to the Africans, and from Africans from the continent to those born on the island and vice versa. Our worldview was formulated in the belief system called Vodou, and we created our own language, known as Creole.

Finally, the revolution was caused by the ultimate depths to which slavers and colonists took their ferocious behaviour, all in the name of God. Yet their arrogance caused them to underestimate the 'thing' that they had engendered; a thing has no knowledge, no tactics, no plans.

Despite the admiration I have for the accomplishments of great men such as Louverture and Dessalines, I cannot limit our ourstory to their accomplishments. I prefer to bring our unsung sheroes to the forefront, who are ignored in most books written with the traditional colonial narrative.

One example is Victoria Montou or 'Aunt Tòya' (1735–1805), who was born in Africa and fought as an officer in the female army of Dahomey before being captured and sold into slavery. She rescued an orphaned baby and brought him up, passing on the knowledge she had brought with her from Africa; as Jean-Jacques Dessalines, he eventually brought the revolution to fruition. She fought with him, creating her own all-male troop and commanding them victoriously in many battles. Her life story illustrates the existence of well-organized nations in Africa prior to the invasion by Eurochristians, and demonstrates that educated Africans could maintain and transmit some of their knowledge even in the worst situations. It exemplifies her beliefs and practices on the continent, as well as her ability to trust in the knowledge she had to overcome adversity and create new situations. She made a plan and worked hard at it over thirty years, until it materialized against all odds. Aunt Tòya was buried on 12 June 1805 in the imperial cemetery in Hayti's new capital, Dessalines.

The memory of Kasikess Anakaona teaches us that, even while facing death as she did in 1503, true leaders must pass on objectives as well as courage and determination to the next generation; the life of Aunt Tòya shows that patience and long-term vision, strategy and planning are vital while educating the next generation; and the story of Marie Sainte Dédée Bazile (d. 1816), who became provisioner to Dessalines' army and who rescued and buried his body after his assassination, teaches us the respect due to the corpses of our dead and that it is sometimes necessary to put one's own life in danger to ensure proper burial of a freedom fighter. The biography of Empress Félicité (1758–1958) – wife of Jean-Jacques Dessalines, who nurtured his many children as well as those she adopted, ministered to the wounded while battles raged around her and urged kindness to people of all colours, including French prisoners – elucidates in bold letters: courage, patience, humility, individual self-sacrifice, protection of the weak and young, sharing of wealth, and to always interact with kindness. Each female and male ancestor has given us different expressions of the principle of empowerment.

Haiti today is a country where people from around the world meddle in every aspect of national life. This is the result of the schooling system imposed by the Eurochristian church. Having ingurgitated a 'his story' written from the point of view of the enemy has diminished our reflecting capacities and created distance between us and our inner selves. It has stopped us questioning and reflecting for ourselves; instead we place value on pleasing others. This school legacy has re-established a colonial and religious mode of operation, based on fear.

But the legacy of the Hayti created in 1804, which took a totally different road, is still alive. However, it is rarely available in books and articles. This Hayti created a constitution that made the imperial crown elective; it defined citizenship as a quality to be acquired, and its people as good children, good parents, good spouses and great soldiers! It also established agriculture as the noblest of all professions.

The term 'Ayitian' refers not just to the people who first occupied this island, but to our nature, that which is engraved in our inner self; in contrast, 'Haitian' expresses attitudes that have been created by the injustices of recent centuries. Ayitians are fundamentally nature lovers and freedom fighters; we fight to exist, to find new ways of doing and inventing. Ayitians don't believe anything is 'impossible' – but 'Haitians' do. Some of us inherit and function with a bit of each. When this happens unconsciously, it creates unrest within that person or in her/his community.

The population of Haiti was decapitated by UN raiding parties in the 1960s, who carried away to work in Africa, Canada and other places a large percentage of Haitian intellectuals, even though the number of educated people was already insufficient for the country's own needs. In the 1980s, an organized programme of boat-people caused us to lose a large portion of our farmers, artisans, electricians and plumbers to US shores. The population continues to haemorrhage – but our legacy of resilience, and of continually finding new ways to resist, keeps Haitians afloat.

Having suffered several occupations and been invaded by practically every religion in this world since the earthquake of 2010, our society is finding many unwanted changes imposed on our value system. Our children, exposed to enemies' positions via the media, tend to lose self-esteem and adopt foreign perceptions of themselves and their society.

In conclusion, thank goodness for our triple Ayitian/Haytian/Haitian legacy. It is rich and diverse. It springs from a cosmic worldview where the astral bodies, animals, vegetables and humans form one family. It gave birth to a most complex ourstory exposed everywhere, in so many forms, while remaining a mystery to most. When, eventually, decision-makers will become conscious of the weakness and the strength in each of us, and set to work making laws to blend them in the right degree while pursuing an aggressive development of the knowledge of self, this process will bring the Ayitian to power again.

Toussaint Louverture

Toussaint Louverture (1743–1803), one of the leaders of the early phase of the Hayti Revolution, was the son of an educated man. He was freed from slavery in 1776, and became involved in the rising against the French in 1791. He trained his own army (his soldiers included Jean-Jacques Dessalines and Henry Christophe), and in 1793 joined the Spanish in fighting against the French. The following year he changed to the French side, arguing that the French National Convention had freed all slaves, and helped in the final defeat of the Spanish forces. He was appointed governor-general of Saint-Domingue in 1796, ending slavery there; in 1801, he also took over Santo Domingo and freed the slaves. In 1802, Napoleon Bonaparte sent a French force to Saint-Domingue; Louverture was tricked, captured and sent to France, where he died in a mountain-top prison.

Jean-Jacques Dessalines

Jean-Jacques Dessalines (1758–1806) may have been born in West Africa and taken to Saint-Domingue as a child. He joined the 1791 rebellion against the French and fought with Toussaint Louverture, leading the Haytian forces at Crête-à-Pierrot in 1802, and at Vertières, 1803. When Napoleon Bonaparte threatened to reintroduce slavery to Saint-Domingue, he led a new revolt and drove the French out of the island. In 1804 he proclaimed the independent state of Hayti with himself as governor-general, and in September 1804 he was crowned Emperor Jacques I. He confiscated the land of whites, and began a campaign of extermination. He was assassinated in 1806.

TIMELINE

1492 Spaniards arrive in Ayiti and establish the colony of Hispaniola

1697 French set up the colony of Saint-Domingue in western Hispaniola

1780s Saint-Domingue peak production of sugar

1791
August Black rising against slavery begins

October Port-au-Prince, capital of Saint-Domingue, is burned

1793
February Toussaint Louverture joins Spain fighting the French in Saint-Domingue

August Slaves liberated in northern Saint-Domingue

September British invade Saint-Domingue

1794
February French National Assembly abolishes slavery

May Louverture changes sides, joining the French forces against Spain

1796 Louverture becomes governor-general

1798 Louverture drives British from Saint-Domingue

1801 Louverture drives Spanish from Santo Domingo, abolishing slavery across Hispaniola

1802
February Napoleonic French army under Leclerc arrives in Saint-Domingue

March Battle of Crête-à-Pierrot; Jean-Jacques Dessalines holds out against much larger French forces

April Louverture and Dessalines agree truce after French promise not to reintroduce slavery

May	Napoleon issues decree reinstating slavery
June	Louverture is captured and deported to France, where he is imprisoned

1803
March	Louverture dies in prison
November	Dessalines finally defeats French at Vertières

1804
January	Independent state of Hayti is proclaimed
March–April	Governor-general Dessalines massacres 4,000 French colonists
October	Dessalines declares himself Emperor Jacques I

1806
October	Dessalines is assassinated

1809 Spain recaptures Santo Domingo

1811 Henry Christophe becomes King Henry I

1825 French recognize Hayti on payment of indemnities for lost property rights

THE YEAR OF REVOLUTIONS: 1848

Axel Körner

The year 1848 saw revolutionaries take to the streets in unprecedented fashion. Barricades sprang up in cities across Europe in the fight against authoritarian, repressive monarchies and empires and in favour of, variously, national rights, constitutional rights, workers' rights, freedom of the press, democracy. Almost every European country was affected. In France, the July monarchy of Louis-Philippe was overthrown and a republic reinstated with universal manhood suffrage; in Austria, Metternich was forced to resign and the Emperor announced a constitution; in Hungary, the revolutionaries won autonomy from Austrian rule. Northern Italy saw uprisings against Austrian rule, while republics were established in Rome, Venice and Tuscany; in the German lands, a National Assembly met in Frankfurt and called for a pan-German constitutional empire with the King of Prussia at its head; in London, Karl Marx and Friedrich Engels published their *Communist Manifesto*, which urged the workers of the world to arise and throw off their chains.

While events in France undoubtedly inspired action elsewhere, there was no single revolutionary impulse, no coordination, no unified set of aims. While many of those on the barricades were workers or unemployed, the leaders were often middle-class liberals, intellectuals, artists, journalists and teachers with little political or military experience, and their disunity proved their downfall. In one centre after another, the established authorities – sometimes calling on help from outside their own borders – used brute force to reassert control and to disperse the revolutionaries. In France, Louis-Napoleon, nephew of the great Bonaparte, got elected president, then seized absolute power in a bloody coup in 1851. The new Austrian constitution was soon withdrawn, though civil rights and the abolishment of feudalism remained in place, while the Austrian army fought back in Italy and the Russians helped crush the revolution in Hungary. In the German lands, the Prussian king rejected the crown. In London, where the huge Chartist movement had demanded universal suffrage, the establishment sat tight and no concessions were made.

The revolutions of 1848 were, therefore, in the short term, failures. Nevertheless, they demonstrated the potential for constitutionalism and stimulated new forms of political organization that would bear fruit in various ways over succeeding decades. Most importantly for Europe's history, they gave powerful voice to the demands for new states based not on dynastic rationales but on those of nationalities. These demands continued to be heard through the succeeding decades and led ultimately to the creation of many new nation states, though they frequently contained tensions of their own that were rarely resolved or even addressed, and were to prove fateful in the 20th century.   PF

The 'Revolution of 1848' was a European, even a global, event. 'All of Europe is in flames', proclaimed a Hungarian pamphlet in April of that year. What had started on the streets of Palermo in January quickly assumed a much wider and more dramatic dimension when, in February, revolutionaries in Paris caused the collapse of Louis Philippe's 'July monarchy' (1830–48). Within a month, revolution broke out in Habsburg Vienna and Prussian Berlin, and soon in the majority of the German-speaking lands – spreading to the principal centres of the Habsburg monarchy, across its border into Russian and Ottoman territory, with repercussions all over the continent, including Scandinavia and the Iberian peninsula as well as the colonies of most European powers. Historians have tended to describe the revolutions as a 'springtime of peoples', as an awakening of national sentiment, usually associated with the idea of establishing modern nation states. Since the late Enlightenment and the French Revolution of 1789, the concept of the nation had increasingly mesmerized first the educated elites, and then growing sections of the wider population.

Over the following century and a half, historians played a decisive role in shaping the memories of the year, the staging of public commemorations, the hagiography of its martyrs and the catalogue of the revolutions' supposed achievements. Some of these historians themselves took part in the uprisings, or occupied political roles in the regimes that succeeded them; for instance, Alexis de Tocqueville (1805–59), who during the second republic supported the Party of Order and later published his memoirs of 1848, or František Ladislav Rieger (1818–1903), an influential leader of the Czech national movement. As a consequence of this intersection between the revolutionary past and later political developments, some events that at the time were widely perceived as European and transnational in scope and content subsequently became part of national narratives, often serving the teleological purpose of justifying the creation of nation states. Most of these nation states were modern creations that shared little with Europe's traditional territorial and dynastic order. Narratives that presented 1848 as a series of 'national revolutions' helped the leaders of the national movements to justify their own political aims and communicate their ideological principles to wider sections of the population, thus turning them into proud members of national communities. A different narrative, but one constructed in much the same manner, made the revolutions' social dimension inevitably lead to the formation of an international labour movement and a natural step in the development of socialism, even though many different ideological sources actually motivated the fighters on the barricades in 1848. Both narratives stand for teleological distortions of historical time that tell us more about the present than about the past.

Most accounts of the 1848 revolutions start in Paris, but the complex relationship of nationalism and transnationalism can be better seen on the periphery – such as in Transylvania. Now part of Romania, it was at the time an independent duchy within the lands of the Hungarian crown, part of the Habsburg Empire. Since the Middle Ages Transylvania had been populated by Romanians, various groups of German and Magyar speakers, Roma and trading communities of different national backgrounds originally from the Ottoman Empire, all divided into a plethora of religious denominations, some of them interethnic. In March 1848, a meeting of Transylvania's so-called 'Saxon Nation' – the representative body of the duchy's German speakers – declared that 'Europe's present situation, and the particular circumstances and conditions of the Austrian monarchy, oblige every people and nation within these glorious lands to take measures to protect our fatherland's territory, its constitution, public safety, individual rights and property.' Yet the Saxon delegates made no reference to an emerging German nation state, abstained from associations with political events in Vienna or Berlin and praised their commonwealth of different peoples. Their concern was not revolution, but the maintenance of public safety and the equilibrium between their duchy's national communities within the larger context of a multinational empire. Behind their fears were the attempts of revolutionary Hungarians – men such as Lajos Kossuth (1802–94), who was leading a national rising in Budapest – to transform their ancient homeland into a Hungarian nation state dominated by Magyar-speaking elites.

Writing later from exile in Walachia, Joseph Bedeus, historian and Saxon mayor of the Transylvanian capital Sibiu/Hermannstadt, paid homage to the European dimension of these events, as did so many of his contemporaries. The Hungarian revolution had forced him to seek refuge in Ottoman territory. Rejecting the attempts at forging Hungary's different ethnic communities into a Magyar-dominated nation state, Bedeus recognized in the Austrian monarchy the only framework where different nationalities could live together peacefully, enjoying the fruits of economic and political progress. Like Bedeus, the present mayoress of Sibiu also belongs to Romania's German-speaking minority, as does the current president of Romania, himself a former mayor of Sibiu. Their backgrounds are relics of the region's multinational heritage. Yet the 'new world order' created in the wake of the First World War imposed nation states on the formerly multi-ethnic territories of central Europe, which over the following century caused millions of people to be expelled from their homelands, to suffer forced assimilation or simply to be murdered – crimes justified by modern concepts of ethnic and religious homogeneity, and by the illusion of national self-determination.

These tragedies notwithstanding, today's rare relics of the region's multi-ethnic past – the fact that in Sibiu's principal Catholic church, mass is read in Romanian, Hungarian and German, and that signs of Jewish life have reappeared around the synagogue near the city's train station – have implications also for the memories of 1848 in post-socialist Romania. Most of central and eastern Europe celebrate 1848 as a year of national emancipation, in tune with the textbook versions of national historiography and avoiding references to the events' wider European dimension, or to the fears associated with the imposition of nation states within an empire that granted its national and religious minorities protection from forced assimilation. Meanwhile, visitors to the small town of Mediaș, fifty kilometres north of Sibiu, will find a pretty park named after Ferdinand I, the Austrian emperor (r. 1835–48), who in the midst of the revolution promised his peoples a constitution, the end of feudalism and the recognition of their nationality – enough for most of them (though not some of the German and Hungarian nationalists) to dismantle the barricades and celebrate their beloved emperor for his concessions. Visitors to Mediaș may also discover the old (formerly German) school, a beautiful Art Deco building named after Stephan Ludwig Roth (1796–1849). During the revolution, Roth, a local pastor and teacher and pupil of Swiss educational reformer Johann Heinrich Pestalozzi, had fought for the rights of Hungarians, Germans and Romanians to use their respective languages in official interactions within Transylvania,

Hungary and the empire. As a supporter of the empire's multinational concept of state, he opposed the pressures of Hungary's revolutionary government to unite the formerly autonomous region with the emerging Hungarian nation state. In May 1849, Hungarian government officials sentenced him to death, creating one of the region's most famous martyrs of the revolution. Roth's monument, prominently placed in front of the school building carrying his name, commemorates a German fighter for the Romanian language, who stood for a multinational concept of state against the emerging national fanaticism.

Pointing to the transnational dimensions of the revolutions, and to the fears associated with the new nation states in parts of central Europe, does not mean denying the crucial role played by national aspirations during the uprisings. Instead, it is the changing meaning of nationalism that is sometimes distorted in the commemoration of the revolutions. In 1848, national demands did not necessarily stand for the formation of independent unitary nation states as they developed later in the 19th and 20th centuries. The kingdom of Bohemia offers a good example. Many German speakers in Bohemia aimed for a union of their crown land with the emerging German nation state, and expected Czechs to assimilate themselves. Yet most leaders of Bohemia's Czech national movement were aware that they lacked the basis for forming an independent Czech nation state: that the kingdom's German speakers, as well as its Moravian and Silesian lands, would oppose the idea of a union with a future Czech nation state; and that any such state would be sandwiched between the much bigger powers of Germany, Austria and Hungary. Since the 18th century, the Czech revival had aimed not to end Habsburg rule in Bohemia, but to affirm the kingdom's binational character and its particular status among the Austrian lands. This is why, in 1848, the historian and widely respected leader of the Czech national movement František Palacký (1798–1876) saw Bohemia's political future as lying within the reformed framework of Austria's multinational empire: 'If it didn't already exist', this empire had to be created 'in the interest of Europe and humanity'. For Palacký, as for the leaders of many of the region's other Slavonic-speaking minorities, the idea of a multinational empire that grants political and cultural rights to its different national and religious minorities represented a powerful alternative to a Europe of emerging nation states.

The situation in Austria's Italian provinces – Lombardy and Venetia – was slightly different, due to the imagined bonds that linked them to the other Italian states; but even here, some of the revolution's protagonists strongly resented the idea that their liberation from Austrian rule would result in annexation by Piedmont-Sardinia – a kingdom that had little in common with the political traditions of Italy's medieval city republics or the Habsburgs' enlightened rule in Tuscany, let alone the Bourbons' historical legacies in the Southern Kingdom. Instead, what had dominated political debates prior to the revolution was the concept, propagated by Vincenzo Gioberti (1801–52), of a confederation of Italy's existing states under the presidency of the Pope. However, the Young Italy revolutionary Giuseppe Mazzini (1805–72) was a fervent opponent of federalism, and his democratic republicanism, seeking a unitary republic covering the entire peninsula, reminded many Italians of the forced centralization that Napoleon had imposed. The military genius of Giuseppe Garibaldi (1807–82), who in 1848 defended the Roman Republic, would have a prominent role a decade later during the process of Italy's unification. Yet the European revolutions had started in the Sicilian capital Palermo: here again the revolutionaries' motivation was not the creation of an Italian nation state, but independence from Neapolitan rule, in the tradition of the island's long history as a separate European power and of the constitution they had obtained under British protection during the Napoleonic wars.

When the histories of these revolutions were later rewritten in nationalist terms, retrospective myth often played an important role. Italy offers a fascinating example of how subsequent events impacted on historical memories. The composer Giuseppe Verdi (1813–1901) has often been presented as the bard of Italy's movement for unification. A central element in this narrative was the idea that Italy's national revolution had started at the opera house, and that Italians had a particular ability to interpret music in political terms. Thus the ancient Hebrews singing about their lost homeland in Verdi's opera *Nabucco* (1842) has often been read as a reference to Italians' own national feelings under Austrian oppression, to the point that the opera's supposedly patriotic reception was seen as having anticipated Milan's revolution of 1848. Despite the story's romantic appeal, there is no evidence that when the opera was premiered at Milan's Teatro alla Scala the audience or critics responded to any of these potentially national references. On the contrary, the Austrians liked the opera so much that they continued staging it throughout their Italian possessions and abroad, including productions in the immediate aftermath of the revolution. During those years Verdi became the new emperor's favourite composer, promoted throughout the monarchy, like Rossini and Donizetti before him. It was only a decade after the revolution, around the years of Italy's unification, that *Nabucco* was suddenly read as a catalyst of Italy's awakening national sentiments; it was an idea promoted by Verdi himself, who had started to openly support the national movement. Ever since, *Nabucco*'s story was told as one of bursting patriotic passions, irrespective of its original reception.

When Germany was eventually unified as a consequence of the wars of 1866 and 1870, the Prussian leadership was not keen on the 1848 revolution's contribution to these political achievements – despite the fact that some of Chancellor Bismarck's close followers, such as the journalist and banker Ludwig Bamberger, had been active supporters of the revolution. In 1849, the Prussian king had refused to accept the offer of an imperial crown from the representatives of a National Assembly, held in Frankfurt, that had emerged from the barricades and whose legitimacy he contested. While democrats and the early labour movement, as well as the more progressive sections of the liberals, continued to celebrate the revolution's memory and its martyrs, the early historians of Germany's unification under Prussian leadership, in particular Heinrich von Treitschke (1834–96), ignored the revolution's and the Frankfurt parliament's contributions to the nation's constitutional development. Official attitudes towards the revolution only changed during the years of the Weimar Republic after the First World War, which saw in 1848 an important step towards the country's democratization. It is not therefore surprising that the Nazis forced the revolution's most prominent historian, Veit Valentin (1885–1947), into exile, where he continued to teach German history first at University College London and then in the United States. After 1945, East Germany commemorated 1848 as an important step in the formation of an international labour movement, associated with the publication of the *Communist Manifesto* in February 1848. West Germany was keen to identify positive references to the country's belated democratization, celebrating 1848 as a moment of political participation and constitutional democracy. But what these commemorations often fail to consider, even today, is the fact that the democratic fight for national unification frequently included disturbing elements of anti-Semitism and of chauvinism towards the national minorities a future German nation state would have included – especially Poles and Czechs, who were widely expected to assimilate themselves within the future political nation. Without much concern for Europe's complicated cultural and linguistic configuration, these democratic nationalists expected the Habsburg Empire to be dissolved into a series of independent nation states, similar to the ideas of the Hungarian revolutionaries and explaining their widespread admiration for Lajos Kossuth.

Different social groups and classes developed their own ways of relating to the events of 1848, depending on specific memories or on the ideological profile of the political movements that represented their interests in the revolutions' aftermath. While in the German-speaking lands, Italy and most of central and eastern Europe the national question determined much of the revolutions' programmes and their subsequent legacies, this was not the case in France, which did not have a national question in 1848 – or was affected by it only indirectly through its colonial possessions, where the revolution had encouraged slaves to rise against their oppressors, as had happened in the British, Dutch and Danish colonies. In the United States it was this connection with the issue of slavery that prompted questions over the revolutions' initial endorsement. Because France did not have to be unified as a nation state, the events of 1848 were mostly remembered in social terms, as a battle over workers' rights and over the legacy of 1789. This particular context posed the question of whether the French nation was best represented by a republican or by a monarchical–imperial form of state. When in 1852 the Second Republic's president, Louis-Napoleon Bonaparte, undertook a coup d'état and established the Second Empire, France's greatest contemporary writer Victor Hugo (1802–85) derided him as *Napoléon le petit* – a minuscule parody of his uncle, who once stood for France's grandeur in the world. For Karl Marx and Friedrich Engels, this coup d'état provided empirical evidence to explain why the predictions made in the *Communist Manifesto* had been premature. The events between 1848 and 1852, followed by the Paris Commune of 1871, delivered the script of the labour movement's political future, a recipe for a historical process that millions of their followers treated as the inevitable course of modern times.

Despite the pressures of the social and of the national question in 1848, the events were also driven by constitutional demands and the recognition of basic political and civic rights. This last point also helps to relate the continental revolutions to the last wave of Chartism in Britain when, fearing a revolution by a huge popular groundswell in favour of universal suffrage, Queen Victoria was evacuated to the Isle of Wight. While there is a strong tradition that sees Chartism primarily within a context of British reformist policies, which successfully prevented any revolutions, contemporaries were fully aware of the ideological and political connections between Chartism and the continental revolutions, just as they related the Irish question and the famine of 1845–9 to the uprisings on the continent.

Looking back at 1848–9, it seems easy to make the argument for the failure of the revolutions. However, the ideas that informed these events forever changed the agenda of modern politics, in Europe and on a global scale. In his 1901 novel *Buddenbrooks*, Thomas Mann (1875–1955) described how in 1848 the dignitaries of the city of Lübeck observed the rather timorous rebellion outside City Hall. The novel tells the story of a family's decline over four generations, standing for a world that was no more, where by the end of the century everything that once defined social status, cultural values and political practice had collapsed. Although partly driven by nostalgia, within this perspective 1848 also stands for the beginning of political modernity. As the great French historian Maurice Agulhon claimed, 1848 worked as an apprenticeship for modern republicanism; and where monarchism continued to retain its appeal, the experience served to familiarize growing sections of the population with the ideas of political representation and popular sovereignty. This is the principal legacy of 1848, which is still shared across national boundaries and ideological divides.

Lajos Kossuth

Lajos Kossuth (1802–94), Hungarian reformer and national leader, was born into an impoverished noble family. He became a political journalist with a powerful passion for liberty and justice of the Magyars, and especially for national freedom based on Magyar dominance. In 1847 he was elected to the Diet, and became leader of the nationalist opposition. In March 1848, inspired by news of events in Paris and Vienna, he dictated a revolutionary programme that was accepted by the King, who also reigned as emperor over the Habsburg monarchy as a whole. He served as minister of finance, and in July called for an army to be raised to defend Hungary, and also to assist revolutionaries in Italy. By late summer he was virtual dictator of Hungary, until August 1849 when he resigned and went to Turkey. In 1851 he had a triumphant tour of Britain and the United States, then settled in London, where he continued to work against the Austrian Empire. He opposed the creation of the Dual Monarchy of Austria-Hungary in 1867, and remained a national hero in Hungary to his death and beyond.

Giuseppe Mazzini

Giuseppe Mazzini (1805–72), an Italian revolutionary born in Genoa, trained as a lawyer. Arrested and exiled for his involvement with the Carbonari secret society in 1830, he went to France, where he campaigned for constitutional reform in the kingdom of Piedmont and the expulsion of the Austrians from Italy. In 1831 he founded the Young Italy revolutionary republican movement to unite the peninsula's states. Moving to London in 1837, he built up contacts among other Italian exiles and British liberals, and returned to Italy in 1848 to support the Milanese in their revolution against Austria. His opposition to Lombard unification with monarchical Piedmont led him to leave and to join the irregular army of nationalist Giuseppe Garibaldi. He was effective head of government in the short-lived Roman Republic in 1849, but after its defeat by the French he returned to London. He continued to support revolutionaries in Italy, and was barely involved in the creation of the Kingdom of Italy in 1860.

TIMELINE

1848

18 January   Uprising in Palermo to demand independent government for Sicily

February   Karl Marx publishes the *Communist Manifesto*

24 February   Revolution in France; Louis-Philippe abdicates; French Second Republic is created

March   Uprisings in German states (including Prussia, Palatinate, Baden, Saxony, Rhinelands, Bavaria)

March   Revolution in Milan; demonstrations in Copenhagen demanding a new constitution; Schleswig-Holstein sets up a new provisional autonomous government

March   Charles Albert, king of Piedmont-Sardinia, declares war on Austria and invades Lombardy; Austrian army driven out of Milan

13 March   Demonstrations and street fighting begin in Vienna

April   Austrian emperor recognizes Hungarian government, dismisses Metternich and issues a constitution; promises constituent assembly in Bohemia

April   Revolutions in the Habsburg Empire spread to Budapest and Prague

April   Hungarian Diet, led by Kossuth, agrees sweeping reforms and effective autonomy for Kingdom of Hungary

8 April   Constitutional reforms are promised in Prussia

10 April   Massive Chartist demonstration for universal male suffrage in London

May   Demonstrations in Vienna lead to more concessions from the Emperor; Slav congress in Prague

18 May   Frankfurt Assembly meets to write a constitution and later proposes the unification of Germany

June	Uprisings of workers in Paris are brutally crushed by the authorities
July	Austria: Convocation of Imperial Assembly for German and Slavonic crown lands; aim to write constitution
August	Austria regains Lombardy and Venetia; Venice declares independent republic
29 September	Hungarian revolutionaries defeat Austrian army
October	Prussia becomes a constitutional monarchy and creates Prussian Assembly
2 December	Austrian emperor Ferdinand I abdicates in favour of Franz Joseph I; invasion of Hungary
December	Louis Napoleon wins presidential election in France

1849

February	Rome declares Republic; revolutionary government in Tuscany
March	Austrian Imperial Assembly dissolved; Emperor grants constitution
April	Delegates of Frankfurt Assembly decide against unification including Austria; Prussian king rejects its offer of German crown
April	French troops defeat Roman Republic and reinstall Papacy; Austria reinstalls Grand Duke of Tuscany
June	German National Assembly finally dispersed
August	Kossuth resigns as Russians assist Austrians to regain control in Hungary; Republic of Venice capitulates

JAPAN: THE MEIJI RESTORATION, 1868

Shin Kawashima

Of all the revolutions in this volume, Japan's so-called Meiji Restoration perhaps fits least well the revolutionary stereotype of the overthrow of a corrupt regime by direct action from the people, or a vanguard party of radicals to enact social reforms. The trigger for the revolution was the forcible arrival of Westerners after a US squadron sailed to Edo in 1853, giving rise to a conviction among Japanese nationalists that the existing military government of the shogun was failing in its duty to protect the country. Following a relatively bloodless civil war within the large and semi-feudal samurai class, the young Meiji Emperor, invisible in the palace in Edo and representative of an office long disempowered, was able formally to restore the long-lost authority of his office by overthrowing the 260-year dominance of the shogun.

Nevertheless, this was in no way a conservative event in the way that may be inferred from the term 'restoration'. While the shogunate was decisively ended, the Emperor did not resume actual power. Instead he remained a relative figurehead, with power transferred to the hands of the modernizing group of daimyo (lords).

But this began the truly revolutionary process of modernizing Japanese society, politics and the economy to meet the challenge of Western imperialism while retaining traditional Japanese values. While the period conventionally described as

the Meiji Restoration continued until the death of the Emperor
in 1912, its significance resonated throughout the 20th century
and beyond as Japan became a world military power and,
after the Second World War, an economic powerhouse as well.

PF

In 1867, the shogunate of the Tokugawa, the military family that
had effectively ruled Japan from its base in Edo since 1603 and
had reduced the office of the emperor to one of political insig-
nificance in Kyoto, was challenged by a number of its regional lords
(daimyo). On 19 November, the instigators of the revolt – young
samurai from domains distant from the main centres of power, who
had spent several years carefully building their alliance – forced the
shogun to resign. Two months later, on 3 January 1868, one of them,
Saigo Takamori (1828–77), led a coup whereby the fifteen-year-old
Meiji Emperor, who had formally occupied the throne for eleven
months, was restored to power as the new ruler of Japan, while Saigo
neutralized any outstanding threat from forces still loyal to the
Tokugawa.

The leaders of this 'Meiji Restoration' – who now effectively
controlled the country – had been distressed by Japan's lack of power
in the face of the 'opening up' by Western forces, notably those of the
United States, which had first arrived in 1853. Adopting the slogan
'Revere the emperor, expel the barbarians', they sought to rebuild a
Japanese state capable of resisting the West, and envisaged a thorough
administrative, economic and social reform to end the feudal system
of hereditary regional lordships. Over the coming decades they succeeded remarkably effectively, despite a brief conflict between the
imperial forces and Saigo himself, who had been driven to rebel over
restrictions to the traditional privileges of the samurai to bear arms
in a state that was creating a conscript army.

By the end of the Meiji Emperor's reign in 1912, however, the
Restoration had transformed Japanese society, introducing Western

technology, universal education and a bicameral constitution. It had made Japan into the predominant military power of East Asia.

The year 2018 was the 150th anniversary of the Meiji Restoration. On its centenary in 1968, domestic Japanese perceptions of the event were mostly negative, with many observers seeing it as the event that ushered in Japan's age of imperialist invasion of Korea and other countries of East Asia – an age that ended with defeat in 1945. By 2018, some voices could be heard, while not necessarily representative of Japanese society as a whole, celebrating the event for the first time. Such shifts suggest that 'Japanese modernity', itself a product of the Meiji Restoration and the values and national ambitions to which it gave rise, are on the verge of transition.

As the event that began Japan's progression to the ranks of the Great Powers, 1868 was a significant turning point in world history. The same is true now, at a time when Japan faces significant challenges in the contemporary world. Can the country effect necessary change on a scale analogous to that of the Meiji Restoration? This is the key issue facing contemporary Japan.

The 18th century had been a time of prosperity for Asia. However, in the late 18th to early 19th centuries, developmental limitations brought an end to this prosperity, and many Asian countries made various efforts to enact reform. Meanwhile, in Europe and North America, the Industrial Revolution brought with it the invention of the steam engine and the 19th century saw steamships and other technologies. Major upheavals also took place in Europe at both the state and societal levels: new national states emerged from civil revolution, and new military technologies arose as a result of the Napoleonic wars.

The European powers, seeking to expand their trading power, began to make advances upon Asia in the mid-18th century. This was the context in which both European powers and America, which had already experienced the transformational power of the industrial and civil revolutions, encountered an Asia that was itself pursuing the path of reform. Yet that encounter – epitomized by the First Opium War (1839–42) between Britain and China – underlined to Asia how much technological progress had been achieved in the West in the previous decades. In the 18th century, the majority of the world's wealth was found in the populous states of China and India. Now, however, wealth was increasingly migrating to the Western world. This shift demonstrated that, irrespective of population ratios, wealth accumulated in countries that possessed advanced technologies and those that had achieved economic, political and military ascendancy. This was the start of the age of modernity.

In the latter half of the 19th century, Japan, previously untouched by this Western expansion and a mere onlooker to the gradual dwindling of wealth in China and India, began making strident efforts to keep pace with the West. The Meiji Restoration embodied these efforts for technological and societal change. It constituted both the beginning of Japan's modernization and its own age of prosperity.

What factors precipitated the Meiji Restoration? One essential characteristic was that it constituted not a class revolution, but rather an internal reform of the samurai class. *Seppuku* (ritual suicide by disembowelment) is often a key focal point of discussions on the samurai class in the Edo period. Mitani Hiroshi, an expert on the Meiji Restoration, refers to *seppuku* in the context of the Restoration as 'social suicide by samurai' – by which he means that the Meiji Restoration was not the kind of revolution in which the lower echelons of society rebelled against the upper echelons; rather, it was a process in which the samurai class actively negated their own social privilege. The Restoration, led predominantly by lower-ranking samurai, caused the breakdown of the feudal shogunate system and the eradication of samurai stipends, and brought about a society predicated on universal equality.

When it comes to describing the Meiji Restoration, then, 'revolution' is perhaps not the most apt of terms. Very few fatalities occurred as a result of it. Furthermore, its ideological underpinnings varied greatly among its proponents. Some argued for the exclusion of foreigners from Japan, while others preferred the opening of the country. Some sought the restoration of imperial rule, while others merely favoured the toppling of the shogunate. These ideas also underwent cross-pollination.

Consequently, the intricate subtleties of the Meiji Restoration cannot be reduced to a simple polarity of conservatives (the Tokugawa shogunate) versus reformists (the Satsuma, Choshu, Tosa and Hizen domains). According to Mitani, the Restoration took place against the backdrop of the cross-pollination of these varying ideologies, as the result of a chain of events that arose according to different circumstances at different moments in time. As such, it ought not to be perceived as a single narrative carved out by a specific historical agent, nor as the realization of targets espoused by a specific social class. Mitani also considers that the chain of events that led to its realization was the product of contemporaneous public debate, and not a result of some lofty decision by a specific person or group. Thus this series of chain reactions led not only to the 'social suicide of the samurai class' but also to the 'restoration of imperial rule'. In other words, while seemingly paradoxical, 'renewal' was generated through the 'revival of antiquity'.

However, what was important was that a consensus existed among the samurai (and likely among shogunal retainers, too): a consensus that recognized the need for an overhaul of the country, and saw the Tokugawa shogunate as incapable of instigating the necessary changes that the country so urgently required. Three key factors precipitated the emergence of this consensus. First, the economy struggled to achieve further growth after the Japanese population had reached thirty million in the 18th century; second, more and more Western ships had begun to ply the seas surrounding the country (particularly in the aftermath of the arrival at Edo of US Commodore Matthew Perry with his 'black ships' in 1853); and thirdly, Qing China had suffered defeat at the hands of the British in the First Opium War. Among the samurai class at least, these factors engendered a shared sense of impending crisis and caused many to ask how Japan's survival could be ensured.

For international society, the Meiji Restoration was not just an indication of Japanese internal reform; it was also a sign that Japan had embarked upon the path of 'modernization'. The Meiji government enacted change across the board: it repositioned Japan as a sovereign state; enacted direct rule over the entirety of the country; pursued the revision of unequal treaties signed with the United States and other Western powers; sought the enrichment of the state; strengthened its military capacity; and supported domestic industry. As a modern state, it also began to seek natural resources and markets abroad. For this reason, people sometimes perceive the Meiji Restoration as the starting point for Japan's imperial invasions of Asia. Within Japan, however, the Meiji Restoration itself is no longer seen as the precipitating cause for the country's imperialist turn. Rather, it is Japan's political diplomacy in the post-Restoration era – its decision to attain the ranks of the Great Powers by challenging other powers such as China and Russia – which is seen as the primary culpable factor.

The Meiji Restoration was highly lauded within East Asia, albeit retrospectively. In the 20th century, modernizing Chinese nationalist leader Chiang Kai-shek (1887–1975) and other leaders in neighbouring countries praised the Restoration for its success in realigning Japan with imperatives presented by world history and, furthermore, for its home-grown nature. Respect for the 'samurai way' and its ability to enact self-reform was implicit in such appraisals. However, contemporary onlookers, at least until the 1880s, were not so quick with their praise. In the 1870s, rebellions spearheaded by discontented samurai continued to plague the Meiji government, and state coffers suffered greatly from the costs involved in their suppression. Indeed, it was not until Prime Minister Matsukata Masayoshi (1835–1924) introduced austerity measures in the 1880s that the country was finally able to alleviate fears about its future. The first positive appraisals of the Meiji Restoration from Japan's neighbours thus did not begin to appear until after Japan's victories over China and Russia in the first decade of the 20th century.

Until the 1970s, the world's developed countries (if we exclude the Eastern Bloc) consisted only of the United States, western Europe and Japan. The Meiji Restoration was widely perceived as the origin of Japan's 'success'. It was often compared with the Tongzhi Restoration (1860–74) and Self-Strengthening Movement (1861–5) that took place in Qing China, but which failed to modernize sufficiently robustly for the Qing to resist the incursions of the West. Historical narratives, too, questioned the underlying reasons why Japan managed in the mid-19th century to adapt successfully to the imperatives of Western modernity, while other Asian countries did not.

On the centenary of the Meiji Restoration in 1968, Japan, apparently miraculously, managed to jump to second place in the world GNP ranking. While the Meiji Restoration was at the time perceived as the origin of Japan's success story, questions about its legacy had also begun to emerge; in particular, whether it also ought to be seen as the catalyst for Japan's turn towards militarism. While the Restoration and Japan's participation in war were not causally related, such questions occupied the minds of Japanese people in 1968. At the time, Japanese public opinion was led by a generation who had experienced the tribulations of war, and this was undoubtedly a factor engendering such a climate.

Since then, however, appraisals of the Meiji Restoration have undergone a dramatic shift, with two trends becoming particularly palpable. The first no longer sees the Meiji Restoration in terms of a success story. The principal reason for this is that China has now outranked Japan as a world economic power, and many other countries are enjoying a new era of prosperity. This view thus posits that Japan's Meiji Restoration in the mid-19th century can now no longer be regarded as a singular success story, and that Qing China, whose response to the challenges of modernity had hitherto been seen as relatively sluggish, can no longer be painted purely in terms of failure.

The second trend is that, since Japan's war generation has retired from the political frontline and the majority of the serving cabinet are of the post-war generation, some nationalists no longer feel hesitant about referring to the Meiji Restoration as a success. Prime Minister Shinzo Abe (b. 1954) was initially elected as a Diet member in a constituency that constituted one of the key areas that backed the Meiji Restoration: Choshu (current Yamaguchi prefecture). Prior to the 150th anniversary, his government was particularly proactive in pursuing a commemorative policy for the Restoration's anniversary. This demonstrates that the view that linked the Meiji Restoration to Japan's turn to militarism has increasingly fallen out of favour; Abe's statement on 14 August 2015, the eve of the seventieth anniversary of the end of the Second World War, clearly reflected this shift in perception.

The latter trend underpins the 2018 commemorative events held for the Meiji Restoration's 150th anniversary, but the first trend, which denied the uniqueness of the event, underpins the reason why larger swathes of Japanese society are not celebrating it.

Japan in the 21st century is struggling to set itself clear goals for the future. Neither the ideology of catching up and overtaking the West nor the ideology of reinstating itself as the leading Asian superpower is relevant to the current age. The Meiji Restoration has hitherto defined Japan's identity. On its 150th anniversary, the nation faces the challenge of overcoming this and defining for itself a new identity. In this sense, a new 'restoration' may well be just what the country needs.

Translated by Thomas Barrett

Meiji Emperor

Meiji Emperor (1852–1912), 122nd emperor of Japan, ascended the throne on 30 January 1867 on the death of his father, Komei Emperor. His given name was Mutsuhito, but this was never used after his accession. Like his predecessors since the 17th century, he lived closeted in the royal palace in Kyoto, with all political power in the hands of the shogun, a hereditary office in the possession of the Tokugawa family. The 1867 Restoration happened in the first year of his reign, when he was just fifteen; he is not known to have had any direct involvement. He travelled to Edo (which was renamed Tokyo) for the first time the following year. Although the profound changes in Japan in the following decades bear his name, his personal responsibility – or indeed involvement or enthusiasm – for them is unknown. It is not even clear how much true influence he had on day-to-day decision-making. His contribution was formal; no diaries, letters or accounts of his opinions are known, only a large collection of poetry.

Okubo Toshimichi

Okubo Toshimichi (1830–78) was a samurai of the Satsuma domain, leaders of the revolt against the shogunate. In January 1868 he was declared a leader of the provisional government, responsible for the police and local government, appointing all the new governors and promoting economic development. In 1871 he introduced a land tax reform, and in 1877 he defeated the Satsuma rebellion led by his former colleague Saigo Takamori. In May 1878, he was assassinated by samurai loyal to Saigo.

TIMELINE

1853   US Commodore Matthew Perry sails to Edo, forcing Japan to open for Western trade

1854   Treaty of Kanagawa signed with the United States, despite opposition from Emperor

1863   Bombardment of Kagoshima by Americans, followed by bombardment of Shimonoseki (1864)

1864   Military coup brings reformist leaders to power as advisors to the shogun

1866   Alliance between the Satsuma and Choshu clans to challenge the power of the shogun; Tokugawa Yoshinobu becomes shogun

1867
30 January   Emperor Meiji ascends to the throne

19 November   Tokugawa Yoshinobu resigns

1868
3 January   Emperor formally retakes supreme authority

7 April   Emperor takes Charter Oath, abolishes feudalism and promises democratic reform, and proclaims he will encourage learning from the West

19 September   Emperor formally moves from Kyoto to Edo, which he renames Tokyo

1869   Reformist daimyos of the Tosa, Hizen, Satsuma and Choshu domains 'return their domains to the Emperor'

May   Armies loyal to the shogunate are defeated at Hakodate

1871   Feudal land system abolished; daimyos forced to return their domains to the Emperor, who divides the country into prefectures run by an appointed governor

1872   Introduction of universal education

1873   Introduction of nationwide conscription; samurai are forbidden to
              wear swords, leading to the short-lived Satsuma Rebellion

1885   Cabinet government introduced

1889   New constitution promulgated, completing the Meiji Restoration

1894–5   Japan defeats China in the Sino-Japanese War

1904–5   Japan destroys the Russian navy in the Russo-Japanese War

1910   Japan annexes Korea

THE YOUNG TURK REVOLUTION, 1908

Mehmed Şükrü Hanioğlu

The 400-year-old Ottoman Empire comprised a multitude of ethnicities, few of whom – including the Turks who had founded it – felt a strong affiliation to the empire. By the late 19th century, it had become unable to meet the political and social challenges of the new industrial age. Frustrations over the Sultan's failure to adopt constitutional reforms led to the emergence of secret societies among young intellectuals and army officers known as the Young Turks, many in exile in Paris.

The revolution occurred when military supporters of the Young Turks, alarmed at the evident impotence of the empire in the face of Russian and British military might, staged a quasi-coup in Macedonia and threatened to march on Istanbul; whereupon the Sultan caved in to their demands to restore the constitution. The upshot was a new parliamentary politics that brought the Committee of Union and Progress, the umbrella organization for the Young Turks, to power; but the tensions of the First World War finally destroyed the empire, and the Young Turk vision of a modern multi-ethnic empire was rendered obsolete.

The Young Turk Revolution was therefore – like the Meiji Restoration in Japan – essentially a constitutional one, its primary aim being political reform rather than social justice. Like the Japanese example, the violence involved was minimal, and so too was the popular passion it aroused. That it failed

ABOVE *William III Landing at Brixham, Torbay, 5 November 1688*, Jan Wyck, 1688. (1)

ABOVE *George Washington Crossing the Delaware*, 25–6 December 1776, Emanuel Leutze, 1851. (2)

BELOW The Réveillon riots, Paris, April 1789. Workers at a wallpaper factory protest against lowered wages. (3)

OPPOSITE ABOVE Burning of the Cap-Français (Cap-Haïtien in present-day Haiti), 1791. (4)

OPPOSITE BELOW Battle between civilians and soldiers during protests. Berlin, March 1848. (5)

ABOVE Surrender of the Satsuma rebels
to Japanese imperial forces, 1877. (6)

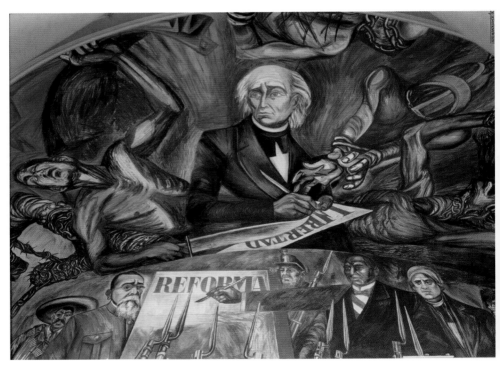

ABOVE Postcard celebrating the Young Turk revolt against the Ottoman Empire, 1908. (7)

BELOW *The Great Mexican Revolutionary Legislation and the Liberty of the Slaves*, José Clemente Orozco, 1948–9. (8)

СМЕРТЬ МИРОВОМУ
ИМПЕРИАЛИЗМУ

ABOVE 'Death to World
Imperialism!' Bolshevik poster,
Russia, 1919. (9)

ABOVE Irish Citizen Army on the roof of Liberty Hall, Dublin, just after the Easter Uprising, 1916. (10)

BELOW Mohandas Gandhi urges Indian troops to unite against the British. Indian Independence League poster, *c.* 1941–4. (11)

to transform the empire in the manner of post-1868 Japan was perhaps less a failure of the revolution and its aims, and more an indication of the structural weaknesses of the Ottoman Empire in an age of burgeoning nationalism.

Curiously, although the long-term political and social legacy of the revolution was strictly limited, it retained a wider cultural impact enshrined in its name: the phrase 'Young Turks' became a common term for confident members of a younger generation seeking to challenge the failing orthodoxies of the past.   PF

On the night of 22 July 1908, the Monastir (modern-day Bitola, in the Republic of North Macedonia) branch of the Ottoman Committee of Progress and Union (CPU) ordered a number of 'national units' hiding in the mountains to storm the town. The CPU was the umbrella organization for the Young Turks: intellectuals, civil servants and army officers who demanded the reinstatement of the short-lived constitutional regime in the Ottoman Empire.

A force of approximately 2,300 men, who had recently mutinied against their imperial officers and been reorganized into the CPU Resen National Battalion, the CPU Ohrid National Regiment, the CPU Monastir unit and two Albanian nationalist bands, entered the town and seized all government buildings. They declared CPU control of Monastir, and announced that anyone who dared to dispute their authority or disobey their orders would be shot on the spot. The CPU Monastir branch, now in control of the telegraph lines, sent messages to local administrators and officials in other European provinces informing them that the Ottoman constitution would be put into effect by force on 23 July 1908, and asking them to prepare accordingly.

The next day, the CPU Monastir branch trumpeted *hürriyet* (freedom) with a twenty-one-gun salute and declared the 1876 constitution restored (Sultan Abdühamid II had suspended its implementation after only fourteen months). As the day went on, in all cities and even small towns in Macedonia, crowds led by CPU officers celebrated this *hürriyet* with public demonstrations and cannon fire. In the meantime, various branches of the CPU, clandestinely established in European Turkey, bombarded the imperial palace with telegrams demanding the reinstatement of the constitution of 1876 and the reopening of the Chamber of Deputies, prorogued in 1878. These telegrams warned the Sultan that in the event of a refusal, they would march on Istanbul with an 'Army of Liberation'. The Sultan grudgingly accepted the *fait accompli* and issued an imperial decree that reopened the Chamber of Deputies, rushing it to the daily newspapers for immediate publication.

This was not a general revolution in the strict sense of the term. It was carried out entirely in European Turkey; the other regions of the empire remained unaware of it until they heard of the restoration of the constitutional regime and, apart from the supposedly self-sacrificing CPU units who assassinated numerous bureaucrats and officers suspected of spying for the palace or organizing loyal military forces to quell the munities, there was no violence or fighting. More importantly, the Sultan, though his neo-patrimonial regime based on loyalty and concentration of power in his position was ended, remained in office, and the transition was carefully managed with little input from those revolutionary abstracts, 'the crowd' or 'the people'. Mass demonstrations in support of the revolution took place only after the matter had been settled. This was no popular revolution of Russia in 1905 or Persia in 1906, but it was not a military coup either – rather, it was the novel hybrid of the two that gave 1908 its peculiar character.

This was the first revolution in modern history to be prepared and successfully staged by an organization composed of civil bureaucrats and military officers. While these individuals carried out a revolution, they were not 'revolutionaries' in the Ottoman context, especially when compared to the members of organizations such as the Dashnaktsutiun (the Armenian Revolutionary Federation) or the VMORO (*Vnatrešna makedonsko-odrinska revolucionerna organizacija* – Internal Macedonian-Adrianopolitan Revolutionary Organization), who were also active at the time. Unlike the Bolsheviks in Russia, who embarked upon the total destruction of the state apparatus to realize their vision of a utopian society, the leaders of the Young Turk Revolution were essentially conservatives who saw their task in terms of preservation and survival. The aim of the Young Turk Revolution was not to destroy, but to restore, to safeguard and to maintain.

Unlike the French revolutionaries of 1789, the leaders of the CPU and, later, CUP (the Committee began to use its previous title of Ottoman Committee of Union and Progress after the revolution) did not end an *ancien régime* to construct a new one in its stead; unlike the Iranian revolutionaries of 1905–6, they did not replace an absolutist monarch with a new constitutional regime. Nor did they inaugurate an innovative consultative body, such as the Russian Gosudarstvennaya Duma that emerged from the 1905 Revolution. The conservative leaders of the CUP brought about a restoration of the constitutional monarchy that had been established in 1876 and subsequently suspended in practice. Despite this, CUP leaders, who hailed the event as 'İnkılâb-ı Azîm' (the Grand Revolution), considered the 23/24 July revolution as the third major modern revolution in history – on a par with the French Revolution of 14 July 1789, and the approval of the American Declaration of Independence by the Continental Congress on 4 July 1776. A more modest picture is painted by the historiography, which views 1908 as one of several constitutional revolutions of the early 20th century, preceded by those in Russia and Iran and succeeded by the Xinhai Revolution of 1911, which ousted the Qing dynasty in China.

The grandiloquent pronouncements of CUP leaders and its significance in shaping the future of the Middle East and Balkans notwithstanding, the Young Turk Revolution was not and did not become an event of global historical importance. Its significance, however, is often underplayed by focusing on the reopening of the Ottoman Chamber of Deputies. The declared aim of the revolution, and the main request of those CPU leaders who spearheaded the uprising in the summer of 1908, was indeed the reinstatement of the constitutional regime, but we should not follow their lead so blindly that we miss the other, incipient demands and effects of 1908.

In fact, we might identify four primary aims of the revolution. First, it wanted to thwart foreign intervention in Ottoman politics, especially a mooted Great Powers reform programme for Macedonia. Second, it expressed a strong desire to impede nationalist-separatist activities of the non-Turkish ethno-religious groups. Third, it wished to strengthen the state apparatus to create a more centralized administration. Finally, although it advanced a passionate Ottomanist rhetoric during its staging, it wanted to reinterpret the official ideology of Ottomanism by casting Turks as the core and dominant element of the empire. In other words, the Young Turk Revolution did not target the state as many revolutions have done, but attempted to save it from seemingly unavoidable collapse and disintegration. Constitutionalism, the overt aim of the revolution, served as a magical catchword, shrouding these other goals in the background.

By paying attention to some of these less obvious aspects of the Young Turk Revolution, we can see that it was a pivotal moment in the gradual emergence of a radical new type of regime that was to become frighteningly familiar across Europe in the interwar period: one-party rule. The CUP retained the Sultan, but reduced him to a figurehead; they reintroduced the parliament, but turned it into an extension of the bureaucracy, churning out laws at the CUP's command. At the imperial court, in the bureaucracy, and within the military, it was the Committee that, working behind the scenes through the existing institutions of the government, came to pull the levers of power.

The phrase 'Young Turk Revolution' calls to mind a 'Turkish' revolution; yet what occurred in the summer of 1908 cannot be described as a distinctly Turkish event. The revolution operated at the level of a polyethnic and multi-religious empire which, even much-diminished by 1908, was still accurately described in school textbooks as stretching from Scutari in Albania (İşkodra/current-day Shkodër) to Basra. Consequently, the impact of the revolution was felt far beyond the confines of modern-day Turkey. Moreover, individuals and organizations of many different ethno-religious groups joined or provided support to the movement. For instance, many Macedo-Romanian-speaking Kutzo-Vlachs (or Tsintsars, who call themselves Aromanians in Macedonia) joined the CPU band network in Macedonia, and the left wing of the Macedonian VMORO supported the revolutionary activity in its final stages.

The support given by Albanians – who formed a majority among the Muslim population of European Turkey – was particularly important. While individuals of Turkish descent dominated the External and Internal Headquarters of the CPU in Paris and Salonica, many of the officers who led the so-called 'national units', and even more of the privates who joined them, were Albanians. On the ground, more Albanians than Turks worked for the revolution, albeit overwhelmingly under Turkish management and command. Likewise, a major anti-interventionist Albanian demonstration held in Firzovik (current-day Ferizaj in the Republic of Kosovo) a few days before the events of 22/23 July helped to lay the ground for the revolution and the reinstatement of the constitutional regime. Thus Albanians, with some justification, initially considered the uprising as an Albanian enterprise, though this identification with the 'Young Turks' was short-lived.

Bitter post-revolution conflict between the CUP and Albanian nationalists, and the eventual separation of Albania from the empire in 1912–13, served swiftly to undermine the importance of the revolution in the eyes of Albanian nationalists. Later, Albanian historiography and popular culture viewed the Young Turk Revolution as a ruse on the part of the CUP, which, according to their interpretation, cajoled the Albanians and exploited their Ottoman patriotism. This historiography, consequently, recast even Albanian Adjutant-Major Ahmed Niyazi Bey – one of the two major military heroes of the revolution – as a gullible scab, outwitted and manipulated by Turkish nationalists. This historical revisionism is not only an Albanian phenomenon. In the Arab provinces, in spite of the real elections, political participation and freedom of the press introduced by the revolution, later developments (especially heavy-handed attempts at centralization, a subsequent punitive policy against Arab nationalists and the disintegration of the empire) led post-war Arab intellectuals to re-narrate the revolution as a coup that had brought a Turkish nationalist organization to power.

In nation states in the Middle East created after the Great War, and in those Balkan states that expanded at the expense of the Ottoman Empire, the memory of the Young Turk Revolution quickly faded. The revolution struggled for relevance in the new nations, and was downgraded to a 'Turkish' event that had transpired in a psychically remote past. Thus, by the 1920s it was long forgotten across the former Ottoman lands, including Albania. The sole exception was the freshly formulated Republic of Turkey.

Even in Turkey, though, the revolution did not leave the long-lasting legacy that its Russian and Persian contemporaries endowed. In the immediate aftermath, the CUP passed a law in 1909 that declared 23 July the sole national holiday of the empire. This reverence continued until the end of the Ottoman state, as public intellectuals and popular culture embraced 1908 as a momentous occurrence that had replaced a rotten and oppressive *ancien régime* with a modern and progressive government. During the Turkish War of Independence (1919–22), leaders of the struggle continued to hold their Young Turk forebears in high esteem, even if they did not have access to the resources necessary to celebrate the anniversary with pomp and vigour. Indeed, the first all-Turkey congress, where the decision was taken to organize a resistance movement against the terms and implementation of the Armistice of Mudros (1918), chose to convene in the eastern town of Erzurum on 23 July 1923 in homage to 1908, and to present the forthcoming struggle as a continuation of that revolutionary project.

After the end of the Turkish War of Independence and the establishment of the Republic of Turkey in 1923, however, a different attitude emerged vis-à-vis the Young Turk Revolution. The official ideology of the new republic, mainly fashioned by its founder Mustafa Kemal Atatürk, was based upon a novel view of history: the Turkish History Thesis (*Türk Tarih Tezi*). This thesis, which posited that proto-Turks had founded world civilization in its Central Asian cradle during the Neolithic age and then spread it throughout the world, attempted to present the Ottoman experience as no more than a negligible footnote to a long and glorious past. Thus, in the new state, especially in the 1930s, the focus of historiography and historical research was on the achievements of proto-Turks, with the aim of erasing any lingering traces of Ottoman history. Likewise, the new regime emphatically rejected any continuation between the Ottoman reforms of the Tanzimat era (1839–76) and the new regime, adopting a language of rupture based upon a dichotomy between the Ottoman state and the new republic. The Young Turk Revolution quickly became an 'Ottoman' event that had occurred in a past that the new republic disavowed.

Though Mustafa Kemal had been a member of the CPU and participated in the revolutionary activity, his role had been marginal. Despite this affiliation, however, he did not allow the remaining CUP leaders to reshape political organizations in his new Turkey. A vague antipathy towards ex-CUP leaders was sharpened when, in the wake of a foiled assassination attempt, Mustafa Kemal organized a kangaroo court that tried these leaders and pronounced death sentences for many of them in 1926. The absolute condemnation of the CUP delivered by the new regime made recognition of the CUP's main achievement, the Young Turk Revolution, even more problematic and politically unwise. Enver Pasha, one of the two major heroes of 1908 and an arch-rival of Mustafa Kemal, was criticized and blamed, portrayed as an adventurist individual who had lost the empire. All of this political manoeuvring contributed significantly to the deterioration of the Young Turk legacy in the national consciousness. Until 1934, the new republic kept 23 July as a national day of celebration, although it was eclipsed when 29 October – the anniversary of the proclamation of the republic – became the main national holiday in 1925. Finally, the national holidays law issued in 1935 dropped 23 July as a day of celebration.

Today, 23 July does not evoke specific memories for the average Turk; nor does it have any place in the collective memory. Even many well-educated Turks would struggle to impart the significance of that date. History textbooks make short, circumscribed references to this event in just a few sentences and, while Turkish journalists still celebrate 24 July as the anniversary of the 'termination of censorship' (after the reopening of the Chamber of Deputies, newspaper editors refused to send proofs to the state censors), this Press Day is marked without reference to the revolution that precipitated this development. Tellingly, even the hundredth anniversary of the Grand Revolution passed in almost full silence in Turkey, the meeting of a few academic panels notwithstanding.

Even the rehabilitation of the CUP leaders by Turkish nationalists after the 1980s did not spark a general interest in the Young Turk Revolution. When the remains of Enver Pasha, who had been killed by the Bolsheviks in the vicinity of Âb-ı Deryâ village in present-day Tajikistan in 1922, returned to Turkey and were buried at the martyrs' cemetery in Istanbul with full state honours in 1996, the eulogies focused not on the hero of the Young Turk Revolution, but on the pan-Turkist who made the ultimate sacrifice.

The events of 1908 remain, then, a long-forgotten revolution that has no purchase or relevance today for Turkey's national self-perception and values. For many Turks, their history starts with the establishment of the republican regime. The 'Turkish Revolution', a phrase coined in the early years of the new state, refers not to 1908 but to the period between the start of the Turkish War of Independence and the death of Mustafa Kemal Atatürk in 1938, presenting these two decades as a gradual and singular Turkish revolution. Others, who embrace the Ottoman past as the part of the glorious history of the Turks, make references to the Young Turk Revolution, but only as a ruinous event that resulted in the eventual dethroning of the last great Ottoman sultan, Abdülhamid II. His political rehabilitation has gained significant momentum in the last two decades, and did prompt a fresh but limited interest in the Young Turk Revolution. Yet it also resulted in conspiratorial revision of 1908 as a Freemason and/or European plot aimed at dethroning a pious, pan-Islamist sultan who had been expending his best efforts to safeguard the Muslims of the world against Western imperial aggression.

Greater, more radical and more substantial revolutions overshadowed the other constitutional revolutions of 1905–11. The Bolshevik Revolution remade the 1905 Russian Revolution as its precursor; the Iranian revolution of 1979 turned the Persian revolution of 1905–6 into historical dust; and the Chinese Communist revolution of 1949 reduced the Xinhai Revolution to a first reaction against Western imperialism.

In the case of the Young Turk Revolution, however, none of the regime changes or revolutions that took place in the former Ottoman realm after 1908 exceeded it in scope, influence or importance. Despite this, it was a barren revolution, especially compared to its generative contemporary peers. The main reason for this lack of afterlife was the dismemberment of the entity that the revolution had attempted to save. If all the Ottoman successor states, with the exception of Turkey, conceptualized their Ottoman past as a tragic subjugation under the 'Turkish yoke', 1908 was, then, a revolution staged to prolong the life of an empire increasingly based in Turkish domination – a state of affairs that was totally alien to these new 'nations'.

The founders of modern Turkey could have embraced the legacy of the Young Turk Revolution, and as CPU members they had all participated in the revolution. However – unlike the Pahlavi rulers of Iran, who attempted to sell their reforms as a continuation of the 1905–6 constitutional revolution; or the Bolsheviks who eulogized the 1905 Revolution as the 'first' one that paved the way to the October Revolution; or Mao Zedong, who praised the 1911 revolution as an anti-imperialist uprising – the Turkish republican leaders chose to begin a new book in 1923 with the Turkish War of Independence as its starting point. In that book, there was no room for the Young Turk Revolution of 1908 – the least enduring revolution of the early 20th century.

Ahmed Niyazi Bey

Ahmed Niyazi Bey (1873–1913), a wealthy Albanian landowner and officer, was one of the leaders of the 1908 revolution. He joined the CPU in 1907 when stationed at Resne (modern-day Resen, in the Republic of North Macedonia). Alarmed by rumours of an impending partition of Macedonia, he created a CPU guerrilla band, raided an Ottoman army post at Resne and issued a proclamation calling for the restoration of the constitution, before taking Monastir on 22–23 July. Widely celebrated as a hero of the revolution, he took a prominent part in defeating the counter-revolution of April 1909. He published his memoirs in 1908, and remained a prominent CUP member until his assassination in 1913.

İsmail Enver Pasha

İsmail Enver Pasha (1881–1922), a Turkish-born soldier, joined the Ottoman Freedom Society which was established in 1906 in Salonica and became the Internal Headquarters of the CPU in 1907. In July 1908, he created a CPU guerrilla band in the mountains of Macedonia. After the revolution he resumed his career in the Ottoman military, serving in Benghazi (modern-day Libya) during the Italo-Ottoman War in 1911–12 and building a political profile before the Balkan Wars (1912–13), in which he reconquered Edirne from the Bulgarians. As one of the triumvirate that ruled the empire from 1913, he built the 1914 Ottoman alliance with Germany. In 1918, he went into exile. There, he established links with the Bolsheviks and attended the Congress of the Peoples of the East held in Baku in 1920, but later broke with them and tried to organize the Turkic peoples against the Bolsheviks. He was killed by the Red Army in Turkistan in 1922.

TIMELINE

1839   Gülhane (Rose Chamber) Edict introduces administrative reforms known as Tanzimat in the Ottoman Empire, and confirms the rule of law

1853-6   Crimean War: Ottoman Empire, allied with France and Britain, defeats Russia

1856   Reform Edict confirms Tanzimat reforms and grants full equality to non-Muslims

1876   Sultan Abdülaziz dethroned and replaced by Murad V, then three months later by Abdülhamid II

1876   Ottoman Empire promulgates a constitution during the Constantinople Conference to stave off international pressure

1877-8   Ottoman Empire defeated by Russia

1878
February   Sultan prorogues the Ottoman Chamber of Deputies

July   Congress of Berlin confirms independence of Romania, Montenegro and Serbia; grants extensive autonomy to Bulgaria; Ottomans lose Bosnia–Hercegovina, Cyprus

1889   Committee of Ottoman Union is established to press for the restoration of the constitution

1895   The Committee is renamed the Committee of Union and Progress (CUP)

1906   The Committee is again renamed the Ottoman Committee of Progress and Union (CPU), an umbrella political organization for the 'Young Turks'

1908
12 June   Summit between Edward VII of Britain and Tsar Nicholas II leads to rumours that Britain and Russia intend to dismantle the Ottoman Empire

June–July CPU rising in Macedonia

24 July Sultan restores the constitution

December Parliament reopens

1909 Failed anti-CUP counter-revolution; CUP-led General Assembly deposes Abdülhamid II, replacing him with Mehmed V

1912–13 Ottoman Turkey loses the bulk of its European territory in Balkan Wars

1914 Ottoman Empire joins First World War on the side of the Central Powers

1919 Turkish National Movement starts to establish an independent Turkish nation state following Ottoman defeat in 1918

1919–22 Turkish War of Independence against Allied forces

1920 Treaty of Sèvres partitions the remaining Ottoman Empire

1922 Abolition of the Ottoman sultanate

1923 Republic of Turkey is established

THE MEXICAN REVOLUTION, 1910–1917

Javier Garciadiego

The Mexican Revolution was one of the first of the 20th century, and among the bloodiest: there were as many as a million deaths, as well as 200,000 refugees, from a population of 15 million. Unlike most of those that followed, it owed little to the thoughts of Karl Marx. Essentially, it was a liberal reaction against the long rule of the outgoing dictatorial president Porfirio Díaz, a fight for liberal democratization, class conflict, a movement for land reform and a regional dispute – all combining in shifting alliances and phases of the revolution. The complexity of the revolution is witnessed by the difficulty in identifying a definitive end date: 1917, 1920, 1929 and 1940 are all suggested.

The upshot was – unlike some of the revolutions that followed it – not an ideological one-party state (even though an avowedly revolutionary party held power for most of the 20th century), but a reformed constitution and a gradual achievement of social and economic modernization. Yet the memory of the revolution, even if in contested form, remains crucial to Mexican identity, and claims to own its legacy are key to success in Mexican politics.　　　　　PF

The revolution of 1910 is the most important event in the modern history of Mexico – and, indeed, modern Latin America before the Cuban Revolution. Although, like many revolutions, it brought promises that remained unfulfilled, its significance lies more in the changes it did bring about. Its enduring importance is rooted in its military and political character, its populist ideology, cultural impact, international significance and even its epic and iconic associations.

Like all revolutions, that of Mexico had a number of phases, and emerged out of a state of total crisis that faced the previous regime. A single government had held power for thirty-four years, between 1877 and 1911; it was known as the *Porfiriato*, owing to its unique and enduring leadership by General Porfirio Díaz (1830–1915). Nineteenth-century Mexico had been a time of chaos and instability until Díaz came to power; he began his lengthy public career in the wars between the liberals – the group to which he belonged – and the conservatives. Historians have called the early 19th century 'the period of anarchy', comprising the war of independence from Spain (1810–21); the loss of Texas (1835–6); war with the United States (1846–8) that led to the loss of half the national territory; and intervention by France (1862–7). On top of these major events were constant rebellions and coups, reflected in a hundred different governments from across the ideological spectrum holding power at different points.

Porfirio Díaz imposed stability and order on Mexico for the first time in the 19th century. This brought, also for the first time, notable and prolonged economic growth, which in turn gave rise to the emergence of modern middle classes and industrial workers. However, the dominant economic model was oligarchic and neocolonial, based on the large agricultural landholdings of a few families and the industrial, railroad, mining and oil businesses of foreign investors connected to the country's leading political figures.

Unfortunately, economic growth did not produce social growth; deep inequality reigned. To top it all, the political system showed no sign of modernization. The constitution was ignored; the division of powers gave way to total domination of legislature and judiciary by the executive; centralized power put paid to any form of federalism;

press freedom disappeared. So too did elections, since political stability became a synonym for continuity, based on a widespread and open-ended policy of re-election. Eventually the political class aged and was rejected by younger generations who aspired to a political role for themselves. Anger and opposition grew.

As Porfirio Díaz grew older – by 1910 he would be eighty years of age – his two principal groups of supporters, the so-called 'Scientists' (who believed in ruling by scientific principles) and the group around General Bernardo Reyes (1850–1913), clashed over the succession of power. In 1904, Díaz created the position of vice president and chose a member of the Scientists to take the role; the supporters of Reyes now became the opposition. Meanwhile, the growing middle class demanded adherence to the liberal principles that Díaz had abandoned. They sought democratization, beginning with the demand that the old ruler commit not to stand for re-election. The growing proletariat was demanding economic benefits and labour rights, which Díaz rejected, giving rise to violent action by miners in the border town of Cananea in 1906 and by textile workers in Río Blanco in 1907, near the strategic port of Veracruz. Both uprisings were repressed – clearly, Díaz could not resolve the problems of modernity. His anachronistic approach was also laid bare by his refusal to grant concessions to the anti-re-election movement. Its leader, Francisco I. Madero (1873–1913), from one of the wealthiest families in the country's north-east, was imprisoned in the middle of the electoral process.

In late 1910, following the seventh successive re-election of Porfirio Díaz, Madero escaped from prison and published the Plan of San Luis Potosí (the town where he had been imprisoned), calling for an armed struggle. Initially, his call received little response, as his anti-re-election sympathizers lacked the profile for taking up arms. Most belonged to the urban middle class, and were inclined towards political opposition rather than armed rebellion – a course of action that appealed only to the few workers who had supported Madero.

Paradoxically, an entirely separate armed movement began to take shape at around this time. This transformed the situation from one of a movement of peaceful political opposition into a revolution. Impoverished rural people, disconnected from the anti-re-election opposition, took up arms, particularly in the northern states of Chihuahua (the most active of all), Coahuila and Sonora. They were followed by peasant groups from the states of Morelos and Guerrero, in the south-centre of the country. They used guerrilla tactics: small groups, unexpected attacks, dispersal and regrouping. The names of their leaders began to win renown: Pascual Orozco (1882–1915), Pancho Villa (1878–1923) and Emiliano Zapata (1879–1919). They faced the Federal Army, with its ageing officer class made up of companions of Díaz and soldiers untested over more than thirty years of internal and external peace. In six months, Díaz was defeated. He agreed to leave his beloved presidential chair in mid-1911.

Madero, a landowner, neither identified with nor trusted his soldiers from the peasant classes, and chose to dissolve the army following the resignation of Díaz. Furthermore, he allowed one of Díaz's collaborators to take up the interim presidency with the single objective of organizing new elections, as the fraudulent vote held in 1910 had been annulled by the resignation of the president and vice president. The exit of Díaz and the arrival of Madero to power did little to assuage the demands of those who had taken up arms. The followers of Zapata, for example, wanted to recover their lands, and decided to maintain the uprising until they achieved their goal.

Madero would soon learn, tragically, that it is easier to overthrow a government than to build a new one. He took over the presidency at the end of 1911, but lacked the necessary experience to govern. His government was weak and erratic, and soon found itself completely isolated. It suffered serious legal opposition in Congress and in the press, together with equally serious illegal opposition; there were at least four major rebellions in less than one year. These were undoubtedly caused by the proposals for political, economic and social reforms, which were seen by the elite as an unacceptable precedent, and by the poor as too moderate or inadequate – a betrayal. Of the four rebellions against Madero, two were led by members of the political elite: one by General Reyes and the other by a nephew of Don Porfirio, Félix Díaz (1868–1945), both seeking to regain power. The two popular uprisings, by contrast, were rooted in social causes: the Zapatistas demanded lands, and the followers of Orozco demanded a range of social reforms.

The rising led by Orozco was the largest, and the most significant. Seeing that sizable contingents of veterans of the struggle against Díaz had also risen up against him, Madero decided that the government army must be strengthened with similar groups of veterans who had remained loyal. These were known as *Irregulares* or *Cuerpos Rurales*, and included Pancho Villa and Álvaro Obregón (1880–1928). There was a tripartite outcome: Orozco's faction was defeated in mid-1912; the Federal Army renewed its officer class, recovered its lost morale and won a new leader, Victoriano Huerta (1850–1916); and finally, the *Irregulares* or *Cuerpos Rurales* remained armed and organized, with links to Madero and the Madero-supporting state governors in the north.

Though Madero was able to defeat these four rebellions, he fell to a coup by the rejuvenated Federal Army, with Huerta at its head. Madero was overthrown and assassinated in February 1913. Co-conspirators in the coup, along with the Federal Army, were the political class from the *Porfiriato* period, as well as the US ambassador Henry Lane Wilson, who was upset by Madero's reforms. The coup leaders quickly won the support of business and landowners – but just as swiftly lost the support of the United States after the Democrat Woodrow Wilson (1856–1924) came to the presidency in 1913, bringing with him a very different, much more sensitive and perspicacious attitude to Mexico.

The struggle against Huerta's coup marks the beginning of the second phase of the Mexican Revolution – known as the constitutionalist phase, as it sought to apply the constitution of 1857 that had been interrupted by Huerta's usurpation. The struggle was based on the Plan de Guadalupe of March 1913, which created the Constitutionalist Army under Venustiano Carranza (1859–1920). Carranza was the governor of Coahuila, and the only one with political experience within the Madero contingent, having been a senator during the *Porfiriato* period as part of the Reyes faction. He built a group around his role as governor and expanded to other states in the north-east. The second-ranking roles were filled by his close collaborators and political allies. The rank and file were the local *Irregulares* and *Cuerpos Rurales* together with workers, miners, cowboys, railroad employees, rural people and lower-ranking state officials. Understandably, their contribution was more political and administrative than military.

The Constitutionalist Army had two other major contingents. The Northwest Army Corps was led by the Sonora-born Álvaro Obregón, Benjamín Hill, Salvador Alvarado, Plutarco Elías Calles and Manuel Diéguez – all members of the rural or urban middle class, with the exception of Diéguez, a former workers' leader in Cananea. Their objective was to retain the political positions they had secured with Madero's victory over Díaz. The rank and file, again, mainly comprised *Irregulares* and *Cuerpos Rurales* along with cowboys, railroad workers, farm workers and employees. They were distinguished from the Carranza-led soldiers of the north-east by two factors: in Sonora the ranks were swelled by the politicized miners from Cananea and by Yaqui and Mayo Indians, who were very able soldiers.

Finally, in the north-central zone the División del Norte was formed under the leadership of Pancho Villa. His principal lieutenants were also of humble origins, some even with a background in banditry – which they shared with Villa himself, and most notoriously his companion Tomás Urbina (c. 1877–1915). The rank-and-file troops were again formed by *Irregulares* and *Cuerpos Rurales*, together with miners, cowboys, farm workers and employees of timber companies; notable in Chihuahua was the inclusion of many veterans of the militarized farming colonies. What they lacked in political and administrative experience, they made up for in military capacity. In addition, they brought popular support to the movement.

The 1913 struggle was more complex in its social make-up, as well as being more extensive in geographic terms. Moreover, across the three regions the 1913 struggle incorporated many more groups from lower social strata than in 1910. Whereas in the north-east, Carranza-led contingent's leaders came from the local political elite, starting with the governor himself, those of the north-west (Sonora) came from the middle class with little political experience; and the Villa-led División del Norte came from the lower classes, without political experience. Meanwhile, when compared with the events of 1910 in the same region, there is a clear distinction in the north-east between Madero and Carranza: the former came from the national economic elite, the latter from the more local political elite. Similarly, in Sonora, Obregón and other members of the middle class could not be compared with the leader of the local struggle in 1910: the great landowner José María Maytorena. Finally, Pancho Villa himself came from humble origins – quite unlike the middle-class background of the Chihuahua leaders of 1910, Abraham González and to a lesser extent Pascual Orozco.

There were also rebel groups of different kinds in many other parts of the country, above all in Morelos and Guerrero, dominated by the Zapatista movement that had remained armed since 1911 with its Plan de Ayala ('Reform, Freedom, Justice and Law!') demanding the return of land seized by the elite, and which became radicalized to fight against Huerta. Faced with such a numerous, extensive, capable and well-equipped army, together with the refusal of support from Woodrow Wilson, Huerta was defeated in mid-1914.

The triumph of the Constitutionalist Army over Huerta ushered in a third phase of the Mexican Revolution. Following failed attempts at compromise between the leading victorious revolutionary factions, violence again broke out in early 1915, with the 'war of the factions' to determine which project for development of the country came out on top. This struggle led to the formation of new alliances, based on a clear social identity. The constitutionalist grouping was formed by the armies of Carranza and Obregón, with a middle-class background and a more mature and comprehensive vision of the country. Meanwhile, the armies of Villa in the north and Zapata in the south formed the conventionist grouping, with a distinctively lower-class character.

Initially the conventionists were expected to prevail, given the strength of the División del Norte and the fear instilled by the Zapatistas, but by the end of 1915 the constitutionalists had decisively triumphed. The reasons were in part military, such as the rising costs of arms and ammunition for the Villa-led troops due to the outbreak of the First World War; or the novel use of barbed wire by Carranza and Obregón's armies, which proved fatal to Villa's cavalry. Economic factors also favoured the constitutionalists, who controlled the oil-producing areas that became strategic in the light of the conflict in Europe. Meanwhile, the conventionists occupied Mexico City, which proved very expensive to maintain. Above all, while the constitutionalists managed to increase their popular support without threatening the middle classes, Villa and Zapata maintained their focus on their own class struggle, a strategy that condemned them to isolation. On top of this, the Zapatistas refused to cooperate with Villa's armies in the 'war of factions', due to their focus on local issues.

The United States adopted a position of 'watchful waiting' in preparation for offering diplomatic recognition to the victorious group. When this turned out to be the constitutionalists, Washington extended de facto recognition in October 1915. Carranza spent the following year expanding and consolidating his power across the country, and at the end of 1916 called a Constitutional Congress of national scope, to promulgate the constitution of 1917. This was a war constitution drafted by the victors, and established the development strategy Mexico was to pursue henceforth. This had also been the case with the constitution of 1824 after the country achieved independence, and with that of 1857, when the Liberals had won their first victory – at the Ayutla rebellion – over the Conservatives.

The constitution of 1917 was drafted on the basis of the social and economic commitments and proposals set out over the seven years of armed struggle. It also took up a number of ideas put forward as early as 1906 by the precursors to the Mexican Revolution, the so-called Magonistas (after their leader Ricardo Flores Magón, 1873–1922) in his visionary Programme for the Liberal Party. Grounded in this constitution, Mexico would be governed by a revolutionary middle class with close ties to the industrial and rural working classes, who undoubtedly remained subordinate but won significant socio-economic benefits, such as agrarian land reform and labour rights.

Giving a precise date for the end of the revolution that had begun in 1910 is a serious historiographical problem. Some veterans of the struggle, together with a number of historians, claim that the correct date should be 1917 – when the new constitution was promulgated, determining the political changes and social commitments of the new Mexican state. Others argue for 1920, when a revolutionary faction from the north-west and seen as middle class took power, and was prepared to embark on concessions demanded by the working classes and to include them in the political operation of the regions. Yet others assert that the right date is 1929, when, following elections in 1920, 1924 and 1928 that had ended in violence among the revolutionary groups aspiring to the presidency, the main factions and groups reached agreement and established the National Revolutionary Party. That year also saw the peace signed with the Catholic Cristeros in the centre and west of the country, who had waged a religious war since 1926. Finally, still others claim that the revolutionary process only ended in 1940 with the conclusion of President Lázaro Cárdenas's term in office, during which the most radical measures of the Mexican Revolution were put into practice: agrarian reform, support for the workers' movement and nationalization of the oil industry.

Regardless of its end date, the Mexican Revolution had a great many consequences and ramifications. The notion of a state governed by the personal dictatorship of Porfirio Díaz and based on an oligarchic structure of landowners disappeared, to be replaced first by a government of revolutionary soldiers and later by a political party of veterans of the armed struggle. The latter, which governed the country for the rest of the 20th century, has been known since 1946 as the Institutional Revolutionary Party (PRI). Significantly, as a result of the calamitous failure of Madero, his successors in the revolutionary leadership did not pursue his democratic tendencies, but established a government that was both authoritarian and notoriously corrupt. As Álvaro Obregón, president of Mexico in 1920–24, cynically commented, 'there was not a general anywhere who could withstand a cannon shot of 50,000 pesos'.

In ideological terms, the Mexican Revolution and the constitution of 1917 involved three social pledges and three major enemies. The pledges were agrarian reform for the peasant farmers; labour rights and social benefits for industrial workers; and a free, secular state education for all. The enemies were the landowners, the Catholic Church and the United States. With regard to the second, Mexican society, which was overwhelmingly Catholic, would have a secular government with touches of Jacobinism (which explains the Cristero war of 1926–9). There was another paradox with regard to the United States: although Mexico's revolution had expressed clearly and constantly its nationalist and anti-American orientation, from the 1920s the United States would be by far the most powerful influence over its Mexican neighbour following the First World War, which left all the European powers seriously weakened.

Finally, the revolution created a new culture, driven by the great educator José Vasconcelos (1882–1959), who had been a Madero supporter and subsequently militated for the conventionists. This nationalist, epic culture – notably expressed in the Muralist movement led by Diego Rivera, David Alfaro Siqueiros and José Clemente Orozco, and in post-revolutionary Mexican literature – gave the country a new identity and positioned the masses as the principal protagonist of history, with their iconic leaders Villa and Zapata, though in reality their role was a subordinate one. In this respect, the Mexican Revolution was less radical in both ideological and programmatic terms than the Cuban Revolution fifty years later.

In the second half of the 20th century, the new governments of the revolution began to reveal their limitations. They were authoritarian and corrupt, and had driven away the leading revolutionaries. Opposition movements began to emerge, such as the student movement of 1968 and the guerrillas of later years. Above all, the PRI split at the end of the 1980s and the Party of the Mexican Revolution (PRD) was created, unifying the Mexican left – whether socialist or communist – with disillusioned groups from the PRI who believed that the revolution was an ongoing process, with clear ideals and pledges to fulfil. Since 1997 this party has dominated Mexico City, and the recurring economic crises of these years led sectors of the middle classes to seek electoral change.

All of this explains how the 2018 election was won by the National Regeneration Movement (MORENA) under the charismatic yet divisive leadership of Andrés Manuel López Obrador (b. 1953). History is always connected to the present, and history is a changing and ongoing process. A century on, are we facing a revival of the Mexican Revolution? Only the future can be the judge of that.

Francisco Pancho Villa

Francisco Pancho Villa (1878–1923), a poorly educated peasant from northern Mexico with a background as a bandit, led a highly mobile and effective revolutionary guerrilla grouping known as the División del Norte. Initially he fought for Madero against Porfirio Díaz and for Carranza against Huerta, and became governor of Chihuahua province in 1914. In August 1914 he entered Mexico City alongside the victorious Carranza; but following tensions with Carranza, he fled to the north, where he provoked the United States into intervening and trying unsuccessfully to capture him. Continuing to fight against Carranza's government, he retired from politics in 1920; three years later he was assassinated by supporters of the president, Álvaro Obregón. His contribution to the revolution was expunged from the official record for many years, but he remained a legendary figure.

Venustiano Carranza

Venustiano Carranza (1859–1920), a northern landowner, eventually became the first president of the new republic (1914–20). As governor of Coahuila province, he opposed the reactionary regime of Victoriano Huerta, leading the Constitutional Army alongside his ally Álvaro Obregón. A politician rather than a soldier, he set up a provisional government after Huerta's defeat and, after also defeating his former ally Pancho Villa, became president under his new constitution of 1917. Despite this, he proved conservative and reluctant to introduce the social and economic reforms promised by that constitution. A nationalist, he resisted US involvement in the Mexican wars. In 1920, shortly before his term of office was due to end, his cautious approach brought opposition from Obregón, and he was assassinated while fleeing from Mexico City.

TIMELINE

1877   Porfirio Díaz becomes president of Mexico

1910
October   Díaz is re-elected president for the seventh time; Francisco Madero
             writes Plan of San Luis Potosí, calling for a revolt against Díaz

November   Madero persuades Orozco and Pancho Villa to join the revolution
             against Díaz

1911
March   Emiliano Zapata leads uprising of villagers in Morelos; armed
             revolts begin in other regions

10 May   Orozco and Villa capture Ciudad Juárez

25 May   Porfirio Díaz resigns power

1912   Orozco leads rebellion in Chihuahua; Victoriano Huerta,
             representing Madero, defeats Orozco and arrests Pancho Villa

1913
18 February Huerta leads coup against Madero, who is shot a few days later

19 February Huerta declares himself president

26 March   Venustiano Carranza, governor of Coahuila, is declared First Chief
             in the fight against Huerta, allied with Villa and Obregón

1914
21 April   US forces occupy Veracruz

15 July   Huerta resigns and flees to Europe

1915
19 October   United States recognizes Carranza as provisional president

1916
9 March   Villa sacks Columbus, New Mexico, in retaliation for US recognition
             of Carranza; General Pershing leads a force into Mexico in search
             of Villa

December	Carranza calls a Constitutional Convention to draw up a new constitution
1917	Mexico adopts the constitution
1919	Zapata dies in an ambush

1920

20 April	Obregón leads a revolt against Carranza, whose support collapses
20 May	Carranza is murdered
26 October	Obregón is elected president

THE IRISH REVOLUTION, 1913–1923

Diarmaid Ferriter

Ireland – the first overseas territory to suffer the English, then British, imperialist yoke – also became the first to successfully throw it off, following a long struggle that began as a parliamentary campaign but eventually used revolutionary tactics and rhetoric. A painful civil war followed between factions with opposing views both on the partition of the island of Ireland that ensured the north remained in the UK, and on the legitimacy of southern Ireland's new status as a dominion of the British Empire. The civil war resulted in the creation of a conservative, church-dominated state and society in the newly independent southern territory.

Although nationalists had long sought 'home rule', complete independence gradually became an objective. The First World War provided an opportunity that was seized by the doomed coterie that briefly took over the General Post Office in Dublin in April 1916. Despite the near-synchronicity between the Irish and Bolshevik revolutions, socialist ideas were only marginal amidst the much louder clamour of romantic nationalism and Catholic separatism. Above all there was a powerful sense of the historic injustice of British rule in Ireland, made unambiguously manifest in the brutal aftermath to the Post Office rising.

The clandestine activities of nationalist and republican groups – whether those of the Irish Republican Brotherhood

(IRB) in 1916, the Irish Volunteers or the Irish Republican Army (IRA), the armed wing of the nationalist party Sinn Féin ('Ourselves'), were important to the nationalists' success both before the British conceded limited independence in the Anglo-Irish Treaty of 1922, and also in the subsequent civil war. Although the new southern 'Free State' accepted that the division of the island could not be ended by violence, it retained the urge and political commitment to unification and to complete the process of ending British rule. The IRA remained a major player in Ireland's history, especially during the thirty-year period of the Northern Irish 'Troubles' from the late 1960s to the late 1990s.   PF

The Irish revolution of 1913–23 was caused by the destruction of the home rule project that had dominated Anglo-Irish relations since the 1880s, and the First World War, which radicalized politics, altered borders and transformed perspectives on British imperialism.

Under the Act of Union of 1800, Ireland was represented by 100 MPs at Westminster, and by the late 19th century, iconic Irish nationalist leader Charles Stewart Parnell (1846–91) had built an alliance between his Irish Parliamentary Party (IPP) and British Liberals that led to an Irish Home Rule Bill in 1886. This was defeated, as was a second Home Rule Bill in 1893; but in 1912, the British government led by Herbert Asquith (1852–1928) agreed to home rule for all Ireland within the empire. Recent political reforms meant that this third bill, unlike the previous two, could not be vetoed by the House of Lords.

Ferocious unionist opposition to home rule was seen in the northern part of Ireland, where the largest concentration of Protestants resided, a legacy of British plantation policies in the 17th century. This was reflected in the formation of the Ulster Volunteer Force (UVF) in 1913, dedicated to resisting home rule, while in the Catholic majority south, the corresponding nationalist Irish Volunteer Force (IVF) sought to secure its implementation. While home rule reached the statute books, its introduction was postponed for the duration of the First World War without a solution to Ulster opposition. The militancy and threatened rebellion of Ulster and the decision by John Redmond (1856–1918), leader of the IPP, to back the British war effort and encourage the Irish Volunteers to enlist in the British army (over 200,000 Irish men served during the war) emboldened a small group of Irish republicans to hijack the home rule movement and infiltrate those Irish Volunteers who had split from Redmond to press instead for complete separation from Britain in pursuit of a thirty-two-county republic.

Partly because of Britain's preoccupation with international conflict but also because of frustration that they were not making enough headway, these separatists decided to stage a rebellion in Dublin in Easter 1916, hoping this dramatic gesture would light a fuse that would lead to an explosion of republican sentiment. Orchestrated by the clandestine, oath-bound Irish Republican Brotherhood, those who resorted to rebellion also included the Irish Volunteers who had split from Redmond, militant socialists in the Irish Citizen Army (ICA) and members of Cumann na mBan, the female auxiliary of the Irish Volunteers. These rebels were rejecting not just an Anglicized identity, but also what they regarded as the conservatism of the political establishment. Their zealousness needs to be seen in a European context, part of the 'generation of 1914' who were almost messianic in their rejection of the established order. Linguistic and cultural nationalism, the language of soldiery preparation and scorn about parliamentarians and their perceived grubby compromises abounded during this period and for this minority of radicals 'physical force' became a fully fledged creed with the outbreak of the First World War.

Notwithstanding those currents, there was no general appetite for rebellion in 1916, which was why deception and secrecy played such an important role in the organization of the Easter Rising. It lasted less than a week, was crushed by crown forces and resulted in the deaths of 450 people, mostly civilians. What changed public attitudes was the growing ineptitude of British rule in Ireland, which historian Charles Townshend has characterized as 'the deep ambivalence about the balance between suppression and provocation', and the degree to which the civil government in Ireland was superseded by the military. Sixteen leaders of the rising were executed in its aftermath; over 2,000 suspected of involvement were interned. A sea change in public opinion generated sympathy for Irish separatism and the building of Sinn Féin (SF, 'Ourselves'), originally established in 1905, as a nationwide political movement.

A British threat to extend conscription to Ireland in 1918 was another turning point, as a combination of clerical, labour and republican opposition further hardened Irish politics. Such was the clamour that conscription was not imposed. Under the leadership of Éamon de Valera (1882–1975), the sole surviving commandant of the 1916 rising, Sinn Féin decimated the IPP in the general election of December 1918, winning 73 seats of the now 105 available to Ireland. Those elected for Sinn Féin were committed to abstention from Westminster and the establishment of an Irish republic. Britain refused to recognize their mandate, as did unionists.

Sinn Féin's political triumph in 1918 brought down the project that Irish constitutional nationalists had promoted since the late 19th century. The War of Independence ensued, with Sinn Féin establishing its own parliament in Dublin and a republican underground government to supplant the British administration in Ireland. In parallel, a military campaign by the Irish Republican Army (IRA), which had evolved from the Irish Volunteers, consisted of sporadic guerrilla fighting – partly orchestrated by the IRA's director of organization and intelligence, Michael Collins (1890–1922), but also propelled by regional dynamics and impulses. The War of Independence, which resulted in the deaths of almost 2,000 people, was no vindication of an astute master plan. Rather, in the words of historian Joost Augusteijn, it was 'a mixture of coincidence, unintended outcomes and local initiatives'. Sources in the Irish Military Archives suggest that the IRA in 1920–21 had a nominal national strength of 115,550, but almost all were part-time, and IRA volunteers had access to only 3,000 rifles during that period. In the region of 40,000 British army soldiers served in Ireland during the War of Independence.

In the midst of this, the Government of Ireland Act of 1920 created a separate parliament for six Ulster counties to constitute the new state of Northern Ireland, thereby partitioning the island. The Act also allowed for the creation of a parliament for southern Ireland, but this was rejected by Irish republicans. It was envisaged that the Act would ultimately lead to Irish unity, but if the two parliaments could not agree to come together they could stay in isolation. There would be no forcing of Ulster to join the south, but neither was there an assumption that Ulster would remain a fully integrated part of the UK. Sectarian violence marred the new Northern state's birth – between July 1920 and July 1922 there were 557 people killed: 303 Catholics, 172 Protestants and 82 members of the police and British forces. Catholics, overwhelmingly nationalist, comprised 33.5 per cent of the population of Northern Ireland in 1926.

The ceasefire of July 1921 between the IRA and the British forces led to negotiations that culminated in the signing of the Anglo-Irish Treaty on 6 December by delegates from the British and Irish governments. This led to the creation not of a republic, but of a Free State, a dominion of the British Empire, for the twenty-six counties of southern Ireland. Irish negotiators did not succeed in undoing partition, instead securing a vague promise that the border would be reviewed independently. Éamon de Valera, though president of Sinn Féin, had refused to be a part of the delegation and denounced the treaty, while Michael Collins reluctantly supported it as part of the Irish delegation led by the founder of Sinn Féin, Arthur Griffith (1871–1922). The bitter and divisive debates that followed the signing of the treaty centred on whether it was a stepping stone to greater freedom, or a gross betrayal of the republic Sinn Féin had fought for. The Irish parliament (the Dáil) ratified the treaty by sixty-four votes to fifty-seven, after which a bitter civil war began in June 1922, leading to approximately 2,000 deaths. The civil war ended with a ceasefire in May 1923, with the anti-treaty republicans decisively beaten by the new Free State Army. The civil war was a conflict that the republicans had neither the resources, soldiers nor popular support to win, but the fighting led to the death of Michael Collins, who had served as commander-in-chief of government forces.

Most of those who participated in the Irish revolution were more focused on the idea of separation from Britain than on any concrete political programme. The revolution was political and military rather than social; one of the supporters of the treaty, Kevin O'Higgins, the minister for home affairs in the Free State government, declared in 1923, '[We] were the most conservative revolutionaries that ever put through a successful revolution.' The Irish War of Independence was not propelled by a great social cause, largely because most Irish farmers owned their own land; some eleven million acres had been purchased as a result of the Land Acts of the late 19th and early 20th century, meaning Ireland's social revolution predated its political one.

Contrasting narratives of the revolution were apparent even before it fully ended, and the 'history wars' of the 1920s were an extension in print of the revolutionary conflict. Unionist historian Walter Alison Phillips came to the task of writing his history early in *The Revolution in Ireland 1906–23* (1923), in his own words, 'as the embers of civil war were still glowing in Southern Ireland'. He insisted the 'Sinn Féin terror' was a 'moral disintegration' underpinned by a 'crude idealism'. In contrast, nationalist narratives focused on 'the destiny of an ancient people' and the righteousness of their cause, which had been betrayed by Britain. Assertions of 'the unflinching support of a civilian population', and IRA Volunteers who came through their ordeal 'with immaculate hands', were also common in early nationalist accounts of the revolutionary period.

In the decades since, the conflict has generated a vast library, much of it controversial and polemical and guided by the winds of contemporary preoccupations. In 1971, eminent historian F. S. L. Lyons noted that the events of 1916–23 'burned so deep into the heart and mind of Ireland that it is not yet possible for historians to approach it with the detailed knowledge or the objectivity which it deserves'. In more recent times, the history of the revolution has been informed by the opening of voluminous archives, generating new perspectives and the revisiting of old assumptions.

It is a period of Irish history still much disputed, but a lot of recent research has sought to highlight those previously sidelined in the revolutionary narrative, including women, the labour movement and the voices of the grassroots who were fuelling the Irish republican engine. Research drawing upon newspapers and private archives, as well as testimony and military pension applications from veterans, has been collected from the 1920s to the 1950s by the state and released between 2003 and 2019. It has generated a multitude of perspectives not only on the political, military and administrative concerns of an elite involved in governance, but also on the personal individual preoccupations with social and economic issues, and Irish death and survival in the trenches of the Western Front. (Up to 40,000 Irish soldiers were killed serving in the British army during the First World War, dwarfing the body count for the Irish revolution.)

There is wide acceptance now that the certainties expressed by so many in the revolution's aftermath were rarely evident at the time. There was a temptation after the events to simplify or romanticize what was a painful period for many: marked by pride, but also by suffering and conflicting allegiances. This was overwhelmingly a revolution of the young and the inexperienced. It was a war fought on different levels; there was often a pitiful shortage of weapons for the republicans, communications problems between IRA GHQ and the regional IRA brigades, and sectarian tensions and killings. There was also an intelligence war fought and a crusade to undermine the Royal Irish Constabulary (RIC), which had been policing Ireland since the early 19th century. There were chilling executions, anger about alleged spies and informers, and sometimes a resistance to the IRA when it was deemed not to be acting in the interests of the communities it claimed to represent.

While crown forces killed more civilians (42 per cent) than the IRA (31 per cent), controversy has tended to be more focused on IRA rather than British violence. Britain's response to its Irish dilemma was characterized by denial of the legitimacy of the republican movement, imperial snobbery and priorities, and contempt for Sinn Féin's mandate, even though it had emphatically won the 1918 election. Auxiliary troops augmenting the RIC and regular British army soldiers were responsible for indiscriminate and brutal attacks, generating considerable embarrassment for the British government.

Much attention is still devoted to the highest-profile Irish casualty, Michael Collins. Historian Michael Hopkinson concludes that 'Through all the speculation, hero-worshipping, and revisionism, Collins can still be regarded as the essential man in the winning of a large measure of Irish independence.' But there is also a recognition that Collins makes little sense divorced from the context of those who surrounded him; as with other revolutionary leaders, he was mythologized and became a blank canvas onto which all sorts of portraits, some fanciful, were painted. The revolution also proved a lottery for leadership; Collins's opponent in relation to the treaty, Éamon de Valera, remained a giant of Irish politics for decades, eventually retiring in 1973 at the age of ninety-one.

The Irish Free State (IFS), like its northern counterpart, experienced a bloody birth. Alongside fatalities, there were 11,480 anti-treaty republicans in jail by the end of the civil war, and 77 had been executed by the state. Battles for legitimacy characterized both parts of the partitioned island in subsequent decades, as unionists in the North created a rotten statelet heavily subsidized by Britain with systematic discrimination against the Catholic minority. After a review in 1925, the Irish border remained unaltered, as it has to this day. The IFS, which became a republic by leaving the Commonwealth in 1949, was remarkably homogeneous, with over 93 per cent of its population Catholic, and the state had a strongly confessional ethos. While the civil war fallout created the two main political parties, Fianna Fáil and Fine Gael, that have dominated Irish politics since, they shared similar, largely conservative values and visions for the new state; the Irish labour movement and its political party were largely sidelined due to the dominance of civil war divisions and a disdain for politics based on class or competing visions about the role of the state, which became one of the most centralized in Europe.

The questions of ownership of the revolution and its legacy were apparent from a very early stage, as was fear about the consequences of some of the radical sentiments it had engendered. Consequently, it was frequently deemed necessary to rein in lawlessness and affirm the need for malcontents to know their place and their status. A struggle to reconcile rhetoric and reality was also relevant to the contested legacy of the period. Adaptation was not easy for many – perhaps because, as was recalled by Ernie O'Malley (1897–1957), a leading figure in the IRA who had the distinction of writing the best literary accounts of the revolution, 'we had built a world of our own, an emotional life but with no philosophy or economic framework'.

The antagonistic elements of the treaty, including an oath of allegiance to the British crown for Irish parliamentarians, were discarded in the 1930s and the state maximized its sovereignty, the ultimate expression of this being the declaration of neutrality during the Second World War. There was remarkable political stability by international standards, but the southern Irish economy, heavily agricultural, floundered, and the 1950s witnessed a staggering 500,000 people emigrate; the southern state had a population of just three million at the beginning of that decade. While there may have been a psychologically damaging isolationism, democracy nevertheless endured, and there was significant pride in Irish independence. The segregation and sectarianism of Northern Ireland, however, were reflected in devastating violence after 1969, a result of native failures, paramilitary violence and British misgovernment that resulted in the deaths of 3,500 people between 1969 and 1999.

Commemoration of the independence struggle was inevitably contentious in the early decades of the state, underlining, in the words of historian Roisín Higgins, how historical memory is 'deeply partial, personal and complex'. Memorializing the revolution was impacted by ideological climate, intergenerational shifts, and later the Troubles in Northern Ireland, but the recent appetite has been for more complicated and inclusive narratives. These have been helped by the peace process in Ireland from the 1990s and by concepts of 'shared history' incorporating, for example, the stories of Irish nationalists and unionists who fought in such iconic First World War theatres as the Battle of the Somme.

In 1997, at the time of the seventy-fifth anniversary of the foundation of the southern Irish state, political scientist Tom Garvin penned a robust defence of politicians' performances in the context of their success in establishing the legitimacy of the state and its democratic institutions, particularly during times when other countries in Europe failed lamentably to do that. 'Despite their mistakes and sins,' he wrote, 'the Irish revolutionaries-turned-politicians got it more right than wrong.' It appeared quite a convincing argument, underlining the achievements of the civil war generation in overcoming the divisions of the early 1920s in order to create stability during difficult times.

But the very impulses that created stability and consensus in the earlier decades of independence also facilitated a fundamental neglect of civic morality. After the laying of the state's foundations, the practice of politics became about the spoils of the system rather than engagement with ideas about the nature of citizenship. It was also about, in a society so homogeneously Catholic, abrogating responsibility to the Catholic Church in too many crucial areas, including education, health and welfare, and that excessive church power created a damaging monopoly. Ireland's membership of the EEC from 1973 broadened the focus of its foreign policy, and membership delivered tangible social and economic benefits. By the centenary of the 1916 rising, Ireland had been transformed and liberalized, economically, politically, culturally and socially; and pride in the revolution was allowed to breathe once again, alongside a vast improvement in Anglo-Irish relations and the lessening of provocative rhetoric about the Irish border.

In the decades after 1920, that border had been cemented by aggressive political ideology, economic policy and harrowing violence, and then its potency tempered by the peace process and economic and political pragmatism. Its future, since the British electorate voted to leave the EU in June 2016, has been under a focus not witnessed in decades, as it is the UK's only land border with another European country. As both Irish states approach the centenary of their foundation, the legacy of the revolutionary period thus remains profoundly relevant to current affairs.

Michael Collins

Michael Collins (1890–1922), Sinn Féin politician and IRA leader, fought in the Easter Rising of 1916, after which he was briefly imprisoned. In 1918 he was elected as a Sinn Féin representative to the Dáil, and became minister for home affairs and minister for finance. As head of intelligence for the IRA, he organized many attacks on the police and British agents and won a reputation for great resourcefulness and cunning. He went to London with Arthur Griffith to negotiate the Anglo-Irish Treaty in 1921 and, while conflicted about its merits and its failure to end partition, secured its passage through the Dáil by arguing that although the treaty did not give nationalists everything they desired, it did give them the freedom to achieve freedom. As leader of the pro-treaty army in the ensuing civil war, he was assassinated in Cork in August 1922.

Éamon de Valera

Éamon de Valera (1882–1975), born in New York and brought up in Limerick, joined the Irish Volunteers in 1913 and was involved in the 1916 Easter Rising, escaping execution because he was not at that stage regarded as a ringleader. After raising funds in the US as president of Sinn Féin and leading the Irish republican government that supported the War of Independence, he led the opposition to the Anglo-Irish Treaty and supported the anti-treaty forces in the civil war. Returning to democratic politics, in 1926 he left Sinn Féin and set up Fianna Fáil, entering the Dáil. He became prime minister (the Irish title Taoiseach was used from 1937) in 1932, serving until 1948 and again in 1951–4 and 1957–9, when he became president until 1973. His vision of Ireland was culturally and politically nationalist, economically self-sufficient and religiously conservative.

TIMELINE

1800   Act of Union between Great Britain and Ireland

1886   First Irish Home Rule Bill is introduced in Parliament, opposed in
             Ulster

1893   Second Home Rule Bill passes Commons but is rejected in Lords

1903   Land Purchase Act is passed, allowing tenants to buy land at low
             prices; a second Act is passed in 1909

1905   Sinn Féin is formed by Arthur Griffith

1912   Third Home Rule Bill passes Commons

1913
January   Formation of Ulster Volunteer Force (UVF)

November   Formation of Irish Volunteers

1916
24–30 April Easter Rising in Dublin

May   Execution of leaders of the rising

1917
July   Prime Minister Lloyd George calls Irish Convention

October   Éamon de Valera elected president of Sinn Féin and the Irish
             Volunteers

1918   Sinn Féin win general election by a landslide

1919   Beginning of War of Independence; first Dáil established; Irish
             Volunteers increasingly referred to as Irish Republican Army (IRA)

1920
November   British forces fire on football crowd at Croke Park

December   Government of Ireland Act creates separate parliaments for north
             and south Ireland; Sinn Féin boycott the southern parliament

1921

July   Truce between IRA and British forces

October   Talks begin in London between British government and Dail
            representatives

December   Anglo-Irish Treaty signed

1922

January   Dail ratifies the treaty after de Valera walks out; provisional
            government is formed, led by Michael Collins; the British leave
            Dublin Castle

June   General election is won by pro-treaty Sinn Féin; civil war begins
            between pro- and anti-treaty Sinn Féin groups

August   Michael Collins dies in an ambush outside Cork

December   Irish Free State formally established

1923

May   Ceasefire ends the civil war

1926   De Valera founds Fianna Fáil

THE RUSSIAN REVOLUTION, 1917

Dina Khapaeva

The Bolshevik Revolution stands as the defining Marxist revolutionary moment of the 20th century. Its leader, Lenin, has served as an inspiration – or a stark warning – for all future revolutionaries seeking the overthrow of capitalism. Challenging Marx's concept of historical inevitability whereby capitalism would collapse under the weight of its own contradictions, Lenin seized the opportunity to secure a revolution even in a country where capitalism and the industrial working class were relatively undeveloped, through the operation of a small, disciplined vanguard party – the Bolsheviks – by seeking power through a well-timed coup. His single-mindeness, authoritarianism and belief that the end justified the means – which led him ruthlessly to destroy not only those who threatened his revolution and those he saw as 'class enemies', but even those who shared his objectives but disagreed on tactics – proved a source of strength in the civil war that followed his successful takeover of power, yet created an intrinsically violent revolutionary state that made possible the inhuman excesses of his successor Joseph Stalin in the 1930s.

While the Bolshevik Revolution was explicitly Marxist in ideology and sought to create a communist state, it was not the first revolution in 20th-century Russia. A popular uprising in 1905 in St Petersburg had come close to overthrowing the absolutist tsarist state, while the collapse of the Russian war effort early in 1917 had induced a bourgeois liberal revolution that caused Nicholas II to abdicate and thereby ended tsarism. The Bolshevik Revolution a few months later involved the overthrow of this nascent, admittedly ineffectual constitutional state, and replaced it with a one dominated by the workers as represented in Soviets (workers' councils).

Whether Soviet Russia could ever have fully achieved its communist ideal is doubtful, and the reasons for this failure are much debated. One aspect was that, as the struggle to secure the regime intensified, it retreated in the 1920s and 1930s from the vision of a Russian-led global revolution to one of 'socialism in one country', invoking a deep nationalism that became vital to the regime's survival in the face of Hitler's 1941 invasion. Nevertheless, the emergence in the late 1940s of the Soviet Union as a rival to the United States for global hegemony meant that Leninism was exported not only to the Soviet Union's satellite states, but much more widely across the globe.   PF

A hundred years after it swept through the country, the Bolshevik or October Revolution of 1917 is still perceived as a cornerstone event in Russian history, a crucial rupture in relation to which the entire Russian past is being re-evaluated and reconsidered by those who inherited it, agonizing over its causes and its effects on the country and its people. This exercise has been part of the daily routine of Russian intellectuals over the past century. However, such pondering of the revolution had never been a matter of unrestrained thinking: the historical memory of the revolution was formed around a set of predetermined ideas and preselected facts that have shaped – and continue to shape – Russian political debates and scholarly discussions.

The historical memory of the revolution was constructed under particular circumstances. After the pre-revolutionary society had been destroyed during the civil war, the Red Terror and the Great Purges, an official Soviet version of history was forced upon Soviet society, to substitute for the absent collective memory of its members and to provide them with a sense of shared identity. Until the death of Stalin in 1953, it was extremely dangerous to keep and share, even with close friends and relatives, memories of the past that deviated from the Communist Party line. Any attempts to alter the official version of history, even with personal memories, were characterized as anti-Soviet propaganda and exposed the offenders to arrest and/or execution. For some, however, even the horrors of repressions by the Soviet secret police (known at different times as Cheka, NKVD, KGB and FSB) were not sufficient to stop them wondering whether what happened in Russia in October 1917 had been inevitable, although it had ruined everything they held dear; or just an unbelievable game of chance, a nightmare from which Russia would one day wake up.

Although all Russian and Soviet history was strictly controlled by the Soviet regime, few historical events were more policed than the October Revolution. For the Bolsheviks, this foundational event legitimized their rule and its 'scientific foundations' – Marxist ideology. The indoctrination of the 'correct way' to remember the revolution emerged shortly after the gloomy night of 25 October 1917 (according to the old-style calendar in use in Russia at the time; 7 November by today's 'new style' calendar), when ruffians and workers armed by the Bolsheviks deposed the Provisional Government. During its brief rule, this government had initiated a wide range of liberal reforms such as freedom of speech and adult suffrage unrestricted by nationality, gender, social class or religion; it had also eliminated capital punishment and established jury trials. The Bolshevik coup d'état ended this brief period of democracy in Russia brought by the February Revolution of 1917, which had allowed Russians to enjoy traditional democratic freedoms for the first time in their history.

The Bolshevik narrative of the October Revolution had to demonstrate that it took place in accordance with Marxist theory, while concealing events and facts that were unflattering to the Bolsheviks. Because the relation between Marxist theory and historical practice has never been unproblematic, numerous paradoxes were born of their marriage. These survived the collapse of the Soviet Union, and still structure political debates in Russia. Incorporated into the propaganda of the current Russian president Vladimir Putin (b. 1952), these narratives play an important role in promoting a new vision of Russia's national future.

Foremost among the paradoxes is that of the inevitability of the revolution. One of the most important dogmas of Soviet Marxism was that a revolution was inevitable and that this event had changed, once and forever, the course of world history. This thesis supposedly proved the Marxist idea that revolutions are, using Marx's metaphor, 'locomotives of history'. The Revolution also served to explain the nature of social change, as class struggle between exploiters and the exploited should inevitably lead to a classless communist society. Karl Marx (1818–83) had prophesied that the communist revolution would happen in the most developed industrialized European countries, which had an educated, progressive proletariat capable of initiating the world revolution. Lenin and his co-conspirators had to prove that Russia – a backward, agrarian, semi-feudal autocracy, a society in which the 1861 abolition of serfdom had left illiterate peasants (more than 80 per cent of the population) with almost no land and where a small number of destitute industrial workers in big cities suffered from abuses owing to inadequate labour politics – fitted the Marxist doctrine. In many essays written during his long exile in western Europe (1900–17, interrupted only by two years' break following the 1905 Revolution), Lenin argued that, paradoxically, Russia's special conditions made it a 'feeble chain' among capitalist countries and that the 'alliance of workers with poor peasants' would overpower the old tsarist regime by the communist revolution.

Marx, who believed that the proletarian masses were the actors of revolutionary liberation, looked down on military coups. Yet Lenin opted for a military coup. It was the Bolsheviks' only chance to seize power ahead of the November 1917 elections to the Constituent Assembly, as they anticipated a loss in free elections. Following the October coup, the Bolshevik government of the Council of the People's Commissars claimed that their role remained provisional until the elections.

The elections took place across the vast country, with a voter turnout above 50 per cent. Despite their demagogical slogans – 'All power to the Soviets! Peace to the People! Land to the peasants! Factories to the workers!' (they only fulfilled the pledge of Russia's withdrawal from the First World War) – the Bolsheviks, with just 24 per cent of the vote, lost badly to the Social Revolutionaries, the peasant party, who won 40 per cent. The Bolsheviks ignored these results, claimed the elections were illegitimate, and dissolved by force the freely and legally elected Constituent Assembly.

Soviet propaganda presented the revolution as 'supported by all people – workers, soldiers and peasants'. The reality was quite different: the Bolshevik coup was met with strikes. In the words of historian Sean McMeekin (2017), 'the world's first proletarian government was thus forced to devote its primary energies to strikebreaking'. The legitimacy of the first proletarian revolution remained an extremely important part of Soviet propaganda precisely because its paradoxically anti-democratic nature had been integral from the very beginning. The illegal military seizure of power, sabotaging the will of the masses, not only contradicted Marxist dogma that revolution serves the interests of the exploited majority against a privileged minority of exploiters; it also undermined the notion that the Bolshevik regime had been inevitable. Lenin's and Trotsky's ruthless cynicism and opportunism, their use of armed gangs against the elected party and their total failure to win the support of the masses shadowed this supposed 'people's revolution'.

According to Marxist doctrine and Soviet propaganda, the proletarian revolution opened a new era and created a new world, a reign of justice, joy and happiness. However, the way to this future happiness was to be paved by a proletariat dictatorship, which would 'preserve the revolution from the counter-revolution by means of revolutionary violence'. The Bolsheviks never shied away from terror, and violence and coercion were their preferred political tools – in theory as well as in practice. Lenin, whom Soviet propaganda dubbed 'the most humane of all people', wrote that if only 10 per cent of the Russian population survived to live under communism, this would be a fair price to pay for

such a bright future. In accordance with Lenin's concept, the implementation of the proletariat dictatorship in Russia resulted in the creation
of one of the bloodiest regimes in human history.

Marxists still blame the crimes and violence of the Soviet regime
on the peculiarity of Russian conditions: the country's backwardness, its
late abolition of slavery, its lack of democratic traditions, the personality
of its leaders and so forth. However, the dictatorship of the proletariat
had been part of Marxist thought from the very beginning. In 1848
Marx had insisted that '[T]here is only one way in which the murderous
death agonies of the old society and the bloody birth throes of the new
society can be shortened, simplified and concentrated, and that way is
revolutionary terror.' His associate Friedrich Engels (1820–95) wrote
in 1874: 'A revolution is certainly the most authoritarian thing there is;
it is the act whereby one part of the population imposes its will upon
the other part by means of rifles, bayonets and cannons – authoritarian
means, if such there be at all;…it must maintain this rule by means of
the terror which its arms inspire in the reactionaries.' Paradigmatically,
on 5 January 1879, Marx said: 'No great movement has ever been inaugurated without bloodshed.' These words, repeated by Stalin, continue
to inspire his contemporary Russian admirers. Despite the evidence to
the contrary, there are constant attempts to dissociate Marxism from
the Soviet experiment by claiming that excesses of violence during and
after the Bolshevik Revolution are 'deviations' from true Marxism. And
this is another paradox: the Bolsheviks, following Marx, used violence
to establish the dictatorship, but this very fidelity to the communist doctrine has given grounds to delegitimize their claims to Marxist heritage.

Marx's idea of human happiness was built upon a denial of traditional humanism, which he called 'false', 'bourgeois' and 'hypocritical', an
ideological support for the existing social class structure, private property
and exploitation. His Bolshevik followers took this further: Maxim Gorky
(1868–1936) articulated the concept of 'proletarian humanism', which
became fundamental to Soviet ideology. In May 1934, Gorky, following
Marx, grounded his concept of proletarian humanism in violence:

> A time approaches when the revolutionary proletariat will step,
> like an elephant, on the mad, the frantic anthill of shopkeepers
> – will step on it and crush it. This is inevitable. Humankind
> cannot perish because it has an insignificant minority that has
> grown creatively decrepit and is decomposing from the fear
> of life and from a morbid yet incurable thirst for gain. The
> demise of this minority is an act of great justice, and this act
> history commands the proletariat to carry out. This great act
> will be followed by the peoples of the world working together
> in friendship and fraternity to create, in beauty, a new life.

Gorky's article received enthusiastic endorsement from Joseph Stalin, who appropriated the concept of 'proletarian humanism' for himself. Emerging as it did on the eve of the Great Terror (1936–8), this concept proved helpful in legitimizing the repressions. So, here is another paradox: the concept of humanism was used by the Bolsheviks to legitimize terror.

The Soviet narrative about the revolution was called into question in a variety of ways by Russian intellectuals critical of the Soviet regime. Among the contesting narratives in Russian debates today are the liberal and the nationalist. Their premises often overlap, and both acquired their current outline during the political liberalization that followed Stalin's death in 1953. Both have survived into the post-Soviet period.

Liberal and nationalist scholars both denied the inevitability of the revolution, seeing it as an illegitimate coup d'état conducted by armed brigands who established control by means of ruthless terror. Both accused Lenin of collusion with the Germans, who financed the Bolsheviks. The liberal narrative blamed the Bolsheviks for ending the Westernization of Russia that had been initiated by Peter the Great (r. 1682–1725), which had made European norms and way of life an existential cultural choice for progressive Russians as opposed to the traditional values and way of life of the peasantry. By contrast, the nationalists reproached the Bolsheviks for the destruction of the peasant world.

The nationalists, many openly anti-Semitic, opposed Soviet 'internationalism' and reproduced claims made by the ultra-nationalists during the civil war, which resemble Nazi propaganda: that the Bolsheviks were Jews, the revolution was a Jewish conspiracy and the Jews were responsible for all the crimes and failures of the Soviet regime. Its proponents counted how many Jews there were among the Bolshevik revolutionary leaders, the NKVD perpetrators, etc. Nationalists accused Lenin of treason for concluding the Brest-Litovsk peace with Germany on 3 March 1918, which resulted in the loss of territories, people, industries and international prestige. In October 2017, on the centennial of the revolution, this opinion was voiced by the Russian minister of culture, Vladimir Medinsky (b. 1970), who described ending the First World War as 'a huge political and historical mistake of the Bolsheviks, which could even be called treason' and blamed the Bolsheviks for 'putting their own interests above those of the state'. Nationalists empathized with the tsarist regime despite its disastrous inefficiency, and created a cult of the counter-revolutionary White Guard officers as models of male chauvinist supremacy. Paradoxically, despite the official Soviet internationalism, many Communist Party and Soviet apparatchiks of the 1970s and 1980s were deeply immersed in this cult.

The liberal narrative stressed that the revolution had been a murderous event that subjected the country to Red Terror and White Terror and a bloody civil war, and led to the Stalinist purges. This narrative offered social evolution in opposition to the Marxist idea of revolution as the only engine of social change: thus Yegor Gaidar, liberal economist and prime minister (1992) of the first post-Soviet democratic government, wrote *State and Evolution*, parodying *State and Revolution*, Lenin's canonic treatise on how to seize power. The memory of the Terror, the bloodshed of the civil war, the millions of lives lost and all the suffering brought by the revolution constitute the core of this narrative, which played an important role in stopping the pro-communist military coup in August 1991. By reminding Russians of the horrors caused by October 1917 and what followed, the liberal narrative was instrumental in turning the collapse of communism into a velvet revolution in Russia, which made

Boris Yeltsin (1931–2007) the first Russian president who peacefully took power, in 1991.

Today, Soviet and anti-Soviet narratives still polarize Russian public opinion, as reflected in the surveys conducted in April 2017. Some 48 per cent of respondents agree that the revolution was historically inevitable, while 46 per cent think that the Bolsheviks' coup was illegitimate. Forty-nine per cent agree that the revolution 'delivered a significant blow to Russian culture', while 48 per cent think that its role in Russian history was quite or highly positive. Thirty-two per cent believe that if the Bolsheviks had not seized power, some 'worse extremists', whose rule would have been even more devastating, would have taken over. Forty-two per cent think that the destruction of the Russian nobility as a social group was a terrible loss for Russia. The survey data also show that mutually exclusive statements belonging to these different narratives coexist in the mentality of the respondents, reflecting clashes of conflicting versions of historical memories of this event at the individual level.

During the centennial year, there was much discussion that Putin sought to discredit the very idea of revolution out of fear of an 'Orange Revolution', or a repetition of the democratic protests against fraud elections of the State Duma (the Russian parliament) of 2011–12. To that end, his ideologists have borrowed fragments from both liberal and nationalist anti-Soviet narratives. On a number of occasions, Putin spoke disapprovingly of the October Revolution, contrasting it to the 'national unity' that he tries to present as his most important political goal. This nationalist idea coexists with the liberal narrative about the October Revolution as an incarnation of abhorrent violence, implying that revolution means terror. His supporter and president of the Council of the Federation, Valentina Matviyenko (b. 1949), expressed this view straightforwardly, saying that 'President Putin...had to rescue the country from chaos, new revolutions and bloodshed.'

However, other comments by Putin about the revolution received almost no attention. Considered separately, they sound paradoxical if not plainly absurd; but taken together, they shed light on his ideology. The 2017 centennial gave him an occasion to promote the messianic

idea of Russia that, ever since his early days in office, has been a building block of the ideology associated with his name. The most politically
important was the claim that Russia sacrificed itself to save the world
from the evil of fascism; hence anyone who opposes Russia's interests
is a fascist. This is why, for example, Ukrainians have been consistently
dubbed 'fascists' by the Russian media following the Maidan revolution of 2014 and Russia's annexation of Crimea. This messianic myth
comprises other claims that have been in circulation since the 17th
century: Russia is the 'Third Rome', the heir of Byzantium and the
saviour of true Christian Orthodox religion; Russia saved Europe from
the Tatar yoke, and later from Napoleon. Then, in 2017, Putin added a
claim that the West benefited from the October Revolution, since many
achievements of the West – the 'rise of the living standards, creation
of the strong middle class, labour reforms and social security, human
rights and rights of minorities, and overcoming the segregation in the
US' – were the results of the challenge posed to the West by the USSR.

On another occasion, Putin blamed Lenin for 'mining Russia with
an atomic bomb that blew it up later on'. This resonates with his statement of 2005, that the collapse of the Soviet Union was 'the greatest
geopolitical catastrophe in human history'. This highly negative view of
Lenin cannot be explained by political rivalry with the Communist Party,
which is completely controlled by Putin's coalition and offers no serious
threat to him today. In accordance with the nationalist narrative, Lenin
is blamed for ending both the Russian Empire and Russia's participation in the First World War. Putin's attitude to Stalin is very different:
in 2017 he said, 'Stalin was a man of his time. On the one hand, he may
be demonized, on the other, his role in the victory over fascism should
be brought into the equation... I think that the demonization of Stalin
is a way to attack USSR and Russia.' He added that his own parents, 'like
everybody else, adored Stalin'.

Russian messianism and nostalgia for the empire, the tributes to
Stalin for expanding the Soviet Empire and establishing a strong state
echo the core claims of the Eurasia movement, which declares Russia a
self-sufficient civilization of a higher order than the West and envisions

the future of the Eurasian continent united under Russian domination. The movement calls for the 'return to the New Middle Ages' and advocates for the reconstruction of absolute monarchy and the society of estates in Russia; but the reconstruction and expansion of the Russian Empire is its main political goal – which makes its adherents admire Stalin and despise Lenin. The leader of Eurasianism, Alexander Dugin (b. 1962), openly praises fascism and allegedly has considerable influence over Putin. He hates Marxism but has paradoxically repeated Marx's formula, in saying about Stalin that no great deeds could be achieved without bloodshed.

Among the indications of the influence this ideology has on Russians are the popularity of the annexation of Crimea in 2014, which boosted Putin's personal approval rating by 20 points to 85 per cent in January 2015, and changes in the public attitudes to Lenin and Stalin. The number of people who consider Lenin and Trotsky 'the most attractive revolutionary leaders' has more than halved since 1990 (from 67 per cent to 29 per cent), while Stalin's popularity has grown three times to 24 per cent; and the proportion of those who dislike Stalin plummeted from 49 per cent to 21 per cent. This liking for Stalin is doubtlessly the result of re-Stalinization, the memory politics, which has been conducted by the Russian government since 2003. Similarly, the number of those who believe that the destruction of Russian autocratic monarchy was a terrible loss for Russia has trebled since 1990, to 34 per cent. Numerous internet petitions to crown Putin as tsar also suggest that this idea has taken root.

To conclude, one more paradox: Putin's Russia still provokes sympathies among the political left in the US and more widely, as if the reflected light of Red October still sparkles on the Kremlin's walls. Some of Putin's fellow travellers keep seeing Russia as the cradle of left politics and the site of a progressive socialist experiment, or as a viable alternative to US imperialism, colonialism and capitalism. Paradoxically, they are not discouraged by the fact that Russia's regime fears and despises revolutions and denounces Lenin and the communist ideology, generates extreme social inequality by unprecedented corruption, conducts aggressive international politics and hallucinates about reconstructing the Russian Empire.

Vladimir Ilich Ulyanov

Vladimir Ilich Ulyanov 'Lenin' (1870–1924) developed his revolutionary views in the 1890s at Kazan University – from which he was expelled in his freshman year, when he was arrested and exiled to Siberia. He then emigrated to western Europe, where he remained until Russia's February Revolution of 1917. With the support of Germany (at war with Russia), he returned to St Petersburg to attack the Provisional Government, take control of the Bolshevik Party and organize the coup of 25 October. He took the position of head of the Soviet government, fighting the civil war against the counter-revolutionary 'Whites' while attempting to transform Russia into a centralized, socialist state with all property nationalized. By 1921, the civil war was won; but with the economy in tatters and the people starving, Lenin pulled back from some of his socialist policies, allowing a limited return to private enterprise. Following the onset of ill health in 1921 his capacity to work was limited, but he remained in office until his death from syphilis in 1924. By this time, his voluminous writings were being published, making his thoughts the most widely accepted extension and updating of Marx's work, both within Russia and elsewhere.

Leon Trotsky

Leon Trotsky (1879–1940), son of a Jewish farmer in Ukraine, became a revolutionary as a young man and, like Lenin, was exiled to Siberia and to western Europe until he returned to Russia in February 1917. He joined the Bolsheviks, and was key to the success of the October Revolution. As War Commissar, he built up the Red Army in the civil war by extreme terror, and organized a countrywide propaganda effort to promote revolutionary ideas. Although he expected to be Lenin's successor, he was out-manoeuvred by Joseph Stalin. After criticizing Stalin's focus on the Soviet Union and what he saw as a retreat from the international values of 'Permanent Revolution' – namely, export of the revolution to the Western world – he was ejected from the Communist Party in 1927 and went into exile, finally settling in Mexico, where he was murdered by Stalin's agent. The influence of his writings remains strong among revolutionary groups in many countries that seek to challenge bourgeois institutions and establish a workers' state, even where capitalism is not well advanced.

TIMELINE

1861   Tsar Alexander II emancipates the Russian serfs

1881   Alexander II is assassinated in St Petersburg

1881-94 Reign of Alexander III

1894   Nicholas II ascends to the throne

1905
9 January   Bloody Sunday in St Petersburg after troops fire on peaceful
             demonstration; 1,000 die

June   Sailors on *Potemkin* battleship mutiny at Odessa

September   Treaty of Portsmouth recognizes Russia's defeat at the hands
             of Japan in 1904–5 war

October   Tsar issues October Manifesto, promising civil liberties and
             elected Duma

1911   Modernizing prime minister Stolypin assassinated

1914
August   Germany declares war on Russia, initiating the
             First World War; St Petersburg is renamed Petrograd

1917
March   'February Revolution' in Petrograd begins with days of
             demonstrations, bloodily suppressed; the Tsar abdicates and the
             Provisional Government is established

April   Lenin returns from exile in Switzerland and prepares for
             military coup

July   Alexander Kerensky takes over as head of the Provisional
             Government, following days of demonstrations by workers and
             soldiers, the 'July Days'; many Bolsheviks are arrested and Lenin
             goes into hiding

September   General Kornilov stages a failed coup to counter the Bolsheviks

October	Bolsheviks seize power in Petrograd and take the Winter Palace
November	Socialist Revolutionaries defeat Bolsheviks in elections to the Constituent Assembly
December	Lenin issues a decree to create the secret police, the Cheka

1918

January	Bolsheviks dissolve the Constituent Assembly and establish the Red Army
March	Bolsheviks make peace with Germany at Brest-Litovsk, ceding much of Russia's land, including Ukraine, and industrial base; Bolsheviks change name to Communist Party
June	War Communism is introduced with nationalization of large-scale industry
July	Nicholas II and family are executed; civil war begins between 'Reds' and 'Whites' (anti-revolutionary forces)
August	Failed assassination attempt on Lenin begins the 'Red Terror' mass arrests and executions

1919

March	Comintern (Third International) is established in Moscow to spread the Bolshevik Revolution globally

1921

March	Lenin introduces the 'New Economic Policy', permitting some private property and markets

1922

April	Joseph Stalin becomes general secretary of the Communist Party
December	Union of Soviet Socialist Republics (USSR) is established

1924

21 January	Lenin dies
December	Stalin introduces policy of 'Socialism in One Country'

THE INDIAN REVOLUTION, 1947

Mihir Bose

The Indian Revolution against British rule saw a mass movement, led by a motivated political party, undermine and then expel a notable military power. Unusually for such a movement in a non-democratic environment, the victory was achieved through the disciplined but widespread use of moral rather than military force – thanks in large part to the personality of its leading spirit Mohandas 'Mahatma' Gandhi and his doctrines of soul-force (*satyagraha*) and non-violence (*ahimsa*). As such, it has continued to inspire idealistic revolutionaries – including Martin Luther King, Jr in the United States civil rights movement – across the world.

Nevertheless, India's revolution was by no means all idealistic, and conflict continued, both before and after independence was achieved in August 1947, between different visions of the future society – whether leftist or traditional, secular or religious – as well as between the different social and communal groupings that made up the independence movement. This was most dramatically demonstrated during the Second World War when Indians were fighting on both the Allied and the Axis sides, each seeing their involvement as a route to independence.

Perhaps the greatest of the anti-colonial revolutions of the 20th century, Indian independence was both a triumph and a disaster, involving the partition of the country with violent and enduring hostilities between the two successor states, India and Pakistan. The competing visions of what independent India should be continue to play out more than seventy years on. This, like so many in this book, is an unfinished revolution.

PF

The Indian Revolution brought independence in 1947. It would never have happened had the British given India dominion status after the First World War, as they did to Australia, Canada, New Zealand and South Africa – but the British could not believe that non-whites were capable of ruling themselves.

On 20 August 1917, the Liberal secretary of state for India, Edwin Montagu (1879–1924), had announced that the aim in India was 'the progressive realization of responsible government'. Some British historians have claimed that this set India on the road to freedom, and the revolution was therefore irrelevant. However, the minutes of the War Cabinet that met six days earlier clearly show that is not what was meant at all.

The cabinet agreed with Lord Curzon (1859–1925), former viceroy of India (1899–1905), who thought it might take Indians 500 years to free themselves. It was, said Curzon, 'the wildest of dreams' that India would ever become a self-governing dominion as the white dominions had become. 'In the march towards the self-governing ideal, the political unity of India may be disintegrated...but of one thing we may be sure, it would disappear altogether if the protecting power [e.g. Britain] were withdrawn.' Arthur Balfour (1848–1930), who within months would promise Jews a national home in Palestine, warned that self-government meant 'parliamentary government on a democratic basis', but the Indians were not the same race as the British, and even with education they could not overcome their racial problems. As Sir Penderel Moon put it in *The British Conquest and Dominion of India* (1989), 'The goal for India as defined in August 1917 did not, therefore, imply India would become a wholly independent state.' Even in 1943, Viceroy Lord

Linlithgow (1887–1952) estimated it would take Indians fifty years to learn to rule themselves but, for that, five or six million British would have to come and live in India and act as tutors. At the height of the Raj only about 150,000 British had lived in India, but Linlithgow felt that, with air-conditioning, more might be tempted to come.

So the seeds of revolution were sown in the first decades of the 20th century, in the conflict between what the British meant and what the Indians assumed they meant. The initial spark was lit immediately after the First World War. The Indians expected to be rewarded for their massive contribution to the war effort – in 1918 even Mohandas Gandhi (1869–1948), leader of the Indian National Congress, forsook his long-standing pacifism to become a recruiter for the British army. But instead of liberty, the British responded with draconian powers for search and arrest without warrant and confinement without trial. The Indians called it 'na dalil, na vakil, na appeal': no argument, no lawyer, no appeal. In response, Gandhi turned into a rebel. On 6 April 1919, he launched the first of his four major campaigns for swaraj (self-government, or home rule). Unlike most revolutionary campaigns, these were based on satyagraha, or soul-force: a commitment to the non-violence of the objective.

Seven days later, on 13 April 1919, General Reginald Dyer (1864–1927) opened fire with no warning on unarmed Indians who had gathered in Jallianwala Bagh, a park in Amritsar, to celebrate the Sikh festival of Baisakhi. His troops killed 337 men, 41 boys and a baby, with up to 1,500 others injured. Dyer also issued an infamous order – that British troops should ensure all Indians who crossed a street where a British woman had been savagely beaten were forced to crawl on their bellies. While Dyer was condemned by the secretary of state for war Winston Churchill (1874–1965), many others in Britain applauded Dyer – with the Archbishop of Canterbury describing him as 'a brave, public-spirited and patriotic solider'. The reaction so shocked the Congress activist and Cambridge-educated Jawaharlal Nehru (1889–1964) that he felt 'how brutal and immoral imperialism was and how it had eaten into the souls of the British upper class'. The massacre convinced Nehru and many

Indians, who until then had believed in what historian Sunil Khilnani has called 'mendicant constitutionalism', that they could no longer rely on handouts from the British to win freedom.

It took another ten years for Gandhi to move beyond his belief in home rule to become an 'independence wallah'. Crucial in Gandhi's conversion was the 1927 decision to send the Simon Commission to India to judge how far Indians had come in learning to rule themselves. The seven members were all white males, one of them a young Clement Attlee (1883–1967), who as prime minister (1945–51) would eventually agree to Indian independence and partition. Attlee left India convinced that the Indians had become anti-British because of 'some social snub which had been administered to them'. He called Indian nationalism 'the illegitimate offspring of patriotism out of inferiority complex' and fretted about the prospect of more 'jobbery and corruption' as self-government advanced.

Gandhi's reaction was to launch the greatest of his non-violent campaigns. On 12 March 1930 he began a walk from his ashram near Ahmedabad to Dandi, a village on the coast of Gujarat, 240 miles away. In his letter to the Viceroy Lord Irwin (1881–1959), he did not ask for independence but the removal of the tax the British had imposed on the manufacture of salt. To gain freedom by making salt by the seaside appeared quixotic, but Gandhi had shrewdly worked out that a tax that weighed heavily on the poor could be made into a symbol of the fight to be free of foreign rule. The campaign rocked the Raj, and Irwin, who had initially imprisoned Gandhi, invited him to talks in 1931.

Unlike the British talks with Irish nationalists, which led to the Anglo-Irish Treaty of 1921, Gandhi's talks with Irwin did not lead to Indian freedom; but even so, as Churchill observed, a rebel was now parleying 'on equal terms with the representative of the King Emperor'. This marked a seminal moment in the Indian Revolution.

Ironically, another aspect of the Indian Revolution recalled the Irish experience: violent uprisings often ran in parallel with Gandhi's pacific soul-force revolution. On 18 April 1930, twelve days after Gandhi broke the salt law, sixty-two young Indians sought to induce an Indian version of Ireland's 1916 Easter Rising. They seized the police and auxiliary forces' armouries and set up a provisional revolutionary government in Chittagong, Bengal. This attempt – which the British called 'an amazing coup' – did not succeed, but the Chittagong rebels represented many in India who rejected Gandhi's pacifist approach.

And just as Ireland had the 'orange card' – in the form of Protestant Ulstermen, who could be relied on to display a determined opposition to independence – so the Indian Revolution had its 'green card': Muslims who had been ruling India when the British arrived. Gandhi, a Hindu, never came to terms with this green card, and his attempts to form an alliance with Muslims were often opportunistic – as in 1919, when he supported the campaign for the Ottoman Sultan to remain the Caliph (titular head of the Muslim world). This proved a fiasco when the Ottoman Empire was replaced by the secular state of Turkey and the Caliphate was abolished. Also, Gandhi's campaign to launch civil disobedience alienated Muhammad Ali Jinnah (1876–1948), the leader of the All-India Muslim League. Once a political colleague, in 1920 he described Gandhi's movement as 'neither logical nor politically sound'.

Gandhi neither sought nor obtained foreign help; yet events abroad eventually triggered the departure of the British. First was Japan's victories across South-East Asia in 1941–2, which destroyed the mystique of white supremacy. Then in 1943, Subhas Chandra Bose (1897–1945) – a former president of the Congress who had fallen out with Gandhi and never subscribed to his policy of non-violence – with Japanese help, formed an Indian National Army (INA) from Indian soldiers taken prisoner by the Japanese. For Bose, the INA was the army of his Provisional Government of Free India, as opposed to the British Indian Army, which subjugated India. The army did not amount to much and Bose died in an air crash in August 1945, days after Japan's surrender. However, when the British court-martialled officers of his defeated army, Bose had an unexpected posthumous success.

The war had split India. Over a million Indians fought for the British, yet Gandhi's Quit India movement of 1942 led to such countrywide protests – with police stations burnt, post offices raided and trains derailed – that

Linlithgow told the War Cabinet that British rule was under the most severe threat it had faced since the revolt of 1857. Some 35,000 men were used to keep India down. Gandhi and most of the Congress leadership were arrested; whipping was reintroduced; troops had to open fire in 538 instances, and on six occasions rebel territories were bombed from the air. On 20 March 1943, Major General Rob Lockhart (1893–1981), military secretary in the India Office, wrote in a secret note: 'For the duration of the War, and probably for some time after, India must be considered as an occupied and hostile country.' The same year also saw a famine in Bengal, South Asia's worst famine of the 20th century. British incompetence and indifference saw an estimated four million Bengalis die.

It was against this background that the INA trials opened in November 1945. The soldiers, charged with treason, were defended by some of India's most brilliant lawyers. Nehru, who had once said he would fight Bose's army, now donned his barrister's robes to defend Bose's soldiers as freedom fighters; and even Gandhi expressed admiration for Bose. There were numerous protests that resulted in the police opening fire. Mutinies broke out in various parts of India, and in Bombay for a few days in January 1946, virtually the whole Royal Indian Navy was in open rebellion. Textile workers joined in what the British-owned *Times of India* called a 'mass uprising in sympathy with the naval mutiny unparalleled in the city's history'. In March 1946 an Allied victory parade in Delhi was abandoned, with the town hall ablaze and mob violence leading to the police opening fire.

Such was the scale of the protests that Claude Auchinleck (1884–1981), the commander-in-chief who had ordered the INA trials and thought he knew the British Indian Army, now confessed, 'there is a growing feeling of sympathy for the "INA"'. The British now accepted that the soldiers were patriots, not traitors, and treated them as prisoners of war. The British could no longer rely on Indian collaborators to sustain the Raj, while British soldiers had no wish to fight to preserve the Indian Empire.

The war had also changed the political equation between the Congress and Jinnah's Muslim League. In 1937 the Congress had taken part in the elections, held on a very limited franchise, for the various provinces of British India (there were no elections in the third of India ruled by the princes). The Congress had won a massive victory that proved it was the only truly national party, with the Muslim League vanquished and often losing to rival Muslim parties. The Congress formed ministers in eight of the eleven provinces of British India. This did not mean freedom, as the British still ruled the central Indian government and ministerial power was limited; but, in effect, at the start of the war the Congress was inside the British tent.

However, Linlithgow declared war on Germany without consulting a single Indian, and – despite saying Britain had gone to war to preserve Poland's freedom – he refused to even discuss when India might be free. Gandhi and the Congress found this hypocritical, and between October and November 1939, Congress ministers resigned from the provincial governments and British civil servants once again took charge. This was the cue for Jinnah to make his game-changing move. As Gandhi walked out of the British tent, Jinnah walked in; throughout the war he curried favour with the Raj, and in 1940 he demanded Pakistan as a homeland for Indian Muslims. By the end of the war Jinnah and his Muslim League, which had looked so bereft in 1939, were a major force. Jinnah was determined to get Pakistan, saying, 'Pakistan is a question of life and death for us.'

In August 1946, Jinnah called for a Direct Action Day to ensure Pakistan came into being. It started with Muslim slaughter of Hindus in Kolkata, followed by massive Hindu retaliation in the kind of religious warfare the country had rarely seen. By this time the British had realized they had to leave, and were trying to get the Congress and the Muslim League to work together in an administration to run the country. A constituent assembly was set up, but the divide was too great; and both the Congress and the Muslim League were finding it difficult to control their followers. In February 1947, Attlee announced Britain would leave by June 1948, sending Lord Louis Mountbatten (1900–79) as viceroy to carry out the transfer of power. But on arrival Mountbatten quickly concluded the British could not hold on, and decided to bring the departure date forward to August 1947.

Historians have long debated whether Mountbatten's decision to cut and run was responsible for the holocaust of Partition, where one million died and many millions more were uprooted, with Hindus fleeing newly formed Pakistan and Muslims the other way. Twenty years earlier, a peaceful transition of power might have been possible. But back in 1925 Lord Birkenhead, then secretary of state for India, had written to the Viceroy saying the Muslims were a 'powerful and virile' community and the British should emphasize the differences between Hindus and Muslims, as it 'illustrated that we, and we alone, can play the part of composers'. By 1947, the British, having ruthlessly played the card of divide and rule for several decades, had become hapless spectators as the subcontinent burned.

At that time many British observers, who had always preferred the Muslims to the Hindus, thought Pakistan would be the more virile state and dismissed India's chances of surviving. However, to the surprise even of some Indians, India has become the world's largest democracy – and, unlike Pakistan, its army has never left the barracks. However, this great achievement cannot conceal the reality that the Indian Revolution remains unfinished. For years Partition was a taboo subject, and it was almost thirty years after independence before Indian filmmakers even tackled the issue.

The Congress Party of Gandhi and Nehru had reluctantly accepted Partition, hoping that Pakistan would collapse and India would be reunited. In 1971, the genocide by the West Pakistan Punjabi army of its Bengali citizens in East Pakistan enabled India to help create Bangladesh and explode the myth that religion can unite people who are culturally divided. However, Pakistan survives, helped by its historic alliance with America; India and Pakistan have fought four wars over the disputed territory of Kashmir, and Indians keep trying to brand Pakistan a terrorist state. The default position in Indian politics is for a politician to pose as the strong man who will stand up to Pakistan.

The shadow cast by Partition means that the story of the Indian Revolution is such a pottage of conflicting ideas that it often resembles kicheree, a popular dish that mixes rice, lentils, vegetables and egg.

Gandhi is revered as the father of the nation, yet his economic ideas of a return to a pre-industrial age built around village life have no relevance in a country that Nehru set on becoming a Western-style industrial society. Only Gandhi's policy of prohibiting alcohol was accepted, with people requiring permits to drink – but even this policy has been largely abandoned. Gandhi built his entire campaign around non-violence, yet Indians who took to violence to achieve independence can today be found on the same moral plane as Gandhi. School textbooks laud both Gandhi and the young revolutionary socialist Bhagat Singh, who killed a British police officer in Lahore and was hanged in 1931. Gandhi had condemned Bhagat Singh's 'revolutionary terrorism', warning that it was 'easy natural step' from 'violence done to the foreign ruler' to 'violence to our own people'. But most Indians now find no contradiction in having Gandhi's image on every rupee note while also having stamps to honour Bhagat Singh.

The most curious kicheree is how independent India has tackled caste. For centuries the hierarchical Hindu caste system had seen the upper castes, led by the Brahmin, despicably treat those they considered untouchable. This is the Indian equivalent of America's original sin of slavery – the American founding fathers did not tackle slavery, and it was nearly 200 years before blacks in the American south got the vote. Independent India's approach to caste and the vote was significantly different. The British electoral system for India was, as the writer Nirad Chaudhuri said, 'as absurd intellectually as it was both inequitable and iniquitous morally'. Only 14 per cent could vote, the rest barred by property and educational qualification. There were twelve separate electorates, and voting took place according to a person's religion, sex, race and seats for commerce, industry and universities. Independent Indians rejected this system and opted for one person, one vote.

This was a major breakthrough for the untouchable castes (now called Dalits): in the polling booth, they were the equal of their former tormentors. They have made the most of this electoral power. As the sociologist Ashis Nandy points out, the Indian political system 'has a much higher representation of the low castes and Dalits...in fact it is much more difficult for you to become the chief minister of an Indian state if you are from an upper caste'. And the Dalits have a champion, Bhimrao Ambedkar (1891–1956), who matches Gandhi. He overcame dreadful discrimination, became a lawyer, played a key role in drafting the constitution and eventually became a Buddhist to escape Hinduism. Today he is honoured with a holiday, and his portrait hangs in public places and banks.

Further, India's founding fathers introduced positive discrimination, reserving a percentage of government jobs and places in educational institutions for Dalits. But it has not worked out as planned. Meant to last just ten years, this system not only still exists but has now been extended, with 2,399 'socially and educationally backward castes' entitled to reservations. It required a ruling in the Indian Supreme Court to restrict reservations to 50 per cent. Amazingly, some higher-caste Hindus, who once would never have even dined with a Dalit, may now claim they are lower-caste in order to qualify for reservations.

Another essential feature of Nehru's vision for India was its secularism. Unlike the United States, where politicians conventionally broadcast their Christian faith, in Nehru's India anyone talking about religion was branded a communalist, the Indian word for a religious bigot. This vision has been challenged in recent decades by the growth of a populist Hindu movement.

Some Hindus had always opposed secularism, and in 1948 Gandhi himself had been murdered by a fanatical Hindu. But in the 1990s they found a winning electoral formula. Hindutva – militant Hindu nationalism – had emerged in the colonial era, and survived Nehru's attempt to wean Hindus away from such religious bigotry. They have now succeeded in convincing many Hindus that Nehru's secularism meant they had lost their country. Hindutva seeks to make Hinduism the state religion, and wants all Indians to accept the Hindu culture of India. Prime Minister Narendra Modi (b. 1950) has shrewdly used Hindutva to win two elections (2014 and 2019). While he himself concentrates on talking of bringing prosperity by helping business, many around him promote Hindutva – which may combine fantastic claims that ancient Hindus had nuclear weapons with growing intolerance of religious minorities. Such has been Modi's impact that supposedly secular politicians are no longer shy to advertise their Hindu credentials, which would have shocked the atheist Nehru. The Hindutva movement has also exploited the distrust of English-speaking Indians who ruled India for half a century, presenting them as an elite that never lost their love for the old colonial power.

It is this fight between Nehru's secularism and Modi's Hindutva that will determine the final outcome of the Indian Revolution.

Mohandas Gandhi

Mohandas ('Mahatma', Great Soul) Gandhi (1869–1948) qualified as a barrister in London before going to South Africa in
1893, where he experienced racial discrimination and began
to campaign for the rights of Indians. During the Anglo-Boer
War (1899–1902) he organized a volunteer ambulance corps
and engaged in religious studies. On returning to India in
1915 he initially supported the war effort, but in 1919 began
a programme of *satyagraha* (soul-force) mass-disobedience
opposition to British rule. By 1924 he was the president of
the Congress Party and sought to bring together its warring
factions. In 1930 he led the Salt March against the British
salt monopoly, and travelled to London for talks on the future
of India. Repeatedly imprisoned, and frequently responding
with a protest fast, he left Congress in 1934 to concentrate on
his vision of rebuilding the traditional, village-based culture
of India. In 1942 he encouraged Congress to adopt the Quit
India Movement. In 1947 he was isolated by the rising tide of
communal violence, and though opposing Partition, sought
reconciliation between Muslim and Hindu communities.
He was assassinated by a Hindu fanatic in January 1948.

Jawaharlal Nehru

Jawaharlal Nehru (1889–1964), Congress statesman and the first prime minister of independent India (1947–64), was born into a Brahmin family. He trained as a barrister in London, practised as a lawyer in India from 1912 and, inspired by Gandhi, joined the Congress in 1919. He underwent several spells of imprisonment, developed an interest in Marxism and was president of the Congress in 1929 when it proclaimed complete independence as its objective. He developed a vision of a secular modern India, distinct from Gandhi's traditionalist view. In 1939 he argued that India should support the fight against Nazism, but only as a free country. Following the Quit India resolution, he was imprisoned from 1942 to 1945; on his release he was recognized as leader of the Congress in its negotiations for independence, and was selected as India's prime minister on independence (15 August 1947). Internally he promoted a secular, democratic socialism; in foreign policy he was a leader of the non-aligned movement, but was drawn into war with China in 1962.

TIMELINE

1885   The Indian National Congress is launched in Bombay

1906   Formation of the Muslim League; Congress calls for *swaraj*
             (self-rule)

1914–18 First World War: 60,000 Indians die in Europe

1915   Gandhi returns to India from South Africa

1919   Massacre at Jallianwala Bagh in Amritsar

1921   Gandhi launches the Civil Disobedience Movement, calling for a
             boycott of British goods

1927–8   The British government appoints the Simon Commission to
             recommend political reforms in India

1930   Gandhi leads the Salt March in protest at the British monopoly
             on salt

1931   Second Round Table Conference in London; Gandhi and Irwin agree
             a pact to end civil disobedience and grant political rights

1935   Government of India Act grants political rights at the provincial
             level

1939   Outbreak of Second World War; the Viceroy unilaterally declares
             India's participation in the war; Congress boycotts the British
             in protest

1941   Subhas Chandra Bose escapes from India, joins with the Axis
             powers in fight against the British

1942
March   Stafford Cripps Mission set up to negotiate India's political status
             after the war

August   The Congress leaders launch 'Quit India' campaign, calling for
             complete independence; the Congress leadership is arrested;

revolts break out across India, and 600 demonstrators lose
their lives

1943   Bose's Indian National Army begins march to India, but is stopped
outside Imphal; widespread famine in Bengal

1945   Labour Party wins British general election

1946   Gandhi–Jinnah talks collapse; communal riots break out

1947   The British, Congress and Muslim League agree to Partition and
Independence

15 August   Independence for India, with Nehru as prime minister, and for
Pakistan, led by Jinnah; communal Partition riots claim hundreds
of thousands of lives

27 October   India and Pakistan go to war over the disputed region of Kashmir

1948
30 January   Gandhi is assassinated by a Hindu nationalist

1952   India holds its first general elections

1962   India and China fight a brief border war

1965   India and Pakistan fight war over Kashmir

1966   Nehru's daughter, Indira Gandhi, becomes prime minister

1971
December   India and Pakistan fight another war over East Pakistan, which
leads to the creation of Bangladesh

1992   Hindu zealots tear down a 16th-century mosque in Ayodhya,
sparking nationwide riots in which about 3,000 people, mostly
Muslims, are killed

1998   Hindu nationalist Bharatiya Janata Party (BJP) forms a coalition
government

VIETNAM: THE AUGUST REVOLUTION, 1945

Stein Tønnesson

The end of the Second World War triggered a wave of nationalist revolutions in the former colonies of the European empires. The Vietnamese revolution coincided exactly with the end of the war in the East, challenging the French, who had ruled Indochina since the late 19th century. While the revolution was initially successful, it was soon crushed in the south by British and French troops; after a period of difficult negotiations, the new regime in the north of Vietnam became involved in a testing war to drive the French from Indochina, followed by a longer, more costly war with South Vietnam and the United States to unite the country.

Combining Marxist ideology with anti-colonial nationalism, revolutionary Vietnam became a model for other independence movements across the world. Despite this, the revolution of 1945 itself soon became eclipsed by the more dramatic and heroic exploits of the country in its two wars, and Ho Chi Minh became an inspiration to revolutionaries and activists worldwide.   PF

The Vietnamese popular uprising of August 1945, in the immediate aftermath of the Japanese surrender in the Second World War, had most of the ingredients needed to qualify as one of the great revolutions alongside the American Revolution (1776), the French

(1789) and the Russian (1917). In the second half of August, young activists seized power in all major cities and towns, setting up People's Committees as foundations for a new republic. A provisional government was established in Hanoi under the veteran communist Ho Chi Minh (1890–1969). Emperor Bao Dai (1913–97), who had been educated in France and installed as a French puppet and for a few months served under Japanese tutelage, abdicated the throne of Annam, to which he had acceded in 1926. The Democratic Republic of Vietnam (DRV) was proclaimed on 2 September at a mass meeting in Hanoi, and its government set out immediately to build a new state with an army to ward off French attempts to reconquer its colony. National elections were held in January 1946, and the National Assembly adopted a republican constitution on 8 November 1946.

Not long after the August uprising unfolded, it was baptized 'the August Revolution' (*Cach Mang Thang Tam*) and analysed in a series of articles by the general secretary of the Indochinese Communist Party, the Marxist ideologue Truong Chinh (1907–88). His ambition was to ensure Vietnam a recognized place in the international revolutionary tradition of the French and Russian revolutions.

Yet this never quite happened. To be sure, Vietnamese children still learn about the August Revolution at school; Ho Chi Minh's declaration of independence is compulsory reading, and every year the movie *The August Star* is shown on TV. Truong Chinh's treatise, compiled for the first anniversary of the revolution in 1946, has been published in multiple editions in Vietnamese, French, English, Russian, Chinese and other languages. A Museum of Revolution in Hanoi takes care of its legacy. Yet the National Museum of History, the Ho Chi Minh Museum and the Museum of Military History are bigger, better equipped and receive more visitors; and the August Revolution is little known internationally. Jack Goldstone's book *Revolutions* (2014) includes a chapter on 'communist revolutions' but fails to mention Vietnam. In 2017, when I complained to a curator at a London exhibition on revolutions that it did not include Vietnam, I was told that Vietnam was a war, not a revolution. Philip Parker in *Revolution: Uprisings that Shaped the Twentieth Century* (2017) tells the stories of eighteen revolutions, including the Cambodian, but does not say a word about the Vietnamese.

Why is this so? The failure of Vietnam to take its proper place in the revolutionary saga has several reasons, only one of which is that its memory was overwhelmed by the tragic heroism of Vietnam's wars with France and America during 1946–75. A more immediate reason was that the August Revolution happened at a time when the world was preoccupied with the end of the Second World War. Not even the international communist press took much notice of it, and when communists around the world heard that a new independent republic had been established under a president called Ho Chi Minh, they did not realize that he was the same man as Nguyen Ai Quoc, a prominent agent of the Communist International in the 1920s and 1930s. By 1945, just after the Allies had won their great victories against German Nazism and Japanese militarism, a communist revolution in a French colony was also not something Joseph Stalin (1878–1953) wanted. He wanted close ties with France, whose Communist Party was a part of the governing coalition.

Another problem for the legacy of the August Revolution was its rapid, easy success. By contrast to the wars that followed, it was virtually bloodless. Some prominent non-communists were murdered, but the insurgents met little resistance. Their seizure of power happened in a power vacuum created by the Japanese emperor's decision of 14 August 1945 to surrender to the Allies. Already, on 9 March of the same year, the Japanese had removed the French colonial regime that had remained in place from 1940 to 1945, serving under the French Vichy government. Japan anticipated an Allied landing in Indochina, which would be supported by the local French forces. However, at this late stage of the war Japan could not replace the French colonial administrators with Japanese, so they had to rely on local collaborators. In 1944–5, north-central Vietnam was ravaged by a horrible famine, causing a desperation that allowed the Viet Nam Doc Lap Dong Minh (Viet Minh) league, which Ho Chi Minh had set up in 1941 in the border region to China, to spread in the Red River Delta as well as down the coast, while other nationalist and communist organizations gained a huge following in the southern

Mekong River delta. When Japan surrendered, local groups seized power in one city and town after the other. The Japanese saw little reason to prevent the revolution from happening, as long as the insurgents did not attack their troops or try to seize the Bank of Indochina and its gold.

Truong Chinh, a voracious reader of French books on revolution, immediately saw it as a challenge to convince people that this seizure of power, in spite of its ease, was a genuine revolution. Hence he titled one of his early articles 'Revolution or Coup?' and strongly argued that it had not been a coup: the goal of the revolution was to generate radical social change, not just replace the governing elite. Hence it was a revolution.

But did it bring social change? Was it really socialist or communist? Or was it just a national revolution in the tradition of the American Revolution, liberating a colonial territory? This question touches on the role of Ho Chi Minh.

Ho had grown up in a patriotic, anti-colonial environment in central Vietnam. As a young man, he left French Indochina, worked his way round the world on ships, took up radical politics in Paris and joined the French Communist Party at its foundation in 1920. In 1923, he left to be trained in the Soviet Union as an agent of the Communist International called Nguyen Ai Quoc (Nguyen the Patriot); settled down for a while in Guangzhou, where he trained a group of young revolutionary Vietnamese exiles; took part in forming communist parties in Malaya and Thailand; and presided over the foundation of the Indochinese Communist Party in Hong Kong in 1930. During the 1930s he was sentenced to death in absentia by a French Indochinese court and imprisoned for a while by British authorities in Hong Kong, but released again so that he could return to the Soviet Union. He survived Stalin's purges and in 1938 went back to China, where he spent time at the headquarters of Mao Zedong (1893–1976) in Yan'an, Shaanxi, before establishing himself in the border region between China and Vietnam. Here he set up the Viet Minh League with a small army of guerrillas, recruited from among the local ethnic minorities.

Most books about Vietnam touch on the question of whether Ho was a nationalist or a communist; most sensible authors reply: 'Both.'

Yet some see him as a nationalist using communist techniques and doctrines to further nationalist goals, while others claim he used nationalism to further communist objectives. During 1945–7, Ho's primary concern was to secure Vietnam's liberation from France so that it could be an independent country. He felt he needed support from all social classes, and thus he downplayed his communism and took no initiative relating to land reform. He even invited former emperor Bao Dai to serve as supreme advisor in his government.

At that time, Ho could not expect any assistance from the distant Soviet Union, and Mao's Red Army was still far away; so he cultivated local US representatives, appealed to the USA for help, and included a reference to the 1776 American Declaration of Independence in his own independence declaration on 2 September 1945. When the Chinese nationalist forces of Generalissimo Chiang Kai-shek (1887–1975) entered northern Vietnam to receive the Japanese surrender, Ho Chi Minh used his diplomatic skills to cultivate their commanders so they would allow him to stay in power. On 22 November 1945, to the dismay of General Secretary Truong Chinh, Ho obtained a decision to officially dissolve the Indochinese Communist Party, which he had set up fifteen years earlier. In March 1946, he formed a coalition government with two pro-Chinese nationalist parties; when foreigners asked about his communism, he said that it was a matter for the future. He brokered two deals with France (on 6 March and 15 September 1946) after it had reconquered South Vietnam, allowing it to establish a military presence also in the North.

Through his moderation, he managed to preserve the new republican state and prove that his authority extended to the population in the French-controlled South. Vietnam's unification under an independent regime, however, was anathema to the local French authorities. They deliberately provoked a crisis that led Vietnam's armed forces to seize the initiative and attack the French in Hanoi on 19 December 1946. This was how the Indochina War began: revolution brought counter-revolutionary intervention, which in turn led to standoff, negotiation and eventually war. In 1947, Ho's moderation turned from an asset into a liability for the Vietnamese communists. They needed foreign support, but their revolution had no high standing in the international communist movement – Ho was seen in Moscow and other communist capitals as a nationalist deviator. In the years from 1945 to 1949, this prevented the August Revolution from acquiring an international status as heir to the October Revolution.

With the outbreak of war with France, the Vietnamese communists were forced to resort to a protracted resistance waged with guerrilla tactics. This put them in a situation similar to the one the Chinese communists had faced after Chiang Kai-shek attacked them in 1927. From 1947, the Viet Minh and the Chinese Red Army fought parallel struggles. Then, with the Red Army's 1949–50 victory and the setup of the People's Republic of China, the war in Indochina was transformed from an anti-colonial war of liberation to a 'hot' war within the broader context of the Cold War between communism and capitalism. In January 1950, China and the Soviet Union recognized the DRV, and Ho could visit Beijing and Moscow. Subsequently, the Viet Minh received huge military assistance from China to upgrade its struggle to conventional warfare and win battles against the French – first in October 1950, when the French were forced to abandon the border region to China, and finally at Dien Bien Phu in May 1954, so an international agreement could be negotiated at Geneva allowing Ho's government to return to Hanoi. The cost was to accept a temporary partition of Vietnam at the 17th parallel, between a socialist North and an anti-communist South, where a counter-revolutionary state had been established by the French in 1949–50 under former emperor Bao Dai. He was ousted in 1955 by his prime minister, the anti-communist Catholic leader Ngo Dinh Diem (1901–63), who became president of a new republic.

The successful Chinese revolution fostered an alternative revolutionary model to that of the October (1917) and August (1945) revolutions. While those had been city-based uprisings leading to the establishment of a republic that would afterwards engage in civil war with counter-revolutionary forces, the Chinese seized power through a People's War, with peasant armies fighting a guerrilla struggle at first, then upgrading it to conventional warfare, encircling cities and conquering them from the outside. From 1950, with help from Chinese advisors, the Vietnamese applied the People's War strategy at a horrendous cost to their people; yet they won against France in 1954, held out against the United States so it would withdraw its troops in 1973 and, finally, triumphed against South Vietnam on 30 April 1975.

Meanwhile, the Vietnamese communists sought to overcome the legacy of Ho Chi Minh's 'mistakes' during the 1945–6 period by founding the Vietnam Workers' Party (Lao Dong) in 1951 and carrying out a brutal land reform in North Vietnam during 1953–6, with tens of thousands of landowners killed. This was a way of proving themselves in the eyes of Moscow and Beijing; but they went too far. It was difficult to distinguish between small and big landowners in northern Vietnam, where few were really big and many just a little more than small. The bloodbath turned out so badly that the senior leaders had to apologize in 1956. Truong Chinh took the blame, and stepped down as general secretary of the party.

It was during the land reform that the Vietnamese Army won the battle of Dien Bien Phu against a US-supported and heavily armed French expeditionary force. The reform, in fact, created an opportunity to promise land to surviving soldiers. This military victory, carried out under the command of General Vo Nguyen Giap (1911–2013) with Chinese assistance and counselling, overshadowed the August Revolution and has been the subject of many books and films.

Yet the August Revolution continued to influence the thinking of the Vietnamese communist leaders. They wanted to prove themselves as true Leninists, and not just copy the Chinese People's War. During the American War of 1964–73 they tried to foster new city-based revolutions in the South – building on the August 1945 experience, yet now in close coordination with military offensives. This was the general idea behind the Tet Offensive of January–February 1968. The Hanoi leadership, now dominated by Lê Duân (1907–86), who had long served in the South, expected that a combination of an offensive by regular forces from the outside and attacks by clandestine cells within the cities would unleash popular uprisings. It must have been a shock when they did not.

The Tet Offensive failed to provoke political change in Saigon, Hue or any provincial capital. Then it came as a relief that the Tet Offensive turned US public opinion against the war. President Richard Nixon (1913–94) 'Vietnamized' the war and withdrew US forces after the Paris agreement of 1973. Then, in 1975, the 'Ho Chi Minh campaign' brought Saigon to its knees, so the South Vietnamese government capitulated. Yet again, there was no uprising. The victory came in the Chinese way. There was never any repeat of August 1945.

Does the August Revolution still have a legacy? Since the fall of the Berlin Wall in 1989, the breakup of the Soviet Union in 1991 and the many anti-communist 'colour revolutions' that came afterwards, there is not much potency in the idea of communist-led revolutions. The August Revolution narrative, as told by the ideologue Truong Chinh, carries little current relevance. Yet attempts have been made – notably by historians based outside Vietnam, above all David G. Marr – to revise the history of the August Revolution by demonstrating that it was far more diverse and spontaneous than is normally imagined in either communist or anti-communist accounts. Young people of many persuasions, often with no knowledge of communist doctrine, took to the streets to win independence and freedom. In fact, the top communist leaders around Ho Chi Minh were not in a position to lead the revolution as it happened. They had not anticipated the sudden opportunity that arose from the Japanese surrender. Hence they were assembled for a congress in a remote place they called Tan Trao, with no means to communicate with the local activists who seized power in the towns. After the revolution had happened, the communist leaders walked into Hanoi, where they were received by local Revolutionary Committees. A more historically accurate, bottom-up narrative of the momentous August 1945 uprising, emphasizing the popular enthusiasm that brought Ho Chi Minh to power, might have a better chance at standing the test of time than the ideological narrative constructed by Truong Chinh.

With the help of Vietnamese friends, I have undertaken a small survey to find out what the August Revolution means for young Vietnamese people today. The result was surprisingly diverse. About half of my respondents were indifferent; it meant nothing to them. Among the other half, some were totally negative; the revolution had killed people, abolished Vietnam's proud monarchy and led to war and misery. Yet a larger group of respondents saw the revolution in a positive light. It brought modernity, independence and freedom. No one praised it for giving power to the people, or for bringing the Communist Party to power. Thus, the legacy of the August Revolution, to the extent that it survives, may fit better into the tradition of the American than of the French or Russian revolutions.

Ho Chi Minh

Ho Chi Minh (Nguyen Ai Quoc and other names) (1890–1969), used many pseudonyms in early life; Ho Chi Minh means 'Bringer of Light'. In the 1910s he travelled as a mariner and lived in Paris, where he became a founding member of the French Communist Party. In 1923 he visited Moscow and China, and in 1930 founded the Indochinese Communist Party (ICP). In 1941 Ho crossed into Vietnam from China and established the Viet Minh, a communist-dominated independence movement; in September 1945 he declared Vietnam's independence and became president of the Democratic Republic of Vietnam (DRV). He led the country in defeating the French at Dien Bien Phu in 1954. 'Uncle Ho' symbolized the ambition to reunite the country – yet he accepted the 1954 Geneva agreement, dividing Vietnam temporarily into North and South. Ho's personal skills helped the DRV to secure massive help from Beijing and Moscow in fighting the French and later the Americans. His funeral in 1969 provided an occasion for Soviet and Chinese leaders to re-establish contact after a frosty period of border war. In 1975, when the DRV launched its final push to defeat South Vietnam and reunify Vietnam, it called this 'the Ho Chi Minh campaign'.

Truong Chinh

Truong Chinh (Dang Xuan Khu) (1907–88), Vietnamese communist leader and ideologue, was general secretary of the Indochinese Communist Party (ICP) and Vietnam Workers' Party 1941–56, and the Vietnamese Communist Party (1986). As a student, he read history and Marxist theory; he worked as a teacher in northern Vietnam during the 1930s. In admiration of Mao Zedong's Long March (1934–5), he adopted the name Truong Chinh ('Long March'). He worked clandestinely in northern Vietnam during the period of French and Japanese repression (1940–45), issued party instructions in March 1945 to resist Japan and prepare for a general uprising, and in 1946 wrote a book to justify the August Revolution of the previous year. He stayed on as party secretary general when the ICP was relaunched under the name Vietnam Workers' Party in 1951, but stepped down after a failed land reform in 1956. In 1986, after the death of Lê Duân (1907–86), who had led the party for the last thirty years, Truong Chinh once again served briefly as general secretary of the party, which in 1976 had taken the name Vietnam Communist Party (VCP).

TIMELINE

1926   Bao Dai becomes emperor of Annam, within French Indochina

1930   Nguyen Ai Quoc (Ho Chi Minh) sets up Indochinese Communist
              Party (ICP) at a meeting in Hong Kong

1940–41   Japan occupies Indochina

1945
9 March   Japan ousts the French colonial regime and sets up nominally
              independent monarchies in Annam, Cambodia and Laos

14 August   Japan surrenders to the Allies; Viet Minh rising follows

25 August   Bao Dai abdicates

2 September   Ho Chi Minh proclaims Democratic Republic of Vietnam (DRV)

23 September Rearmed French troops take control of Saigon

1946
6 March   Having reconquered southern Vietnam with British help, the
              French land troops in the north but are compelled to sign a deal
              with the DRV

19 December   War breaks out between the DRV and France

1949–50   French set up the State of Vietnam under Bao Dai, whose
              government in Saigon is recognized by the UK and USA; China
              and the USSR recognize the DRV

1954   French forces are defeated at Dien Bien Phu; Geneva conference
              divides Vietnam temporarily into North and South

1955   Ngo Dinh Diem, prime minister in the State of Vietnam, ousts
              Bao Dai, sets up Republic of Vietnam with himself as president,
              compels the French to leave and invites US advisors

1960   National Liberation Front (NLF) formed in South Vietnam to lead
              the struggle against Diem and his US advisors

1964–5   US bombs North Vietnam and lands regular troops in the South

CHINA: THE COMMUNIST REVOLUTION, 1949–1976

Mobo Gao

The communist accession to power in China in 1949, following victory in a long civil war against the nationalists, was merely a precursor to the thoroughgoing revolutionary socialism that they introduced across the country once in power. In the previous century, the huge country had already seen several revolutionary movements: the Taiping Rebellion of 1850–64, which left over twenty million dead; the Boxer Rising of 1899–1901; the Xinhai Revolution that overthrew the Qing dynasty in 1911 and introduced a republic; the anti-imperialist Shanghai strikes of 1925–7 that brought the nationalist Kuomintang to power. Together, these had gone some way to transform China from a traditional Confucian empire to a republic that embraced Western values, nationalism and capitalism.

But the triumph of the Red Army was swiftly followed by a root-and-branch transformation of China into a fully revolutionary state, controlled by the Communist Party and following the Marxist–Leninist ideology of Chairman Mao Zedong. Without concern for the human cost, the country was able to modernize – sometimes chaotically but ultimately decisively – while traditional patterns of authority were totally overthrown, especially during the Cultural Revolution of the

1960s. The revolution's ideas were spread throughout China and worldwide through the unconditional repetition of Mao's aphorisms in the 'Little Red Book', which was understood to contain all the knowledge needed for the vast majority of people. Yet their meaning, ethics and legacy are today unresolved in a country where the Party remains in uncontested power only by having abandoned the Maoist ideology of its revolutionary years.   PF

T he Chinese Communist Revolution and establishment of the People's Republic of China (PRC) in 1949 changed China beyond recognition and forever. Looking back after seventy years, its achievements are remarkable by any standard; but not without controversy.

The establishment of the Chinese Communist Party (CCP) in 1921 was the essential precursor to the revolution, and Mao Zedong (1893–1976) was the individual who decisively made the CCP the nation-changing body that it became – even though he was not its unchallenged leader until the 1930s. His role, particularly in two traumatic events – the Great Leap Forward (1958–62) and the Cultural Revolution (1966–76) – means that debate continues over the assessment of Mao, and is at the heart of the controversy surrounding the revolution itself.

Widespread poverty and famine had for centuries given rise to rebellions among the Chinese peasantry, and these occurred more frequently in 19th-century China. Some – such as the Taiping Rebellion of 1850–64, in which an estimated twenty million died – were exceptionally bloody and violent.

Life for the Chinese peasantry had always been precarious due to the very low availability of arable land to support the population, and a precarious natural environment that brought frequent floods and droughts. What was new in the 19th century was the penetration of China by the West, following China's defeat by the British in the Opium War (1839–42) and subsequent defeats at the hands of the Western powers and the Japanese; China was in real danger of being carved up by colonialists. In order to generate the ever-increasing revenue required to defend the empire and pay for the indemnity demanded by foreign powers, the authorities imposed heavy taxes on the peasantry. Land rents were rising while the government was bankrupt. These problems were exacerbated by a trade imbalance caused by the large-scale illicit import of opium and competitive industrial commodities from the West.

A modern Chinese nation state was desperately needed, but instead of reform, or even revolution, the 19th century saw a series of great rebellions. A rebellion – essentially a protest movement – is distinct from a revolution, which offers a wholesale socio-economic programme and has an ideological narrative to deal with societal problems. The Taiping Rebellion, whose leader Hong Xiuquan (1814–64) claimed to be the younger brother of Jesus, had an ideology of a sort: Hong set up the Heavenly Kingdom of Harmony in Nanjing, and proclaimed a programme of returning the land to those who tilled it. He even advocated the idea of gender equality. However, his Heavenly Kingdom did not have the capacity to implement its societal programmes; and in any case, his rebellion was crushed by the Qing government with the help of foreign intervention.

China required a more thorough revolution, one that could deal with societal problems and build an effective state. And a more radical revolution did take place, without much bloodshed, in 1911 when, under pressure from a republican movement and provincial warlords, the Qing imperial dynasty was forced to abdicate and China was declared a republic.

Two political parties emerged: the Nationalist Party (Kuomintang, or KMT), with a background of wealthy landlords and urban capitalists; and the CCP, which based its credentials on rural land reform. When, in the 1920s, the KMT under Chiang Kai-shek (1887–1975) became the ultimate power-holder of the Republic of China, its central government was unable to carry out an effective programme of social reform. While it tried to build industrial infrastructure, it had no solution to rural issues related to land ownership. Meanwhile it had to fight the CCP, which established its own revolutionary bases where it began to implement rural reform.

While the KMT adopted a capitalist model of development, the CCP took a Marxist approach. Marxism claims to be based on a historical law known as dialectic materialism, according to which society's structures (including law and order, values, education and arts) reflect its economic base, but in a dynamic manner, driven by contradictions between social classes. Class conflict eventually leads to new forms of society: so, in a capitalist society, conflict between the workers and the capitalists will inevitably bring socialism. This suggests that socialism can take only place in advanced capitalist societies; but in 1917 Lenin had shown that Russia, where capitalism was poorly developed, could still experience a socialist revolution through a party of vanguard revolutionaries, the Bolsheviks. Such a party, armed with a knowledge of the truth of histori-cal laws as well as with strong organization and discipline, could instil sufficient spirit and consciousness into the proletariat to bring about a working-class revolution. The CCP initially followed Lenin's lead.

They attempted to organize workers' movements in cities such as Shanghai and Wuhan, but when this repeatedly failed to work, they resorted to an armed struggle for power, fighting the KMT in urban centres. This too ended in failure. It was at this point that the CCP turned its attention to Mao and his comrade Zhu De (1886–1976), who had begun to organize armed struggle in rural areas, adopting the tactics of guerrilla warfare. Most importantly, the revolutionary rural bases carved out by the CCP's Red Army implemented social programmes of land reform, along with other projects such as the liberation of women and working to increase literacy rates among the poor.

The Red Army might have been routed completely if not for the Japanese invasion of, first, Manchuria (1931) and then China. In the early 1930s, the Red Army was threatened by KMT military encirclement and forced to abandon its bases in Jiangxi in south-eastern China. The Red Army escaped to the north of China in the Long March – a march of some 10,000 kilometres, during which it incurred heavy losses and Mao emerged as undisputed leader. The force was reduced to about a tenth of its original size by the time it reached Shaanxi in the north-west. What happened next proved fatal for the KMT, but vital for the CCP: in 1936, instead of fighting the Red Army as ordered by Chiang Kai-shek, one of Chiang's top generals, Zhang Xueliang (1901–2001), arrested Chiang in Xi'an. He released him only after Chiang agreed to form a united front with the CCP to fight the Japanese invasion.

After the Japanese surrender in 1945, the CCP and its army were strong enough to defeat the KMT. They forced the KMT government to withdraw to Taiwan in 1949. This victory allowed Mao to claim to have advanced Marxism and Leninism by applying the scientific truth of historical dialectic materialism with Chinese reality: that China was largely an agrarian society. The successful recipe was that the revolution should start with the rural poor and not the urban proletariat, because there was not much of an urban working class to be mobilized.

Following the victory of October 1949, the PRC, administered by the CCP with military-style discipline, started a political programme with two umbrella projects: the first economic, involving land reform and the nationalization of the means of production in urban centres; the second social. Land was confiscated from landlords and rich peasants, and redistributed to households on a per capita basis. Capitalists and entrepreneurs were forced to give up their ownership of means of production, with little or no compensation. In what was called 'socialist transition', land was rapidly collectivized during the mid- and late 1950s and peasants were organized to work as members of communes. The social reform project carried out mass programmes of women's liberation, education of the poor and welfare for the urban working class including full employment, free housing, free schools and medical care.

These two umbrella projects were successful enough for the CCP to build up a state with the capacity to defend China's interests in, for instance, the Korean War, which broke out in 1950; the border war with India in 1962; and another war with the Soviet Union in 1969. China established a credible national defence industry, and in 1964 it claimed to be a nuclear power.

An indisputable achievement was the dramatic rise in the status of women. One of the first decrees of the PRC was the marriage law protecting women's rights and status. Gender equality was officially proclaimed, and as a result the rate of Chinese female work participation outside of the home is today one of the highest in the world. Mao's slogan 'Women prop up half the sky' remains an inspiration for many women today in the world. Other non-controversial achievements include the dramatic increase in literacy, not only in urban but also in rural China – and in life expectancy, which rose from 39 to 69 by the end of the 1970s.

However, the most noticeable achievement of the 1949 revolution is land reform. Though poverty remains, there is little in the way of extreme poverty, such as children hunting for food on rubbish dumps or massive urban ghettos. Land reform has provided China with a huge and cheap labour force without placing any burden on the state. Rural migrant workers can leave their families behind to work in urban centres, but they can always return to their land if they cannot find work.

The revolution also laid a solid infrastructure for China's economic take-off. In 1949 China's industrial capacity was roughly equivalent to that of Belgium; but by the end of the 1970s, China was the world's sixth-largest industrial power. It is no accident that by the late 2010s everything could be made in China, because China had the most comprehensive industrial and manufactory network of skills and platforms.

Even with the policy of one child per family which was in place from the late 1980s to 2016, China still has 20 per cent of the global population, although its arable land represents only around 10 per cent of global availability. Food production therefore remains vitally important – not only for China itself but for the world, because the rest of the world cannot afford to feed the Chinese people. The revolution laid a sound foundation of agricultural infrastructure, including all kinds of irrigation projects, over many years and involving the participation of hundreds of millions of people – maintaining the mighty but often destructive Yangtze and Yellow rivers, building dams, dikes, wells and pumping stations. Whereas famines had been frequent before 1949, the Great Leap Forward famine of 1959–60 was the first and last in the history of the PRC.

The Great Leap Forward (1958–62) was one of two events that have tainted the history of the PRC. It started with an overly ambitious programme of national economic build-up, intended to catch up with the West in a great leap. A large number of industrial projects mushroomed, and around twenty million rural people were recruited in this huge industrialization programme. Meanwhile, a nationwide collectivization took place in rural areas, with household farming phased out and villagers organized into communes; people were even urged to eat in public canteens instead of cooking household meals. All kinds of experiments, such as deep ploughing and close planting, were encouraged to find new ways of raising food production. One outrageous project – of increasing iron and steel output by means of self-made ad-hoc furnaces – not only turned out useless products but also wasted time, energy and resources: forests were cut down for the furnaces, while in some villages cooking utensils and even nails were melted down to fulfil production quotas. The result was a great decline in food production during 1959–60, leading to shortages and eventually to famine; the estimated death toll of the famine ranges from several million to fifty million (the latter estimate including those who might have been born but, owing to the famine, were not). As Mao was leader of the CCP, and the post-Mao authorities would not point a finger at themselves, today Mao alone is blamed – implicitly or explicitly – for the folly of the Great Leap Forward.

The Cultural Revolution (1966–76) was the second great stain on the Chinese revolution. The CCP had launched a critique of what it called Soviet Russian Revisionism, arguing that bureaucratization and elite privilege in the Soviet Union led to its deviation from socialism. Mao then turned his attention to domestic development in China, such as the de-collectivization that followed the Great Leap Forward; the negligence of rural healthcare; the focus on academic merits in school; the emphasis in literature and arts on themes of wealth, fame and beauty, and on the past; and the increasing privileges of the Party officials. The programme to rectify the situation was so called because the power-holders inside the system needed a *cultural* revolution to change their mentality. It was meant to target those who had not really changed their old mentality, and those who might slide into a capitalist way of life.

Liu Shaoqi (1898–1969), president of the PRC, and Deng Xiaoping (1904–97), general secretary of the CCP, were particularly singled out as 'capitalist roaders' and accused of leading China into capitalism. Students, organized into the Red Guard, were called on to rebel against their teachers, and the populace was encouraged to criticize their superiors by writing up posters and airing their opinions. Although the Cultural Revolution direction documents (the Sixteen Articles) stressed that 95 per cent of Party officials were very good or good comrades, almost anyone in a position of authority in any work unit was under some pressure to offer self-criticism and to be criticized in public. While many used this unprecedented freedom to let out their anger at official corruption, perceived injustice or abuse of power, some took it as an opportunity to express personal revenge. Most of the Red Guards' violence against the professionals and the supposed old-class enemies of capitalists and landlords was in fact carried out by the 'princelings' – sons and daughters of veteran Party officials and army officers who themselves were meant to be the targets of the Cultural Revolution. Many were traumatized. In 1967, factions started to form due to differences in politics or personal networks. Violence in cities such as Wuhan and on campuses such as Qinghua University became so out of hand that Mao had to call out the army to restore order. Finally, about seventeen million urban students were sent to remote rural villages or borderline state farms, and white-collar professionals such as artists and academics, Party bureaucrats and officials were sent to villages, factories or special schools to be engaged in labour. Many stayed until after 1976.

Analysis of the Cultural Revolution involves a number of issues, including that of whether Mao launched it as part of power struggle within the CCP. The post-Mao official line is that it was less a power struggle than a result of Mao's mistaken belief that revisionism (capitalist opposition) existed in China and 'capitalist roaders' existed in the CCP itself. To avoid a direct condemnation of Mao, these capitalist roaders blamed the people surrounding him, such as the so-called 'Gang of Four' – which included Mao's wife, Jiang Qing (1914–91), who committed suicide in prison, as well as the radical theorist Zhang Chunqiao (1917–2005) – for abusing power and victimizing the Party elite. Another issue for debate is the extent to which the Cultural Revolution damaged China's economic development. Although production had been badly affected by the widespread disruption of the years 1967–8, growth started to pick up after 1969. In memoirs or official historiography, the Chinese intellectual and political elite tend to dwell on the turmoil and personal experiences of the first three years of the Cultural Revolution while avoiding the subsequent constructive development, such as the great improvements in education and healthcare in rural China.

In September 2018, the visiting Venezuelan president Nicolás Maduro (b. 1962) paid homage to Mao, who was lying in state at the Mao Memorial Hall on Tiananmen Square, calling him a 'giant of the homeland of humanity'. No Chinese media except Phoenixnet, based in Hong Kong, reported the news; the CCP mouthpiece the *People's Daily* shyly mentioned (but only on its website) that the Venezuelan president paid homage to the Monument of the People's Heroes outside the Mao Memorial Hall. This reticence was unusual, but not surprising. By the late 2010s, the Chinese authorities – despite ruling through the CCP – almost wanted the memory of the PRC's first three decades, until Mao's death in 1976, to disappear. When the Olympic Games were held in Beijing in 2008, the glamorous opening ceremony narrating thousands of years of glorious Chinese history did not even mention Mao's name.

The Chinese authorities are unsure about the legacy of Mao and, by association, of the 1949 revolution itself under his leadership. There are many reasons for this; one is that some of Mao's policies and administrative decisions cost many lives. Yet even the rural people, who suffered the most (the vast majority of the Great Leap Forward famine victims were rural), do not generally hold a grudge against Mao himself or the revolution as such. They tend to interpret the Great Leap Forward as a genuine policy error on part of the wider leadership, especially at the local level.

What caused the most elite backlash against Mao was the Cultural Revolution – especially during 1966–8, when most Party officials and many professionals went through some kind of hardship and personal victimization. It had been almost two decades since the 1949 revolution, and they thought they deserved to benefit from this effort. It was and remains very difficult for the Chinese political and intellectual elite – who have the means to construct the historical narrative – to understand the Cultural Revolution ideology that targeted them. Therefore, for them both emotionally and intellectually, the Cultural Revolution not only left a scar but also planted the seed of doubt about the value of the revolution itself.

This perplexity about the revolution was greatly exacerbated by the reforms promoted by Deng Xiaoping after Mao's death. The pragmatic Deng proved to be a 'capitalist roader' – exactly what he was accused of being during the Cultural Revolution – and, in the name of economic development, he led China onto the road of capitalism. Abandoning the narrative of 'Only socialism can save China', he moved the national narrative in the direction of 'Let some get rich first, whatever it takes.'

Today, the CCP leadership in particular and the Chinese authorities in general are caught in a dilemma. To disown the 1949 revolution would mean the removal of the intellectual foundation of their very existence; but to own it runs contrary to the policy practice since the death of Mao.

What do the ordinary Chinese people, the workers and farmers, think about this? It is difficult to source reliable information on this issue under a political system that restricts free speech, but the impression given by the occasional survey and the evidence of social media is that the rural people and the urban working class have a largely positive evaluation of the 1949 revolution, and of Mao.

Some argue that, before 1949, agrarian Chinese society was not sufficiently advanced for a socialist revolution. In the 1980s, this argument was supported by the then PRC premier Zhao Ziyang (1919–2005), who was later put under house arrest until his death because of his sympathy with the pro-democracy demonstrators in Tiananmen Square in 1989. Zhao presented a narrative of China being at the primary stage of socialism, so as to justify capitalist development under the leadership of the CCP after Mao's death.

Xi Jinping (b. 1953), the current leader of the CCP, was one of the educated youth sent to rural China at the tender age of seventeen. He lived and worked alongside poverty-stricken villagers for seven years, and has stated that the history of the three decades since Mao should not be used to denigrate the thirty years of Mao's era. This was an indirect rebuttal of those among the elite who wanted the Mao era to be entirely forgotten.

Xi now has the Herculean task of reconciling the two legacies – that of the revolution up to the death of Mao, and that of the post-Mao economic reform that has developed a capitalist market economy. The essential dilemma is: how does the CCP (which apparently holds as its creed the communist ideology of 'from each according to their ability, and to each according to their need') control the profit-seeking capital that has transformed the country from being one of the most equal in the world to one of the most unequal?

Mao Zedong

Mao Zedong (1893–1976), communist general and chairman of the PRC (1949–76), was born into a peasant family in Hunan and had a basic education before joining a revolutionary army in 1911. He worked at Beijing University prior to the May Fourth Movement of 1919, and joined the Communist Party in 1921. From 1925, he saw the revolutionary potential of the Chinese peasantry; from October 1927 he built a revolutionary army in remote Jiangxi, and developed effective guerrilla tactics. In October 1934 he was driven out of Jiangxi by Chiang Kai-shek and embarked on the Long March, arriving in Shaanxi province in autumn 1935. He then became the dominant figure in the Communist Party, wrote several books and pushed the Chinese Party away from toeing the Soviet line. After leading the CCP to victory in the civil war (1949) he proclaimed the Chinese People's Republic and, as chairman, enjoyed supreme power. Seeking to harness the revolutionary potential of both the urban working class and the peasantry, he comprehensively attacked the traditional elite in the Great Leap Forward (from 1958) and the Cultural Revolution of the late 1960s. His philosophy, published in the 'Little Red Book', became required learning for every Chinese person, and he kept China closed to any outside influence. He has been held responsible for the deaths of tens of millions of people in the course of his career.

Deng Xiaoping

Deng Xiaoping (1904–97), son of a landowner, studied in France in the 1920s, where he became involved with the Communist Party. After returning to China, he worked with Mao to build communist strength in Jiangxi, and participated in the Long March. He led an army during the civil war, and later became vice-premier of China (1952) and general secretary of the CCP (1954). His pragmatic policies brought him into growing conflict with Mao's more radical vision, and he lost his government posts during the Cultural Revolution. After Mao's death in 1976 he was reinstated, and by the late 1970s he had become the most influential figure in China, although he was never head of state nor head of the government. His period in power was marked by market-economy reforms and gradually opening China to Western influence; seeking 'socialism with Chinese characteristics', he introduced China's one-child policy in 1980. In 1989, he used force to suppress students and others calling for reform in Tiananmen Square, Beijing.

TIMELINE

1842   Defeat by Britain in Opium War marks beginning of Western influence in China

1850–64   Taiping Rebellion against Qing rule

1899–1901   Boxer Rising, supported by Qing government, against foreign influence in China

1911   Abdication of last Qing emperor

1912   Declaration of the Republic of China, with Yuan Shikai as president; foundation of the Kuomintang (KMT)

1919   May Fourth student movement for reform protests China's treatment by Western powers

1921   Formation of Chinese Communist Party (CCP) in Shanghai, with Soviet support

1924–7   CCP and KMT work together to build a Nationalist Revolutionary Army and end warlordism

1927   KMT sets up provisional national capital in Wuhan, takes Shanghai with CCP help, then turns on CCP; Mao writes report on revolutionary potential of peasants in Hunan

1928   Chiang Kai-shek's government receives international recognition

1929   CCP under Mao establishes a base in Jiangxi province

1931   Japan invades Manchuria and sets up a puppet government

1934
October   Mao and the Red Army leave Jiangxi and head westwards on the 'Long March', ending in Shaanxi (October 1935)

1936   Chiang Kai-shek kidnapped, forced into anti-Japanese alliance with CCP

1937   Beginning of all-out war with Japan (to 1945)

1945   CCP endorses Mao Zedong's thinking as the Party's guiding
                ideology; US attempts to broker peace between Nationalists
                and CCP (truce collapses June 1946)

1947-8   Communists launch offensives against Nationalists in north

1949
January   CCP take Beijing, also Nanjing (Nationalist capital) in April

October   Mao proclaims People's Republic of China (PRC); Chiang
                Kai-shek withdraws to Taiwan

1950   PRC and USSR enter into alliance; social reform and land reform
                programmes begin

1953   Start of first Five-Year Plan

1958   Start of second Five-Year Plan (Great Leap Forward),
                collectivizing agriculture and promoting 'backyard furnaces' for
                steel production

1959-60   Widespread famine following drastic fall in agricultural output

1964   Publication of *Quotations from Chairman Mao Zedong* ('Little
                Red Book')

1966   Beginning of Cultural Revolution to root out 'imperialists' from
                government, bureaucracy and Party; students denounce teachers
                and parents

1968   Students and intellectuals relocated to countryside

1973   Moderate economic reform programme agreed; Deng Xiaoping
                rehabilitated as vice-premier

1974   Four modernizations announced (agriculture, industry, national
                defence and technology)

1976   Death of Mao Zedong; Deng Xiaoping becomes more powerful;
                Gang of Four denounced as responsible for China's ills

THE CUBAN REVOLUTION, 1959–2006

Luis Martínez-Fernández

The Cuban Revolution – in which a small band of urban and rural guerrillas defeated and removed the corrupt, US-backed regime in the largest island of the Caribbean and, a few years later, installed a Marxist state that has endured for sixty years – has had enormous resonance around the world. The images of its most charismatic figures, Fidel Castro and Che Guevara, became instantly recognizable both to radical Westerners and to people engaged in liberation struggles in the Third World; and the macho romance of their success in achieving their military objectives, in maintaining the revolutionary state and in spreading their form of guerrilla-based Marxist revolution to other countries of Central America and Africa has been remarkable. The virulent, overt and enduring opposition to the Cuban Revolution from Washington rendered its survival extraordinary, and at the same time enhanced the David and Goliath myth that appealed to many revolutionary and anti-imperialist movements elsewhere.

Before he took power, Castro's message had focused on reform, opposition to corruption and the restoration of the liberties that had been taken away by the dictatorial Fulgencio Batista; however, soon after he achieved power the revolution was swiftly supported, politically, militarily and economically, by the Soviet Union. Revolutionary Cuba became a one-party communist state and the scene of some of the most dramatic moments of the Cold War – notably the Missile Crisis of October 1962 that brought the world to the brink of nuclear conflict. Castro saw Marxist revolution to overthrow capitalism as a global necessity, but the economic and social challenges of improving living conditions for the Cuban people while the country remained shut out of Western markets meant an ever-increasing focus on internal affairs to the exclusion of external relations. In many ways, the revolution brought greater equality and welfare provision to Cubans, at least as long as the economy could be subsidized from Moscow. But this came at the cost of political liberty, as dictatorial one-party – indeed, one-family – rule was strictly enforced.   PF

What came to be known as the Cuban Revolution started shortly after Fulgencio Batista (1901–73) grabbed power through a coup on 10 March 1952. A wide range of groups, including students, civic organizations, opposition parties, factions within the military and revolutionary movements, sought to re-establish democratic rule. Some favoured civic dialogue and electoral solutions; leaders of the leftist parties were split, some preferring ballots, others bullets. Progressive and revolutionary armed groups engaged in guerrilla warfare. Among these was the group that would become known as the 26th of July Movement, led by Fidel Castro (1926–2016).

The first organized armed action took place on Easter Sunday 1952, when sixty-five members of the National Revolutionary Movement staged a futile attack against Camp Columbia. Several participants joined Castro's budding rebel group, which on 26 July 1953 attacked the Moncada army garrison and three other targets in eastern Cuba. Nearly a third of the 160 combatants were killed in action or tortured to death; the rest were sent to jail.

Castro's speech in his own defence, 'History Will Absolve Me', outlined his plan for a new Cuba. This included restoring the constitution of 1940, granting property rights to landless peasants, establishing profit-sharing for industrial workers, guaranteeing compensation for sugarcane growers and confiscating all ill-gotten property and gains. He also promised agrarian and urban reform, comprehensive education reform, nationalization of foreign-owned utility companies, industrialization, expansion of job opportunities and clean elections.

After eighteen months in prison, Castro, his brother Raúl (b. 1931), Argentine Ernesto ('Che') Guevara (1928–67) and seventy-nine others launched an invasion from Mexico on board the *Granma* yacht. Organized by the País brothers (Frank and Josué), 26th of July Movement fighters revolted in Santiago in part to distract government forces from the *Granma*'s landing. The vessel, however, arrived late, by which time army and police forces had smashed the uprising and killed 300 rebels. Sixteen or seventeen of the invading insurgents regrouped and climbed the Sierra Maestra mountain range.

Urban fighters in Santiago and Havana (*el Llano*, the lowlands) faced greater dangers and casualties than their counterparts in *la Sierra* (the highlands). By attrition, almost by default, Castro and his mountain guerrillas were the last men – and women – standing. Another independent guerrilla force, meanwhile, operated the Second National Front of El Escambray mountain range.

In 1958, highland rebel troops and hundreds who joined them along the way marched towards Havana. Government troops were demoralized, and desertions ran high. In the United States a chorus of voices censored Batista's actions, leading to an arms embargo and the withdrawal of US support. In the early hours of 1 January 1959, the besieged president fled with his relatives and associates.

Military victory turned Castro into the undisputed leader of whatever would come next. With virtually unanimous popular support, the revolutionary government passed a flurry of legislation, some of it in fulfilment of promises Castro had made in 1953: confiscating fortunes gained through corruption and graft, an agrarian reform, and cutting rents, utility rates and the price of medicines. Other measures went further: nationalization of oil refineries, private banks, medium and large businesses and large agricultural estates. A massive and successful literacy campaign in 1961 served as foundation for future investments in education that ran parallel to the expansion of free healthcare for the entire population.

These revolutionary political transformations produced mixed results. Batista's allies were persecuted, their illegal fortunes confiscated; some went into exile, but those who could not escape were imprisoned or killed. Traditional parties (except the PSP, Communist Party) were banned and labour unions and the media fell under state control. The promised return to the constitution of 1940 and elections were postponed and later discarded. Revolutionaries offered an alternative form of 'democracy', legitimized by popular acclamation and widespread citizen participation in mass organizations such as the Federation of Cuban Women, the National Association of Small Farmers and the Young Communists Union.

The revolution's initial political leadership included moderate president Manuel Urrutia (1901–81), Prime Minister José Miró Cardona (1902–74) and a largely moderate cabinet alongside an increasingly influential shadow government composed mostly of communists led by Guevara and Raúl Castro. By the end of 1959, virtually all moderates were out of office, many in exile. Soon, *Fidelistas* and communists controlled almost all government and civil society institutions.

Increasing authoritarianism, mounting human rights abuses and property nationalizations sparked opposition among growing numbers of Cubans on the island and exiles concentrated in South Florida, as well as the US government. The opposition included pro-Batista civilians and members of the defeated military/police forces, disaffected progressives and even revolutionaries such as Eloy Gutiérrez Menoyo, Pedro Luis Díaz Lanz and Huber Matos, who had fought against Batista. In 1960 several hundred peasants formed a new guerrilla front in El Escambray. The exiled opposition, meanwhile, established anti-Castro organizations of diverse political colours. Tensions escalated as Cuba confiscated more and more American-owned properties. The US retaliated by cutting Cuba's sugar export quota, carrying out propaganda and sabotage operations and imposing a damaging trade embargo. In April 1961, a 1,500-strong army of CIA-backed exiles launched an invasion on the Bay of Pigs. It ended tragically for the invading forces, and cemented Castro and his regime's prestige at home and throughout the world.

Almost overnight, Cuba's revolutionary government was forced to rearrange its international strategy, making new alliances and trade deals with the Soviet Union and its eastern European satellites. China, whose radical revolutionary formula appealed to Guevara, was also supportive, becoming the island's second biggest trading partner and benefactor. Soviet–Cuban relations hit a bump, however, in the aftermath of the Missile Crisis (October 1962), when Castro viewed the unilateral decision to remove Soviet missiles as an affront.

Guevara, a proponent of revolutionary internationalism, supported anti-imperialist movements in Latin America, the Caribbean, Africa and Asia. Cuba also invested large amounts of resources in building schools and water wells, providing vaccinations and other medical services, and deploying essential equipment and materials.

Following the recession of 1962, with the revolutionary government firmly in control, Cuba's leadership embarked on the 'Great Debate' over rival socio-economic formulas: a gradual and pragmatic reformist approach in line with the USSR, or a radical China-inspired idealistic route seeking immediate social equality and complete government control of the economy. The debate was meshed into other dilemmas: forging a strong primary alliance with the USSR or China; emphasis on industrialization and food crops or on export staples such as sugar; application of moral or material incentives to motivate worker productivity; and the extent to which Cuba should support guerrilla and liberation movements abroad.

The Great Debate's main voices were, on the one hand, Guevara and those who favoured close ties with Mao's China – embracing its fast transition-to-communism formula and pushing for economic diversification and industrialization fuelled by the 'new man' motivated by volunteerism and a spirit of sacrifice. On the other hand, *Fidelista* communists favoured alliance with the USSR, and reformist policies that included government firms self-financing, opportunities for private employment and the use of material incentives such as salary differentials and bonuses, championed by Raúl Castro and Carlos Rafael Rodríguez (1913–97).

The Great Debate continued until around 1966, by which time Cuba was definitely under Soviet influence: the USSR was the stronger military power, and able to provide more aid and larger loans. It also had a seemingly insatiable appetite for sugar, which benefited Cuba's trade but had adverse consequences – such as discarding industrialization while obsessively building a monocrop economy that was expected to yield a ten-million-ton sugar harvest in 1970. Economic dependency eroded Cuba's ability to pursue an independent foreign policy, something made painfully patent when Cuba was coerced into accepting the Soviet Union's justification for its invasion of Czechoslovakia in 1968.

In the domestic realm, Guevarist socio-economic policy preferences prevailed, pursuing egalitarianism through policies aimed at reducing income inequality and guaranteeing appropriate levels of nutrition through the rations system. Education, childcare and healthcare policies also followed egalitarian goals. This was consistent with the second agrarian reform of 1963 and the so-called Revolutionary Offensive of 1968, which nationalized all land units larger than 167 acres and almost all private businesses.

Thus the Great Debate produced pro-Soviet foreign and international trade policies, but Sino-Guevarist social domestic policies. This compromise exposed the contradictions of elevating the standard of living of the masses while subjecting hundreds of thousands to the brutalizing labour demands of sugar. The regime's justification of the back-to-sugar strategy – as the source of capital that would enable Cuba to pursue economic diversification and industrialization – lost credibility when the heralded 1970 harvest fell short of its goal. It sealed Cuba's dependence on one product for one market, and eroded the island's ability to follow an autonomous foreign policy and a nationalist revolutionary agenda at home.

The 1970s witnessed increasing Soviet influence in almost every aspect of the economy, government and society. The revolution shifted towards reformist and pragmatic social policies and the institution-alization of Soviet-aligned legislation and government and military structures. Cuba's economy became fully integrated into the Soviet-led Council for Mutual Economic Assistance (CMEA) in 1972. The Soviets also guaranteed multi-year trade agreements that valued Cuban sugar at above-market prices and protected it from downward price fluctua-tions. Soviet oil bought at highly subsidized prices further sweetened the deal, along with generous trade credits and loans. The economy was secured in five-year plans aligned with those of the Soviet Union. These arrangements allowed Cuba to remain afloat and even prosper, at a time when most Latin American countries suffered paralysing inflation rates.

Soviet influence was also evident in government structures. The Cuban Communist Party became increasingly powerful; at its first Party Congress in 1975, delegates established the basis for the revolu-tion's first constitution (ratified in 1976). Partially copied from the 1936 Soviet constitution, it enumerated civil rights. Women's rights were codified in the 1975 'Family Code'. These developments represented the institutionalization of the revolution: doubtless, institutions were strengthened, but they remained subordinated to the Castro brothers and a few communist leaders, virtually all white and male.

The armed forces also received large shipments of Soviet mili-tary supplies. Cuba fought numerous Cold War proxy wars against US allies, including in Yemen (1972, 1976), the Middle East (1973), Angola (1975–88), Ethiopia (the Ogaden War, 1977–8), and Grenada (1983). Cuba also supported, trained and equipped left-wing movements and governments during the prolonged Central American crisis that started in 1979.

The domestic realm now saw a swing away from idealism. Material incentives were expanded, and self-employment decriminalized. Productivity consequently increased. These changes, however, created a wealth gap that hurt Afro-Cubans most. Dark-skinned Cubans were over-represented among those who took part in the Mariel exodus of 1980.

From 1985, profound changes raged through the Soviet Union. Originally meant to save the Soviet economy from collapse, these had profound global reverberations, among them the end of the Cold War. Sharp reductions in Soviet trade, subsidies and aid, along with pressures to have Cuba pay up its past-due debts, triggered a recession crisis in Cuba, beginning in 1986.

Rather than follow Gorbachev's reformism in the Soviet Union, Castro went in the opposite direction, promising, 'We are going to build socialism'. What followed was a package of counter-reforms – the so-called Rectification of Errors – that reversed many of the reforms of the past decade and a half; it was a swing back to orthodox Marxism, collectivism and political centralization.

Economic setbacks threatened the regime politically. The US government passed anti-regime legislation, including an enhanced embargo that punished foreign companies for trading with Cuba. In the domestic arena, Castro asserted his primacy by rounding up and imprisoning scores of members of the Revolutionary Armed Forces and Ministry of the Interior.

The recession that had begun in 1986 deepened as Soviet Union subsidies to Cuba dried up. This was revolutionary Cuba's most profound crisis. Castro christened this the 'Special Period in times of Peace' – Special Period, for short. It proved Cuba's lengthiest economic crisis; it began in 1991, and by 2007 Raúl Castro recognized that it was not over yet.

In 1993, the economy hit rock bottom. GDP had fallen 35 per cent in two years, and the budget deficit had tripled. Productivity levels fell as international trade withered. The population, meanwhile, fought for survival as basic food, medicines, housing, electricity, transportation, and other goods and services became scarce. The tightening US embargo made matters worse.

The government experimented with different foreign and domestic strategies. At first, it embraced a radical survivalist strategy along orthodox Marxist models. From 1993 it shifted to pragmatism, allowing market mechanisms, foreign investments and individual entrepreneurship.

In 1997, with the worst of the crisis over, these reforms were slowed down or reversed.

Largely owing to lack of resources, the government withdrew from many of its social obligations, resulting in inadequate food distribution, healthcare, education, housing and transportation. Malnutrition and infectious diseases soared, while education and health indicators declined. Pragmatist measures such as opening Cuba up to international tourism, welcoming remittances from Cuban exiles, expanding self-employment and dollarizing the economy brought counter-revolutionary repercussions: prostitution, anti-black racism, a sharp growth in income differences and massive illegal emigration.

In July 2006, Fidel Castro became disabled and was replaced by his brother, who became interim president of the Central Committee of the Communist Party and the Council of State. Formal transition occurred in February 2008, when the younger Castro was elected president. He introduced pragmatic reforms aimed at expanding the private sector and reducing the state's responsibilities as a provider of employment, social services, even food. The government also laid off thousands of workers and distributed land to farmers. The resurgence of material incentives and unequal opportunities for blacks, people of mixed race and women led to sharper racialized and gendered income gaps.

However, economic reforms were not accompanied by an increase in political freedoms and democratization. Repression persisted against the disaffected and growing opposition in which women, young people and people of colour were over-represented. After decades of domination by greying military officers of Fidel's generation, Cuba's leaders tried to diversify by electing a larger percentage of women, younger people and civilians. In 2013, fifty-two-year-old civilian Miguel Díaz-Canel (b. 1960) rose to become vice president, the second in command after Raúl Castro.

Internationally, Cuba became increasingly dependent on Venezuela's trade and subsidized oil shipments; it also developed relations with China, Iran and Russia. Barack Obama's entry into the White House in 2009 offered an opportunity for rapprochement with the United States. On 17 December 2014, Castro and Obama announced their intention to normalize relations, but progress slowed when Donald Trump ascended to the US presidency in 2017. Fidel Castro died in 2016 at the age of ninety. Two years later, Díaz-Canel replaced Raúl Castro as president.

The official narrative of the Cuban Revolution, like most state-generated historical narratives, is selective and politically driven, partial in the sense of being incomplete and biased, and a reflection of the perspectives and goals of Cuba's ruling elite. Strict censorship, moreover, has silenced alternative views.

This official narrative follows a classic dramatic structure of prologue and three acts; the epilogue is yet to be written. The prologue comprises Cuba's liberation struggles up to the 1950s. The first act covers 1953–70, the rebellion years and the first decade of revolution: a time of youthful idealism, guerrilla warfare and martyrdom, culminating in military victory in 1959, then war against the legacies of neocolonialism, corrupted democracy and a host of social and economic ills. The second act covers 1971–85, the period of Sovietization, pragmatism and institutionalization that witnessed the reversal of many of the revolution's early goals. The final act, from 1986 until the present, begins with the recession of 1986 and the Rectification of Errors, goes through the Special Period, and closes with the years when Raúl Castro ruled Cuba.

During the prologue, the earliest struggles for liberation, there were no triumphant founding national myths to draw on – Cuba's is tragic: the torching to death of Taino chieftain Hatuey by Spanish conquistadors in 1512. The wars of independence from Spain in the late 19th century, while undoubtedly heroic, were no more triumphant, as they had either failed or been thwarted by US intervention.

With no victorious foundational myths to turn to, Cuba's leaders cast the revolution as the third of three heroic struggles for national sovereignty and social justice. First had been the wars of independence of 1868–78 and 1895–8, the latter frustrated by US intervention and the imposition of neocolonial rule from Washington. Second, the revolution of 1933, when non-commissioned officers and progressive forces overthrew the dictator Machado. That generation's aspirations went unfulfilled, again courtesy of US intervention – though this time in 'good neighbour fashion', without gunboats firing. But finally, redemption had been achieved via the triumphant revolution that began in the 1950s.

Just two days after the toppling of Batista, Castro took to the airwaves and vowed that 'our Revolution will go forward….It will not be like 1895 [sic] when the Americans took over….Nor will it be like 1933.' A few days into the revolution, the editors of the newspaper *Revolución* wrote that the war against Spain had failed because of the intervention of the United States, and in 1933 'the good fortune was short-lived'. Filmmaker Humberto Solás used that structure in the film *Lucía* (1968), a three-part masterpiece with three different women named Lucía: one in 1895, another in 1932, and the third, a selfless young woman who volunteers in the Literacy Campaign of 1961.

Act one, the years 1953–70, comprised less than a third of the revolution's chronology, but forms the centrepiece of the revolutionary narrative. Books published in Cuba pay disproportionate attention to this period of victorious guerrilla warfare and against-all-odds regime survival, during which the revolutionaries accomplished most of their domestic goals. The official narrative seems to end here, frozen at its climax.

These early years of revolution were the stuff of good literature: an eventful, nearly apocalyptic context; a photogenic geographic setting; an array of perfectly cast characters (heroes, villains and the occasional traitor); and a plot unfolding as part David and Goliath, part Spartacus, part Robin Hood and part *Paradise Regained*. There are few more suspenseful episodes in the history of the Americas than the Bay of Pigs Invasion or the Missile Crisis.

The revolution's own historiography is overwhelmingly limited to pre-1959 and the early 1960s. Yet one is hard pressed to find actual works of history published on the island; most are autobiographies, chronicles, speeches, memoirs and diaries. Instead, the revolution has been captured by artists such as pop-art painter Raúl Martínez; poster designers Alfredo Rostegaard and René Mederos; singer-songwriters Carlos Puebla

('Y en eso llegó Fidel', 1960), Sara González ('Girón, la victoria', 1962), and Pablo Milanés, Noel Nicola and Silvio Rodríguez ('Cuba Va', 1970); film-makers Tomás Gutiérrez Alea (*Historias de la Revolución*, 1960) and Octavio Cortázar (*Por primera vez*, 1967); photographers Korda, Osvaldo Salas and Raúl Corrales, who captured iconic black-and-white images of bearded guerrillas and thousands of anonymous Cubans at mass rallies, in the countryside, and fighting off the Bay of Pigs attack; cartoonists; writers; and even ballerina Alicia Alonso, who, in *The Advance Guard* (1964), wore olive green fatigues and army boots.

Although the rebellion actually started in 1952, the official narrative only begins with the attacks on the garrison at Moncada and other targets the following year. Moncada produced a pantheon of martyrs. That day's assault on an army camp in Bayamo, however, is erased from memory; it was led by Raúl Martínez Ararás, who later broke with Castro.

The evolving narrative immortalized the Sierra fighters with massive murals and billboards, but recognized clean-shaven *Llano* leaders such as País and Echeverría merely at the level of postage stamps and an occasional anniversary speech. The revolutionary pantheon also excluded anyone deemed a traitor: the editor of *Revolución*, Carlos Franqui (1921–2010), for example, was airbrushed out, Soviet-style, from a photograph of him next to Castro. Exiles were derided as *gusanos* (worms), and the peasant guerrillas in El Escambray scorned as *los bandidos*.

This narrative focused mostly on the celebration of the physical prowess of fighters, builders who poured cement to build hospitals and schools, and workers who cut millions of tons of cane. It was a macho story that relegated women to supporting roles. Only a handful were included: Vilma Espín (1930–2007), the wife of Raúl Castro and founder and long-time president of the Federation of Cuban Women; Celia Sánchez (1920–80), Fidel Castro's close friend and secretary; and Haydée Santamaría (1922–80), director of the cultural organization Casa de las Américas. All three had taken up arms against the Batista regime.

From the beginning, revolutionaries laid out a Manichean before-and-after narrative, with 1959 separating hell (neocolonialism, oppression and poverty) from heaven (national sovereignty, freedom and prosperity). A 1961 manual for literacy campaign workers stressed the 1959 watershed: 'Before, the people were unarmed and only reactionaries and agents of imperialism had weapons. The Revolution armed the people, the workers, and peasants….[It] put an end to embezzlement.' Many of Castro's speeches were similarly structured.

In 1959, the government began the practice of giving an emblematic name to each year. These year names serve as an index for the revolution's unfolding narrative. Thus, the first three, Year of Liberation (1959), Year of the Agrarian Reform (1960) and Year of Education (1961), reflect the period's primary goals and accomplishments. The Great Debate period continued to mirror the course of the revolution: Year of Planning (1962), Year of Organization (1963). From 1966, the names reflected the contradictions resulting from the Great Debate: radical internationalism (Year of Solidarity, of Heroic Vietnam and of the Heroic Guerrilla Fighter) and the feverish Ten-Million-Ton goal.

Artists and intellectuals turned to historical heroism to galvanize workers, soldiers, students and anyone who could swing a machete in the struggle for those ten million tons. They spoke of 'one hundred years of struggle', presenting the revolution as the culmination of a struggle that had begun in 1868. This leitmotif was widely exploited in 1968–70 with posters, stamps and a record of revolutionary anthems by Esther Borja, all connecting 1868 and 1968. The dominant narrative was exported to Algeria, the Congo, Bolivia and elsewhere by workers who re-enacted the revolution as guerrillas, military advisors, physicians, teachers and construction workers. It was welcomed in the Soviet Union and socialist bloc; and, curiously, it was uncritically embraced by academics, writers and artists in Paris, London, New York and every other major city – with the exception of Miami, with its large community of exiles.

Domestic counter-narratives were silenced. The regime monopolized all media and censored alternative views of past and present, with ideological cleansings in which hundreds of artists and intellectuals were persecuted, ostracized or sent to jail. Particularly harsh was the treatment of gay artists, many of whom were confined in labour camps.

Exiles, meanwhile, failed to produce their own effective counter-narrative, at best offering a return to the time before Batista's corrupt system. Manolo Alonso's documentary *La Cuba de ayer* (Yesteryear Cuba, 1963) is particularly egregious. It portrays a pre-1959 Cuba without problems, drowning in wealth, schools with swimming pools – a lily-white Cuba, a paradise lost.

Throughout the 1970s and 1980s, many of the year names commemorate landmark events: Year of the Twentieth Anniversary of Moncada (1973) and Year of the Twentieth Anniversary of the *Granma* (1976). Others reflect the regime's agendas: the Communist Party congresses, and the Year of Institutionalization (1977). These decades provided little by way of enthusiastic or inspiring history; they had increasingly bland protagonists and a flat plot lacking tension and climax.

The revolutionary thrust had shifted to the global stage, and so did the official narrative. Cuba's foreign policy followed two complementary channels: military intervention and foreign aid. Cuban troops arrived in Angola in 1975–6, and Ethiopia the following year; these were accompanied by civilian armies of doctors, nurses, teachers and engineers. Historian Manuel Moreno Fraginals published an essay in *Granma* (1976) about an Angolan slave who had lived in Havana three centuries earlier. The article's purpose needs no explanation; neither does the publication timing of César Leante's historical novel *Los guerrilleros negros* and Tomás Gutiérrez Alea's film *The Last Supper*, both in 1976.

Cuba's Special Period made for a disappointing third act. The official narrative now focused on the aggressive, damaging actions of the United States: the embargo, the 'kidnapping' of seven-year-old Elián González after his mother died trying to reach Miami, and the imprisonment of the five Cuban 'heroes' – who were actually spies. In 2004, the official slogan for schoolchildren, '*Seremos como el Che*' ('We shall be like Che') was changed to one alluding to these 'five heroes': 'One. Two. Three. Four. Five. Thank you.'

The revolution's first act had now lost whatever glow and glamour it once had. The youthful rebels of the 1960s were now in their late sixties or seventies, and their familiar before-and-after stories felt stale.

Younger generations were unreceptive to a mythology that ran contrary to their everyday experience.

Funding for the arts virtually disappeared. Some writers and artists turned to alternative co-productions with foreign partners; others went into exile. The authorities lost control as increasingly subversive films were released. The literature of the 1990s was bitter and critical, sometimes nihilistically so. Some artists and musicians produced openly irreverent works: Eduardo Ponjuán and René Francisco Rodríguez painted Castro in drag; rap lyrics by Los Aldeanos insulted the Castro brothers, and so did Gorki Águila's punk rock band, Porno Para Ricardo. Others expressed their criticism through blogging.

The state tried to respond by founding the Cuban Rap Agency (2002) and creating unit of 'cyber-soldiers' code-named Operación Verdad (Operation Truth), whose tasks included writing counter-blogs. Uniformed policemen and policewomen praising Castro's government to the tune of rap represents the nadir of state-sponsored arts.

Yet the established narrative of the revolution has reflected and buttressed the agendas of the Cuban state. Six decades on, its heroic first act still remains central to the revolutionary story inside and outside the island. The second act, while unimpressive domestically, had profound international reverberations that elevated Cuba's image around the world. The third has provided little reason for celebration, but the overall narrative is still embraced the world over – understandably so in impoverished countries, less justifiably among American and European intellectuals, artists and academics.

Fidel Castro

Fidel Castro (1926–2016) was born into a prosperous sugar-farming family, and took up radical politics while training as a lawyer. In 1953 he created and led a guerrilla group, the so-called 26th of July Movement, against the Batista regime. By 1959 his group, with a coalition of parties, movements and labour unions, took power, transforming his country into the first communist state in the western hemisphere. He held the title of premier until 1976, when he became president of the Council of State and the Council of Ministers. Renowned for his physical dominance and lengthy speeches, he controlled the revolution for forty-seven years, reputedly surviving more than a hundred attempts at assassination. Health problems forced him to make a provisional handover of power in July 2006; he formally gave up the presidency two years later, being succeeded by his brother Raúl. Throughout his career he challenged US power and ideology, and internationally was a leader of the Non-Aligned Movement.

Ernesto 'Che' Guevara

Ernesto 'Che' Guevara (1928–67) was an Argentinian-born doctor and revolutionary who joined Castro's 26th of July Movement in 1956, and quickly became one of Castro's closest advisors. Following the takeover of power in 1959, he became a Cuban citizen and served as minister of industry and president of the national bank. In his writings, he developed the ideology of the revolution; among other things, he wrote a manual of guerrilla warfare that became highly influential internationally. His essential message, backed up by his austere, hard-working lifestyle, was one of selfless commitment to the revolution, which – together with his film-star looks – made him the pin-up of idealists across the world. Disappointed with Castro's increasing reliance on Moscow, in 1965 he went to the Congo, then to Bolivia to support a guerrilla group. He was killed in action in October 1967.

TIMELINE

1868–78 Ten Years War of Independence

1886 Slavery abolished

1895–8 José Martí, Antonio Maceo and Máximo Gómez lead a second war of independence; US declares war on Spain

1898 US defeats Spain, which cedes Cuba to the US

1902 Cuba becomes independent; US claims right to intervene in Cuban affairs

1924 Gerardo Machado institutes programmes to support mining, agriculture and public works; he later establishes a dictatorship

1933 Machado overthrown in a coup

1934 The US abrogates its right to intervene in Cuba's internal affairs

1940 Ratification of a new progressive constitution

1944 Fulgencio Batista is replaced by Autentico Party candidate Grau San Martín

1952 Batista seizes power again and establishes an oppressive regime

1953 Fidel Castro attacks the Moncada Barracks in an unsuccessful revolt

1956 Castro lands in eastern Cuba and moves to the Sierra Maestra mountains to wage guerrilla war

1959 Castro's army enters Havana, after Batista flees; Castro becomes prime minister, with Raúl Castro as deputy

1960 US businesses in Cuba are nationalized without compensation

1961 The US sponsors an abortive invasion by Cuban exiles at the Bay of Pigs; Castro proclaims Cuba a communist state and begins to ally with the USSR

1962   Cuban Missile Crisis: Castro allows USSR to deploy nuclear missiles on the island; Organization of American States (OAS) suspends Cuba

1965   Cuba's sole political party is renamed the Cuban Communist Party

1970   Ten Million Ton sugar harvest target missed

1972   Cuba joins the Soviet-based Council for Mutual Economic Assistance

1975   The Family Code is introduced, providing enhanced women's rights

1976   Cuban Communist Party approves a new constitution; Castro elected president by members of parliament

1976–81 Cuba sends troops to help Angola's left-wing MPLA and, later, to help the Marxist Ethiopian regime

1980   El Mariel exodus: 125,000 Cubans flee to the US

1986   Rectification of Errors Campaign begins

1991   USSR collapses; Soviet military advisors leave Cuba

1993   The US tightens its embargo; Cuba introduces some market reforms

1998   The US eases restrictions on the sending of money to relatives by Cuban Americans

1999   Cuban child Elián González is picked up off the Florida coast after the boat in which his mother and stepfather tried to escape to the US capsizes

2000   US approves the sale of food and medicines to Cuba

2006   Fidel Castro undergoes surgery and temporarily hands over government to his brother, Raúl

2007   Fidel Castro fails to appear at Havana's May Day parade

2008
February   Raúl Castro takes over presidency

May   Bans on private ownership of mobile phones and computers lifted

2009   US Congress lifts restrictions on Cuban-Americans visiting
             Havana and sending back money

2011   US president Obama relaxes restrictions on travel to Cuba

2014   Presidents Obama and Castro announce plans to begin formalizing
             relations

2016   Death of Fidel Castro

2018   Raúl Castro steps down from the presidency; Miguel Díaz-Canel
             replaces him

THE STUDENT REVOLUTION, 1968

Stephen Barnes

The year 1968, like 1848, saw an inchoate host of revolutionary activity and rhetoric in different countries, inspired for
the most part by middle-class idealistic youth protesting the
'old order' without clearly defined purpose, leadership or
organization. With the slogan 'the personal is the political',
the revolutionaries of 1968 used music and art, street theatre,
placards, slogans and body decoration to express their mainly
peaceful messages: rather than fight the establishment with
guns or even with logic, they sought to expose and ridicule it
mercilessly. Revolution was openly discussed, its meanings
explored far beyond the rational strictures of Marxist orthodoxy.
Even so, in some countries, notably France, the establishment's
control was seriously loosened.

Just as in 1848, the year ended with the 'old order' firmly
back in control in most affected countries. But in a further
parallel with 1848, the immediate failure of the revolution did
not mean that all that had occurred was in vain – the legacy
was the achievement. The attempted political revolution may
not have brought down the pillars of the establishment, but the
new individualist mentality, rejection of authority and opportunities for social reform that accompanied it had permeated
the mindset of a generation and would influence personal and
political decision-making for the next thirty years or more.

PF

n the Western mind, the year 1968 rings out like a fire alarm. Vietnam; student riots; Paris and the 'May events'; New York; Chicago and the Democratic Convention; civil rights; Black Power; Mexico and Tlatelolco; the Prague Spring; feminism; environmentalism; the worldwide counterculture. There was, as the British band Thunderclap Newman sang, 'something in the air'. But what exactly was in the air? Can we make sense of all these disparate events? How much of that meaning remains with us today?

The political revolutions threatened in so many countries failed to occur; by the year's end, conservative governments were mostly in control while the revolutionary climate was cooling. But something *had* happened. Abruptly, the world before 1968 looked grey, constrained and dated. Youth-led and on an ever-rising wave of cultural consciousness, 1968 broke through the walls of normality and didn't need history to call it a revolution.

The year started quietly. A new president, Alexander Dubček (1921–92), was appointed in Czechoslovakia. France was said to be 'bored'. In the United States there was optimism that the war in Vietnam could be won. And on the night of 30 January, US forces in Saigon were relaxing as they celebrated the Lunar New Year and a military truce. But unseen, the Viet Cong – Vietnamese communist fighters – were moving into position. Explosions and gunfire shattered the night: the Tet Offensive had begun. The US embassy compound was breached, Saigon was an instant battlefront and other cities across South Vietnam were simultaneously attacked. The American fightback was swift and effective: Tet was largely repelled within a week. But it was the TV news that did more damage. There was coverage of Viet Cong seizing a city (Hue), of US confusion and its servicemen being killed. Until then, ordinary Americans believed that this was a war being won. And the graphic image of a young Viet Cong soldier cold-bloodedly shot in the head by a South Vietnamese police chief seemed to capture the inhumanity of this distant war.

Facing a loss of public confidence, the Democrat president Lyndon Johnson (1908–73) announced he would not seek re-election. Meanwhile, ever-larger numbers of young men were drafted into the Vietnam campaign

– a force of 20,000 in 1965 had grown to half a million. The anti-war movement had existed since the early 1960s, but now it went mainstream. Efforts to bomb North Vietnam into submission – Operation Rolling Thunder – were obviously failing, but the official view remained that insurgent communism in South-East Asia could and would be crushed.

In 1968, students and universities became a political force. In all Western countries, student numbers had grown rapidly as the demand for highly qualified personnel increased. Steadily through the 1960s, students had become more radical, challenging the assumptions of the official worldview. They attacked racial discrimination, economic inequality, big business. They urged participative democracy and advocated non-violent civil disobedience.

This was a generation born during and just after the Second World War. Brought up on technological and economic progress, they were taught to have huge expectations, but found their pathway blocked by the mindset of the wartime generation: conservative, dutiful, self-denying and entitled to be in control. The new generation had new values, new ideals and new consciousness. It was in flagrant collision with the old order.

The University of California's Berkeley campus had been the setting for mid-1960s civil rights protests and the movement for free speech on campus. Berkeley students triggered radicalism across America and provided the template for protests to come. In 1968, trouble erupted at Columbia University in New York. Like so many protests that year, it started as a relatively minor affair. The university had a ban on indoor demonstrations; the students defied the ban, and were disciplined. The protest widened in numbers and in its demands, and links were discovered between Columbia and the Pentagon. With their militant leader, Mark Rudd (b. 1947), the protestors stormed the administrative building and broke into the president's office. More buildings were seized, and the police were called. Violence erupted, with 150 people injured and over 700 students arrested. Yet another occupation in May brought full-scale battle with police and improvised barricades. Middle America was deeply shocked.

Opposition to the Vietnam War had become a rallying call every-where. In London's Grosvenor Square, mounted police had prevented demonstrators from reaching the American embassy; injuries and mass arrests were the outcome. Protests in Berlin spread across West Germany, culminating in May with a mass demonstration that united university students with trade union members. The same pattern of protest engulfed cities across Europe as campus anger hit the streets and students clashed with police. And in Japan an extraordinary inten-sity of rage and rebellion fired an explosion of student protest against university administrators, the war in Vietnam and authority in general. Fluid networks of activists staged mass demonstrations, occupied and closed key universities and fought riot police.

Mexico was a particular tragedy. With the Olympic Games approach-ing, the autocratic government of Díaz Ordaz had good relations with the United States. Conflict between the government and radical students had been simmering before '68. Then, in Mexico City, a student skirmish triggered police violence in a spiral of intensifying protests. These quickly transcended their specific causes and, without obvious coordination, a summer of unrest saw students appealing directly to the people. It was an incipient revolution, everything that Díaz Ordaz feared.

The showdown came ten days before the Games opened. A gathering of 10,000 students was deliberately trapped by the army in Tlatelolco plaza. A signal brought the start of a shooting massacre, with 300 people killed and many others arrested. There was no more protest. The Olympics went ahead as planned.

In France, at the start of the year, student radicalism was still latent. The universities, though expanding fast, were authoritarian and formal in character, based on didactic teaching and passive learning. The Nanterre Campus on the edge of Paris, bleak and overcrowded, became the unlikely flashpoint. Protests began in late January and fol-lowed what became an archetypal pattern: an escalator of protest and repression tipping towards violence. The charismatic Daniel Cohn-Bendit (b. 1945) led anarchists, Marxists, Maoists and newly radicalized ordinary students to the Sorbonne Campus, where violent clashes with police spread and intensified. The 6th of May saw raging battles between students and riot police. Demonstrators tore up the cobblestones for ammunition and created barricades. The largest pitched battle occurred on the night of 10–11 May, as 40,000 students faced ranks of brutal and well-equipped police.

Crucially, public sympathy now flowed towards the students, who were joined by young workers. On 13 May the key unions called a strike, and over a million marched through Paris. The next day factories were being occupied as wildcat strikes spread. France was gripped by a revolutionary fervour. Conversations everywhere challenged the state, but also the whole nature of a capitalist and materialistic society. Subversive posters appeared: 'Imagination is power, take your dreams for reality' and, more ambiguously, 'Under the paving stones, the beach'. By 23 May an unprecedented ten million workers were on strike and the normal economy had ceased to function. With the government close to collapse, President de Gaulle (1890–1970) left Paris by helicopter. Prime Minister Georges Pompidou (1911–74) assumed that he had fled.

Actually, this was the moment when the revolution faltered. De Gaulle had flown to the French military headquarters in Germany, where General Massu (1908–2002) confirmed army support. Much reassured, he returned to France, announcing elections and ordering strikers back to work. It was over.

In America, the civil rights issue was a recurring factor in almost every protest movement. Racism was visibly entrenched in US society, but also invisibly present in attitudes and social behaviour. And the greatest civil rights leader, Martin Luther King, Jr (1929–68), was finding his Christian belief in non-violent civil disobedience under contest from a new wave of militant leaders. But in April, King was assassinated by a racist gunman in Memphis. Arson and rioting broke out in 125 cities across the USA. Despite the physical damage in many ghettoes, the disturbances were short-lived. Crucially, the 1968 Kerner Report on the race riots of the previous year had recommended police restraint, which now helped prevent the usual 'protest escalator' from operating. From a high point in 1967, race riots gradually declined.

Meanwhile, the growing Black Power movement diverged from the civil rights tradition, stressing black pride, black separatism and black consciousness. This tendency gained worldwide exposure at the Mexico Olympics, when US athletes Tommy Smith and John Carlos raised black-gloved hands at their medal-awarding ceremony. But despite links with the radical left, the new movement drifted into terrorism and crime, becoming marginalized in the 1970s.

November's presidential elections were approaching. Pro-war vice president Hubert Humphrey (1911–78) was the leading Democrat contender for the candidacy but challenged by Eugene McCarthy (1916–2005) and Robert Kennedy (1925–68), both on an anti-war ticket. Then in the early hours of 5 June, while celebrating victory in the California primary, Kennedy was shot and died the next day.

Now Vietnam was the key issue. As the candidates arrived in Chicago for the Democratic Convention, anti-war protesters also gathered in Lincoln Park. They included many 'Yippies' – political hippies – whose leaders, Abbie Hoffman (1936–89) and Jerry Rubin (1938–94), nominated a live pig for the presidency. More ominously, they were confronted by riot police, who violently enforced a curfew. On 28 August the Democrats held a debate on Vietnam while 15,000 protesters rallied in Grant Park. Chicago mayor Richard Daley (1902–76) called up the National Guard. With tension rising, the 'peace plank' was defeated. Outside, what was described (even in an official report) as a 'police riot' erupted. Demonstrators were surrounded in front of the Conrad Hilton Hotel, whose front windows collapsed under crowd pressure, and hundreds were injured in the ensuing chaos and violence. Inside the convention, Humphrey was selected but Democrat disunity was obvious. And as so often in 1968, the tide of radicalism then reversed. Republican Richard Nixon (1913–94) won the November election; the war dragged on.

On a very different battlefront, 1968 was the year of the Prague Spring. This began in January when conservative communist leader Antonín Novotný conceded power to the more liberal Alexander Dubček. Within a month, the laws on censorship were loosened and a torrent of political debate and cultural activity was released. Prague quickly became a crossroads for young people exploring the radical terrain of 1968.

In April a wider programme of liberalization announced 'socialism with a human face' and moves towards a more competitive economy, with greater production of consumer goods. The new programme offered a 'fuller life of the personality than in any bourgeois democracy'.

By July the reforms were still advancing, but in the Kremlin, Leonid Brezhnev (1906–82) was losing patience. At the Bratislava Conference with eastern European leaders, Marxist–Leninist orthodoxy was affirmed and a military option to 'assist' Czechoslovakia moved up the agenda. On the night of 20–21 August a Soviet and Warsaw Pact invasion began with 200,000 troops and 2,000 tanks. A shocked Dubček urged no resistance, and was arrested the next morning. Heroic and often youthful protest persisted as the tanks took up positions in the capital. Protracted argument ran on in Moscow with an exhausted Czech leadership. Finally Soviet leaders secured agreement to a formal Protocol that ended the revolutionary Prague Spring. Dubček was allowed to resume his leadership but was soon deposed.

In the early 1960s, two books by women had been published that each lit a revolutionary fuse: by 1968, these were making contact with their explosive charge. The first was the environmentalist manifesto *Silent Spring* by Rachel Carson (1907–64); the second was *The Feminine Mystique* by Betty Friedan (1921–2006). The latter argued that women were imprisoned by stylized gender images and corresponding roles. The time had come to resist sexist power structures and to look for equality beyond suffrage.

In September 1968, women gathered in Atlantic City, New Jersey for the annual Miss America contest. Outside the hall, 400 protesters also gathered to challenge this annual spectacle. In ongoing street theatre, they crowned a live sheep, displayed a woman's figure marked out as a side of beef and paraded a life-sized Miss America puppet. Four protesters bought tickets for the event and during the outgoing Miss America's speech they unfurled a Women's Liberation banner before being ejected by the police. Back outside, there was the 'freedom trash can' into which they flung mops, high-heeled shoes, sexist magazines, curlers and false eyelashes. The wider revolution for women's consciousness had begun.

Carson's book had a long fuse. On television, Americans had watched the increasing despoilation of their natural environment by the march of material progress. The Great Lakes were dead, and some rivers were so polluted that they could catch fire. The first environmental campaigning began. Meanwhile the Club of Rome, comprising high-ranking statesmen and scholars, was founded in 1968 and argued that the environment was a key dimension of the world's interrelated challenges. And in the autumn of 1968 the first *Whole Earth Catalog* was published. Ecology, self-sufficiency and alternative education were its distinctive values.

Since the mid-1960s, waves of hippies had begun arriving along the Californian coast. Evolved from the Beat Generation, the movement urged peace and harmonious coexistence with nature while exploring communal lifestyles, mysticism, experimental art and music and the use of 'mind-expanding' drugs. The hippies affirmed a kind of tribal empathy in the search for heightened awareness that would transcend the banality and barely concealed violence of the rationalist worldview. 'Do not adjust your mind. There is a fault with reality', instructed a slogan of the era. This was the counterculture: a spontaneous generational rejection of industrial imperatives. Life as a grey, monotonous and time-driven sequence of mechanical and inauthentic obligations, rewarded only by the consumption of endless disposable consumer goods: this was a form of bondage to be broken. However, the chains being snapped were not those proclaimed by Marx, but the self-imposed manacles of a deadening bourgeois consciousness.

Unsurprisingly, the arts reflected the political and cultural climate. About all the 'events' of 1968 there was a sense of theatre, a feeling that these often extraordinary scenes were some kind of situationist 'happening'. Many artists became political activists. And everywhere there was a breaking down of boundaries: the strictures of modernism were challenged as art was stripped of its formal clothing. Meanwhile the old distinction between popular and 'classical' artistic expression was dismantled by pop art and op art, by art cinema and by pop music that jumped genres. And as in the new street politics, artists and audience could contingently engage to create a unique performance.

Inner truth was the new touchstone as objectivity was pushed from its plinth. Reality was no longer an inexorable fact but a contestable point of view. And the time had come to liberate art from its traditional custodians. No more baleful glances from classical busts, no more silken ropes and hushed reverence. Art was to be touched, danced around and directly experienced. Blow open the doors of the museum and let art escape...

The '68 phenomenon was like outbreaks of fire: unpredictable, often unstoppable surges of events, surges of history. It could not be extinguished because there was no beginning or end, no single or identifiable cause, no figurehead to blame, no HQ to close down. Its leaders were ad hoc, impromptu, acting with no planning. A 'cause' would begin as a singular issue and then morph into allied causes or sub-causes. No list of grievances was ever complete. Those in authority could not understand this kind of revolution: it was outside their mindset.

A kind of collective learning process drove events along: posters, marches, magazines, leaflets, speeches, teach-ins all raised understanding and awareness. The learning was chaotic, spontaneous, unplanned, uneven, open to chance. Paris '68 is remembered for the barricades and the general strike. But the people there, the 'soixante-huitards', remember it for the 'conversations', for the feeling of solidarity, for the euphoric sense of possibility. And the scenario was not confined to the front page or the TV news: '68 happened across countless cities and communities, colleges and schools, flats and suburban sitting rooms.

But for what? Where was the revolution? Even in France, the Gaullists comfortably won the June elections, conclusively ending the revolutionary moment. Capitalism was back in control. In America, it was as much military failure as political protest that eventually brought the Vietnam nightmare to an end. Civil rights did gradually improve, but the ghettoes deepened and darkened. While student protest in the West rumbled on into the 1970s, in Mexico it was crushed.

And the prison door closed on protest in Prague: resistance flickered for a while, then disappeared underground. Poland's nascent protest movement was similarly silenced. The revolution was coming, but not for another twenty years.

So was there really a revolution in 1968? The answer is yes, and it is with us every day. Most obviously the legacy is cultural and social, but it has many political dimensions. The year 1968 inaugurated a far more informal society, one in which morality became personal choice and democracy jumped out of the ballot box.

The women protesting the Miss America contest launched a new wave of feminism. Thousands of women began the quest to find an authentic identity. Sexism remains endemic in Western society, but it is far more widely challenged. And attitudes towards the environment are not unrelated. Before 1968, nature was a subject for conquest through ever more sophisticated transmission of science into technology. Yet within months of '68, Friends of the Earth and Greenpeace were founded and America had signed off the Environmental Protection Act. A revolutionary ecological paradigm emerged, recognizing that nature was an intricate, interdependent system of which human beings were not owners but stewards. Symbolically, it was Christmas 1968 when the crew of Apollo 8 took the world's most famous photograph: 'Earthrise' – a lonely blue planet seen whole for the first time. The environmental revolution is still unfolding.

Revolutionary movements such as feminism and environmentalism are not about a change of regime, but a change of consciousness. And that takes us to the heart of '68. The year saw a change of consciousness that masqueraded as a political revolution. 'Ho, Ho, Ho Chi Minh', chanted the protesters; 'A true nature's child, I was born, born to be wild', sang Steppenwolf in that same year. Together they reflected the words of Mario Savio (1942–96), student leader at Berkeley in 1964: 'There's a time when the operation of the machine becomes so odious, makes you so sick at heart, that you can't take part! And you've got to put your bodies upon the gears and upon the wheels…upon the levers, upon all the apparatus, and you've got to make it stop!'

And the identity of that machine? A vast technocracy that had taken control of the Western consciousness in the name of science, objectivity and rationality. The paper charge against the bourgeoisie concerned capitalism and exploitation, but the existential charge was far greater: the denial of the human spirit; the reduction of life to the logistics of greed and destruction, blind enslavement to the hierarchies of power.

The spirit of 1968 affirmed the centrality of what the machine had made peripheral: imagination and creativity, mutuality and spirituality, improvisation and spontaneity. In a new understanding of the world as a living, organic whole, 1968 was the beginning of the beginning. But for the view of the world as an industrial machine, it was the beginning of the end.

Revolutions don't come much bigger than that.

Jerry Rubin

Jerry Rubin (1938–94), American counterculture activist, was born in Cincinnati. He attended University of California, Berkeley, where he became involved in radical politics, campaigning for the legalization of marijuana and opposing the war. He was a founding member of the Youth International Party ('Yippies') with Abbie Hoffman, and appeared before the House Un-American Activities Committee (HUAC), using these as opportunities for political theatre. Active at the Chicago demonstrations of 28 August 1968, he and other Yippie leaders were convicted the following year for incitement to riot. He published *DO IT!: Scenarios of the Revolution* (1970). In the 1970s he ceased involvement with politics and became a businessman, investing in Apple Computer.

Alexander Dubček

Alexander Dubček (1921–92), Czechoslovak politician, was the first secretary of the Czech Communist Party (1968–9). A wartime partisan fighter against the Nazis, Dubček was a member of the Czech National Assembly from 1951. He became first secretary of the Slovak branch of the Party in 1963, introducing liberalization and encouraging expression of Slovak national identity. Appointed first secretary to the Czechoslovak Party in January 1968, he began to liberalize the government, introduce 'socialism with a human face' and relax censorship. Following the Warsaw Pact invasion of August 1968, he was taken to Moscow, but returned in late August to resume his duties. Forced to resign in April 1969, he then worked in the Slovak Forestry Service until 1989 when, with Václav Havel, he supported the mass demonstrations of Civic Forum and was elected chairman of the Federal Assembly.

TIMELINE

1961
4 May   'Freedom Riders', an interracial group of protesters, travel
             from Washington, DC to the South to test President Kennedy's
             commitment to civil rights

1962   Rachel Carson's *Silent Spring* is published; Port Huron
             Statement or 'Agenda for a Generation' – manifesto of Students
             for a Democratic Society (SDS)

1963
28 August   During the Civil Rights March on Washington,
             Martin Luther King, Jr delivers his 'I have a dream' speech

1963   Betty Friedan publishes *The Feminine Mystique*

1964
7 August   US Congress passes Gulf of Tonkin Resolution, allowing the
             President to wage war against North Vietnam without a formal
             declaration of war

2 July   US Civil Rights Act is passed, outlawing discrimination on basis
             of race, colour, religion, sex or national origin

1965
21 February Nation of Islam leader Malcolm X is assassinated in Manhattan

2 March   US president Johnson approves Operation Rolling Thunder, a
             massive bombing campaign of North Vietnam

5 September *San Francisco Examiner* introduces the word 'hippie'

1966
30 June   National Organization for Women is founded in the US to bring
             'women into full participation in the mainstream of American
             society'

15 October   Bobby Seale and Huey Newton found the Black Panthers,
             a militant group prepared to use violence for defence

1967   'Summer of Love' in San Francisco

1968

30-31 January Tet Offensive launched by Viet Cong; within days, US forces retake most areas; a battle for Hue rages for twenty-six days

22 March French students occupy Nanterre University administration building

4 April Abbie Hoffman protests against capitalism at New York Stock Exchange by throwing fake currency from the gallery; Martin Luther King, Jr is assassinated

2-3 May Student demonstrations begin in Paris

10 May Night of the Barricades in Paris

13 May General strike in France

6 June Senator Robert Kennedy assassinated in Los Angeles

20-21 August Warsaw Pact troops march into Czechoslovakia, ending the Prague Spring

25-29 August Anti-war demonstrators beaten by police outside the Democratic Party convention in Chicago

2 October Tlatelolco massacre: hundreds of protesting students killed in Mexico City

5 November Republican Richard Nixon wins US presidential election

1969

20 July US astronaut Neil Armstrong becomes first human to walk on the moon

15-17 August Woodstock rock festival attracts 400,000 in New York State

15 October The Peace Moratorium, the largest demonstration in US history, attracts two million protestors nationwide

PORTUGAL: THE CARNATION REVOLUTION, 1974

Filipe Ribeiro de Meneses

Portugal's near-bloodless revolution won its colourful name from a moment when the people of Lisbon gave flowers to the soldiers engaged in their coup against the long-standing right-wing regime. In a gesture that perhaps owed something to the iconic photographs of anti-Vietnam protestors in the US putting flowers in the rifle barrels of troops drawn up against them just a few years earlier, the Portuguese military placed the carnations into the muzzles of their own guns.

This unusual revolution, which took place in western Europe at the height of the Cold War, was in some respects part of the ongoing reshaping of the world in the wake of the Second World War. The Estado Novo ('New State') regime had been founded by António Salazar in 1933, and was a direct legacy of the era of Hitler and Franco; as well as sweeping this away to replace it with representative democracy, the revolution also brought a sudden but long-needed end to Portuguese imperialism in Africa and elsewhere. PF

O
n 25 April 1974, troops loyal to the Movimento das Forças Armadas (MFA, Armed Forces Movement) overthrew the government of Marcelo Caetano (1906–80), who six years earlier had replaced António de Oliveira Salazar (1889–1970) at the helm of Portugal's 'New State'. The MFA, made up of mid-career officers – hence its sobriquet the 'Captains' Movement' – had a number of important aims, not least of which were instituting a democratic regime and putting an end to the colonial wars in which Portugal had been embroiled since 1961. Their action – which came to be known as the Carnation Revolution – unexpectedly gave rise to a revolutionary process which lasted for a year and a half (some would say longer) and whose ultimate outcome became, for a time, entirely unclear: different political parties and military factions vied for supremacy, resting their claims on diametrically opposed assertions of legitimacy. Although Portugal eventually emerged from this process as a parliamentary democracy, it did so with constitutional contradictions which would take time to correct. Meanwhile the decolonization process failed to prevent a number of catastrophic outcomes: the occupation of East Timor by Indonesia, civil war in Angola, and the headlong flight out of Africa of over half a million Portuguese.

By April 1974, Portugal had been fighting a number of colonial wars which, in the case of Angola, stretched back over thirteen years. There, as well as in Mozambique and Guiné-Bissau, Portuguese forces found it increasingly difficult to halt incursions by foreign-backed liberation movements such as the MPLA, FNLA and UNITA (Angola), FRELIMO (Mozambique) and the PAIGC (Guinea-Bissau). What was worse, for national servicemen and professional officers alike, was that no political solution could be discerned on the horizon. Unlike Great Britain and France, which had also faced anti-colonial violence, Portugal was a dictatorship, whose legitimacy, such as it was, rested on a nationalist reading of the country's history. According to this viewpoint, the alienation of any portion of Portuguese territory was out of the question. The country thus found itself in a cul-de-sac, even after Salazar's replacement by Caetano, whose arrival had been greeted with relief and even hope. A long-time defender of a federal structure for the Portuguese Empire – in contrast with Salazar's integrationist, centralizing vision – Caetano found it, however, impossible to do anything other than continue the war. This failure dented the political impact of his domestic reformist agenda, built on modernization and economic growth. And as the fighting continued, with mixed success on the field, Portugal found itself increasingly isolated on the world stage – apart from two friends with whom it shared little other than the desire to keep as much of southern Africa as possible under white rule: Rhodesia and South Africa. Their long-standing hopes for a political solution dashed, mid-ranking officers formed the MFA, resolved to upend the regime. Only its disappearance, they now believed, could bring about the war's end.

At dawn on 25 April 1974, the MFA struck. Its troops converged on Lisbon, seizing the airport, radio and television stations, and other key points of the city. There was little in the way of a government reaction – troops thought to be reliable switched sides rather than confront their comrades in arms. Only the secret police, once known as the PIDE but rebadged Direção Geral de Segurança (DGS, Directorate-General of Security) by Caetano, resisted, killing four people outside its headquarters. Elsewhere, though, celebration was in the air: civilians and soldiers fraternized, and the latter were quickly bedecked with the red carnations that would come to symbolize the day. The Prime Minister holed up at the headquarters of another police force, the Guarda Nacional Republicana (GNR, Republican National Guard). Outside it, in the small Carmo square, a crowd gathered, sang the national anthem and cheered the MFA forces surrounding Salazar's heir. It took the arrival of General António Spínola (1910–96), a former governor-general of Guinea-Bissau, to secure Caetano's surrender. The day belonged to the MFA, but it was the well-known Spínola who grabbed the headlines. Earlier that year he had shaken the government to its core by publishing a book, *Portugal and the Future*, which stated openly that the war in Africa could not be won – that a political solution was necessary. The book led to the dismissal of the general – the second-in-command of

Portugal's armed forces – and his sole superior, General Francisco da Costa Gomes (1914–2001), who had approved its publication. Both men were then contacted by the MFA, which favoured Costa Gomes; but on 25 April he could not be found, and the more elitist Spínola, complete with his trademark monocle, seized the day. Popular approval of the MFA's actions was confirmed on 1 May, when enormous demonstrations took to the streets, calling on the new authorities to deliver improvements to living and working conditions.

Although a National Salvation Junta, composed of senior officers and headed by Spínola, was immediately formed, and although this body chose Spínola as the new president of the republic, the MFA did not disband. Neither did it do so once a civilian government, which included the leaders of political parties old and new, was appointed. The 'captains' increasingly distrusted Spínola. His desire for protagonism was impossible to disguise, as was the antipathy he directed both to the communists, whose commanding hand he now discerned everywhere, and the African liberation movements. Spínola remained wedded to the colonial programme unveiled in *Portugal and the Future*: the gradual handover of sovereignty to the 'overseas provinces' (as the Portuguese called their colonies), whose respective electorates would freely determine their own future. According to Spínola, there was still time to ensure each population would vote for independence in a commonwealth-like 'Lusitanian Confederation'. There wasn't: the liberation movements sensed that complete military victory was in their grasp, and refused to make peace until they were recognized by Lisbon as the sole legitimate voice of their respective peoples. There would be no elections, no lengthy transition periods. The rest of the world agreed with them, as did most Portuguese politicians, eager now to debate their country's future in Europe, not to pursue a lost cause in Africa. And few soldiers were willing to fight on now that Caetano was gone: in such circumstances, thwarting the liberation movements' intent became impossible, despite the threat their rule posed to Portuguese lives and investments in the colonies. Just as the military split into different factions – with the MFA's commitment to immediate independence of the colonies proving far more popular within the army's ranks than Spínola's less immediate solution – so too political parties split over this and key domestic issues. However, because the oldest and best organized of these parties, the Portuguese Communist Party (PCP, Partido Comunista Português) had a head start over the others, its influence was out of proportion to its actual size. This influence began to exert itself within military circles, more and more officers coming to the conclusion that Spínola had to go in order to achieve peace in Africa. He would fall in September 1974, to be replaced by Costa Gomes.

There is a number of different readings of the events in Portugal between April 1974 and November 1975. The most commonly accepted one falls into the category of 'transition to democracy'. According to this view, the Portuguese Armed Forces shepherded the country from the 'fascist' New State regime (as it would be described in the preamble to the 1976 Portuguese Constitution) to a parliamentary democracy, with the help of the political parties, be it those already in existence, notably Partido Socialista (PS, Socialist Party) led by Mário Soares (1924–2017), or others created after 25 April 1974 – Francisco de Sá Carneiro's Partido Popular Democrata (PPD, Popular Democrat Party, soon to be rebaptised Partido Social Democrata) and Diogo Freitas do Amaral's Centro Democrático Social (CDS, Social Democratic Centre). The legacy of forty-eight years of dictatorship meant that this was a bumpy process, with spanners being thrown into the works by a number of groups: on the one side, the PCP far-left parties and those factions within the military aligned with them; on the other, the shadowy forces of the far right. General Spínola played an ambiguous role before and after his resignation. The 'transition to democracy' explanation places great weight on the unambiguous result of the constituent elections, held on 25 April 1975, which gave an overwhelming majority to the parties committed to the democratic process (PS, PPD and CDS), to the detriment of the communists and their fellow travellers – and on the help given to these formations by foreign supporters, notably the socialist and Christian democrat parties of western Europe.

The PCP and its supporters remember events differently. They focus on the importance of the links forged by the Communist Party with progressive officers (the most important one of whom was Lieutenant-Colonel Vasco Gonçalves (1921–2005), who headed five 'provisional' governments between the summer of 1974 and that of 1975). This alliance between the 'people' and the MFA was able to achieve a number of social, economic and diplomatic victories – as much as could be asked in a NATO member located on the western tip of Europe during the Cold War (with a still-Francoist Spain as neighbour). The PCP's leadership was decisive, communist commentators argue, in breaking up monopolies, nationalizing key industries and financial services in general, pursuing an agrarian reform that looked after the interests of the landless peasantry of southern Portugal and handing over Portugal's African colonies to the liberation movements which had contributed so much to the eventual defeat of the New State. In so doing, they broke the back of those social and economic groups that had propped up the Salazar regime. The 1976 constitution is celebrated as a document which, especially in its original state, enshrined these popular victories.

A third reading of the Portuguese Revolution is that of the far left, which claims that the army's actions on 25 April opened the road for a genuine popular revolution capable of setting the country on a dramatically new course, whatever the interests of the international community. This aim was actively pursued by civilian elements and their military backers (the most famous of whom was Brigadier General Otelo Saraiva de Carvalho, b. 1936), who together wished to create a genuine popular democracy with radical and far-reaching economic and social goals. This, they claim, was a genuine possibility, thwarted in the end by the combined forces of national and international reaction and, crucially, the PCP itself, which preferred to consolidate and secure its limited gains rather than join forces in an attempt to carry out a deeper transformation of the country. Although this rift – which grew out of existing bitter differences between, for example, the Moscow-loyal PCP and more recently established Maoist groups – would leave a legacy of bitterness on the Portuguese left, it was generally ignored at the time by centrist and conservative forces, which lumped all communist factions together and believed them to be acting in unison. Die-hard supporters of this cause would be behind the Forças Populares 25 de Abril (FP-25, Popular Forces of 25 April), a short-lived terrorist movement active in the early 1980s.

All three readings of what happened in 1974–5 agree on one point: that the events taking place in Portugal transcended the country's borders. It could not be otherwise, given the Cold War and all that was at stake, both in Europe and in Africa. On the one hand, whoever was in power in Portugal would be in a position to affect directly the outcome of the decolonization process in Angola and Mozambique, which shared borders with the remaining white-governed territories in the region: Rhodesia, Namibia and South Africa. This entire region, it seemed, was up for grabs. On the other, the West could not afford to see Portugal – and its Atlantic island groups of the Azores and Madeira – fall into hostile hands. US secretary of state Henry Kissinger (b. 1923) may have for a time despaired of the situation in Portugal, but his ambassador, Frank Carlucci (1930–2018) – a man with known ties to the CIA – did not. Kissinger encouraged Carlucci to be bold – to take risks, as he put it – in order to support anti-communist forces in Portugal; the extent to which he did so is still to be determined. Also important were European political parties and their umbrella organizations, such as the Socialist International and the European Union of Christian Democrats, which channelled funds and political know-how into the pro-democracy parties, helping these to overcome the gulf in experience and structure that separated them from the PCP. As for the Soviet Union, its leadership did not believe, it seems, in the possibility of a communist Portugal. It did, however, have high hopes for Angola, increasing massively the aid delivered to the Marxist MPLA – the movement favoured also by much of the MFA and the Portuguese left in general.

The legacy of the Portuguese Revolution was profound, even if the actual events that shaped its evolution continue to be disputed to this day. The 25th of April has become a national holiday (Freedom Day), with a by now familiar ritual during which parliament pays homage to the men who took power in 1974. The revolution, once completed, left in place a democratic regime, in many ways Portugal's first (the First Republic, displaced by Salazar's New State, had restricted the suffrage to literate male adults). Soon after it was over, Portugal applied for membership of what was then the European Economic Community (EEC), thus sealing the reorientation away from empire which had led the country to its African wars. The change of regime made possible the establishment of a national health service and greater educational opportunities, thus broadening the life options of an ever greater number of Portuguese. So profound has the transformation of the country since April 1974 been that it is tempting to dismiss the importance of the actual events of 1974–5, and the apprehension felt by many in the country about a revolutionary process whose ultimate outcome was by no means clear. At a number of key moments Portugal veered decisively to the left (notably after 11 March 1975, when a right-wing coup was thwarted by the MFA and supporting civilian groups), leading both to the so-called 'institutionalization' of the MFA – the grafting of its increasingly convoluted decision-making machinery into the state itself – and the adoption of radical economic measures. Intellectuals flocked to Portugal to see a popular revolution in action; landed estates were occupied by those who worked them, while in the cities empty houses were occupied by those who had none. By the so-called 'Hot Summer' of 1975, and in spite of the electoral results of April 1975, the Portuguese government was made up of communist and far-left militants. And when this was replaced by a more representative cabinet, which included socialists and Popular Democrats, revolutionary activity was actually stepped up, rendering the country ungovernable. In one infamous incident, parliament was surrounded and held hostage until protesters' complaints were upheld. Demanding protection from the President and the MFA against such incidents, Prime Minister Pinheiro de Azevedo (1917–83) then declared his cabinet to be on strike. By this time, indiscipline was rife in the barracks, with a new group, Soldados Unidos Vencerão (SUV, Soldiers United Will Triumph), calling on enlisted men to cast aside their obedience to officers in defence of popular goals.

On 25 November 1975, amidst increasing talk of a Lisbon Commune and civil war, matters came to a head. Moderate army forces seized the initiative and defanged the most radicalized military units, putting an end to any more talk of revolution. Celebrated as the end to a troubled period in the country's history, this counter-strike did not mark the end of the military's involvement in politics, which would be enshrined in the 1976 constitution. A Council of the Revolution would remain in place for a number of years, acting as a military-staffed supreme court; the commander of the November action, Brigadier General António Ramalho Eanes (b. 1935), was elected president of the republic in 1976, combining the role with that of chief of staff of the armed forces; and successive governments' ability to supervise the military was very restricted. Many believe that the CDS's Adelino Amaro da Costa (1943–80), the first post-revolution civilian minister of defence, paid with his life in 1980 for his attempt to shine a light on the murkier edges of military affairs. An aeroplane in which he and Prime Minister Sá Carneiro were travelling crashed shortly after take-off from Lisbon, killing all seven people on board. Successive parliamentary investigations have concluded that the crash was caused by a bomb.

November 1975 was also the month in which independence was finally granted to Angola. By then, this country was in the midst of an all-out civil war which the divided Portuguese forces had not managed to contain. Other Portuguese colonies had already received independence. The revolutionary politics of Samora Machel's FRELIMO, in Mozambique, alongside the complete breakdown of law and order in Angola, led to the mass flight of hundreds of thousands to Portugal, many of whom had initially been tempted to remain in the countries where they had long resided, or been born. Their plight tends to be ignored in the celebratory accounts of the period. And the colonial reckoning was not yet complete: in December 1975, before its independence had been granted, Portuguese (East) Timor would be invaded by Indonesia, eager to incorporate it and to snuff out what Jakarta described as a locus of revolutionary infection. The ensuing occupation, which would last until 1999, was marked by extreme brutality towards the Timorese.

Mário Soares

Mário Soares (1924–2017) was one of the founders of the Portuguese Socialist Party, imprisoned and exiled several times under Caetano. After the coup of April 1974 he became foreign minister in the provisional government, overseeing independence for Portugal's colonies. A committed democrat, he resisted the communist attempt to take over the country, and in 1976 he was elected prime minister of a minority government (until 1978), hampered by hostility between the socialists and the communists. Elected again in 1983, he took Portugal into the European Economic Community (EEC); in 1986 he became the country's first civilian president.

Vasco Gonçalves

Vasco Gonçalves (1921–2005), who came from a wealthy background, was an army officer and member of the Communist Party. He was involved in planning the coup of 25 April 1974, and served as prime minister from July 1974. In the spring of 1975, following a failed right-wing coup, he nationalized much of Portugal's industry and media. Following elections won by the more moderate Socialist Party, he was denounced as extreme and forced out of office in September 1975.

TIMELINE

1933   António Salazar establishes the fascist New State regime

1949   Portugal becomes a founder member of NATO

1956   Independence movements founded in Portuguese colonies Mozambique and Guinea

1961   Angola war of independence begins

1968   Salazar retires, and is replaced by Marcelo Caetano

1970   Death of Salazar

1973   Guinea-Bissau unilaterally declares independence

1974
25 April   Carnation Revolution; Caetano is exiled to Brazil

1975   Most colonies granted independence

March   Failed right-wing coup against the revolution

1976   A democratic constitution is introduced

1980   Prime Minister Francisco de Sá Carneiro and Minister of Defence Adelino Amaro da Costa killed by a bomb in their aircraft

1982   Civilian government is formally introduced

1986   Portugal joins the EEC

CAMBODIA: THE KHMER ROUGE REVOLUTION, 1975–1979

Sorpong Peou

The Khmer Rouge Revolution of 1975–9 is perhaps the most ruthlessly thorough, radical and inhumanly urgent revolution in history. A group of guerrillas naming themselves after the Khmer, Cambodia's main ethnic group, took inspiration from Mao's turn to the peasantry and his belief in self-sufficiency, combining this with a nativist belief in Cambodia and its people. They sought to remove all vestiges of ethnic or religious minorities and urban culture. Phnom Penh and other towns were forcibly emptied as soon as they fell under Khmer Rouge control, and any perceived foreign influence on the country was rooted out while an egalitarian, nationalistic Cambodia was built, based on reformed, collectivized agriculture and without private property, trade, religion or modern medical facilities. The country was entirely cut off from the outside world. All this was done at lightning speed.

The resulting chaos brought widespread famine, while many of those who had been forced out of the cities, now seen as useless to the new society, were deliberately starved to death or suffered mass execution. The regime's paranoia met the slightest hint of criticism with torture, imprisonment or execution.

Yet unlike many other revolutionary regimes, it neither built a cult of personality around its leadership – Prime Minister Pol Pot remained a shadowy figure until his death – nor publicized its ideological underpinnings. Although the Khmer Rouge emerged from a long-standing communist movement, it prized secrecy and kept this fact hidden for several years. And although its four-year nightmare revolution was swept away by invasion from Vietnam in 1979, the Khmer Rouge did not collapse but returned to its roots – a continuing guerrilla struggle based on the Thai border. Eventually some former Khmer Rouge leaders were incorporated within the political system that sought to rebuild the country, while others were prosecuted for crimes against humanity by a UN-backed court constituted for this purpose.   PF

In April 1975, a group of radical Marxists known as the Khmer Rouge (Red Khmer) succeeded in overthrowing Cambodia's pro-US republican government, with the aim of building a 'new Cambodia' that would be democratic and just (Cambodia was then officially called Democratic Kampuchea). Instead, however, they created a killing field. The regime presided over the deaths of between one and two million people, and then self-destructed. It was driven out of power in late 1978 by an invading army of more than 100,000 Vietnamese troops.

The Khmer Rouge Revolution left a deep impact on Cambodian society and politics. In spite of a UN intervention in the early 1990s to transform the country into a peaceful, democratic and prosperous country, factional politics and social divisions remain the bitter legacies of the revolution. Survivors of the killing field remain deeply traumatized. The pursuit of democracy and justice remains elusive, despite the fact that most people share a strong collective identity and are proud of their nation's ancient glory.

Whether the Khmer Rouge Revolution was based on Marxism–Leninism or Maoism, or driven by nationalism/racialism, is a subject of academic debate, but what it is clear is that its ideological roots can be traced back to the 1950s. What is also clear is that the regime was bloodthirsty: it committed mass-atrocity crimes. Let's turn to each of these points.

Cambodia remained part of French Indochina until 1953, when it was declared an independent kingdom under Prince Norodom Sihanouk (1922–2012). Two years earlier, the Khmer Rouge movement had been formally launched when the Khmer People's Revolutionary Party (KPRP) was founded. Until this time, few Cambodians saw themselves as communists. No Cambodian joined the Indochinese Communist Party (ICP) founded in Hong Kong in 1930. Only a few had joined the party by the end of the Second World War. Much of the effort during this period was driven by a resistance to French colonial rule. Subsequently, however, a number of resistance members turned radical. More joined the movement under Vietnamese leadership and formed their own party when the ICP was dissolved in 1951.

Early during the Cold War, radical intellectuals also participated in parliamentary politics but did not succeed in consolidating their political influence because of repressive violence by Prince Sihanouk, who had abdicated the crown in 1955 but became head of state in 1960 and famously coined the term 'Khmer Rouge'. Top Khmer Rouge leaders had pursued their education in France, where they became radicalized and began an underground guerrilla movement against the royalist Sihanouk regime. The underground communist movement was also constrained by the fact that the communists in North Vietnam did not support any armed struggle against Sihanouk when he was still in power, but took advantage of the Prince's downfall in a US-supported coup by Defence Minister Lon Nol in 1970 and used Sihanouk's popularity among peasants to build their own power base. The US, fearing a Marxist regime in Phnom Penh, undertook extensive bombing raids on Khmer Rouge zones over the next three years, fuelling anger among Khmer Rouge survivors against the incumbent regime and resulting in massive flows of refugees into urban areas. The bombings failed to stop the advances of the revolutionary army or prevent its victory in 1975.

The ideological force of the new Khmer Rouge regime derived from anti-colonialism, anti-monarchism, anti-intellectualism, anti-capitalism and anti-imperialism, while its obsession with building a utopian society meant it began to implement its programme at lightning speed. The leadership was motivated by the idea that, having used violence successfully to win power in 1985, the way to further victory was by resorting to more violence. The new regime, led by Pol Pot (1925–98), adopted a policy of autarky (economic self-sufficiency) and self-isolation inspired by dependency theory. It began a civil war against all its enemies, targeting for destruction all those branded as enemies of the revolution. It moved quickly to destroy all existing state, political and social institutions and classes – as well as royalists known as Sihanoukists, former government officials, intellectuals, and even wealthy peasants and anyone else branded as treacherous or treasonous. It also abolished money, private property (in favour of collectivization), the existing educational system and all religions (condemned as the 'leech of the masses', echoing Marx's phrase, 'opium of the people'). Overall, Pol Pot was in good company with Lenin, Stalin and Mao. The mass atrocities extended beyond 'class war': the regime aimed to build a totalitarian atheist state by destroying all those, including party members, suspected of posing a threat to the top leadership's radical agenda.

But the Khmer Rouge reign of terror was more extensive even than the terror led by Lenin and Stalin in the Soviet Union or Mao in China, given the level of destruction and mass-atrocity crime that took place in less than four years. In that period, up to two million Cambodians – a quarter of the total population – died at their hands, compared with some twenty million who perished under Soviet rule and the sixty-five million Chinese who died in Maoist China (roughly 10 per cent of the total population in each case). The Extraordinary Chambers in the Court of Cambodia, established in 2006 to bring the top Khmer leaders to justice, charged the leadership with three types of serious crime: war crimes, crimes against humanity and genocide. The regime's war crimes and crimes against humanity are beyond dispute, though the alleged crimes of genocide with which its leaders were charged are debatable.

Pol Pot and his group were not primarily driven by racialism nor by lust for power in their violent push to control the country. Rather, the regime was ideologically blinded by the need to build a classless society in the shortest period of time possible, and it was driven by its unrestrained willpower to realize its revolutionary dream at all costs. Its crimes might be best described as motivated by a belief that the socialist end justifies all means.

Extreme regime insecurity caused much of the violence. The movement only grew to become a fighting force after the 1970 coup that overthrew Prince Sihanouk, and it had to rely on the support of the Prince and Vietnamese communist fighters in major battles in the early years of the war; yet it won its military victory just a few short years afterwards. The 60,000-strong revolutionary army was small in comparison to some 200,000 surviving republican troops, and was led by a small group of administratively incompetent ideologues. Although it grew quickly, it was mostly made up of poor peasants who had no administrative experience. Many had initially joined the revolution because of their loyalty to Prince Sihanouk and/or their resentment towards urban dwellers, whom they regarded as looking down upon them. In a clear sign of the nascent regime's extreme insecurity, the role of the Communist Party in the Khmer Rouge movement was kept hidden until 1977. Ordinary Cambodians only heard about the faceless *Angka* (organization), which was made known to them as a way of keeping everyone in constant fear, suggesting it had 'eyes like the fruitlets of a pineapple'. The excessive use of violence also resulted from the total destruction of existing state and social institutions, which left the country in the worst 'state of nature' that exacerbated the paranoia of the Pol Pot group and permitted it to destroy anyone it branded an enemy. Enemies of the revolution were found both within society and in the party itself, as evidenced by the intraparty purges that led to armed rebellions and a massive Vietnamese military invasion.

A border conflict with Vietnam began soon after the Khmer Rouge victory, and resulted in 1978 in the Vietnamese invasion and its occupation of Cambodia until the end of the 1980s. The People's Republic of

Kampuchea (PRK) was now set up by the Vietnamese, with the support of the Soviet Union; it was led by the Khmer People's Revolutionary Party (KPRP), whose official ideology was based on Marxism–Leninism and aimed to build socialism based on the people's wishes. Despite this, the country remained divided and internally at war.

The KPRP regime had to be built from scratch and had no choice but to rely on the support of socialist states in the Soviet bloc. A new constitution was adopted in 1981 and state institutions were quickly established with the support of fewer than 30,000 party members, who represented about 0.36 per cent of the population. The regime was led by a number of former Khmer Rouge officials – the most well-known of whom were Pen Sovann, Chea Sim, Heng Samrin and Hun Sen – who then engaged in a power struggle that led to the rise to power of the latter three. Pen Sovann was seen as a nationalist, and was arrested and then imprisoned in Vietnam; Chea, Heng and Hun, however, were regarded as pro-Vietnam.

Factionalism within the party continued, with one group led by Chea and the other by Hun. Nevertheless, it did not resort to extreme violence. Overall, the regime was institutionally weak: it enjoyed limited political legitimacy, partly because of the political background of its top leaders, their embrace of socialism, and their complete dependence on Vietnam and the Soviet Union for regime survival. From the KPRP's perspective, the regime was legitimized by the notion that it was waging the war of 'national salvation' from the 'genocidal' Pol Pot clique. It devoted much effort to fighting the Khmer Rouge remnants and their anti-communist allies, painting itself as the only legitimate party capable of fighting to prevent Pol Pot from returning to power.

In its effort to enhance its legitimacy, the regime sought to downplay its socialist image. In 1989, the PRK was renamed the State of Cambodia; in 1991, the KPRP further polished its political image by renaming itself the Cambodian People's Party (CPP).

On the other side of the civil war of the 1980s was the resistance movement, made up of armed groups, the most important of which were the Khmer Rouge faction (which had survived the overthrow of the regime and continued to control parts of the west of the country, still under the leadership of Pol Pot); the so-called republicans, formally known as Khmer People's National Liberation Front (KPNLF); and the royalists, officially known as National United Front for an Independent, Neutral, Peaceful and Cooperative Cambodia, or FUNCINPEC, which was initially led by Prince Sihanouk and subsequently by his son, Prince Norodom Ranariddh. Together these three formed a coalition government in 1981, known as the Coalition Government of Democratic Kampuchea (CGDK), whose international support came from China, Western states and members of the Association of Southeast Asian Nations – particularly Thailand, whose objective was to drive the Vietnamese forces out of Cambodia. Unlike the KPRP, which viewed Vietnam as its principal ally, the CGDK regarded Vietnam as the aggressor violating international law by invading and occupying Cambodia as a sovereign state. Yet the CGDK factions were never really united. Their marriage of convenience was based on the idea that Cambodia must be liberated from Vietnamese domination, but they never trusted each other. They went their separate ways after the Paris Peace Agreements were signed on 23 October 1991, ending the war with Vietnam and establishing a temporary role for the UN in managing the triple transition to peace, democracy and market-friendly economics. They turned into three different political parties, competing for power in the national election scheduled for 1993 and organized by the United Nations.

As a result, it is fair to say that deep and enduring factionalism was one legacy of the Khmer Rouge Revolution. The total destruction of existing state and social institutions carried out by the Pol Pot leadership had left the state institutionally weak and extremely fragile. As a result, the warring factions had such mutual distrust and so little ability to find common solutions that they tended to operate according to the logic of 'kill or be killed'. This tendency only began to end when the Cold War had thawed sufficiently to allow the Permanent Members of the UN Security Council, notably China, the USSR and the United States, to push for a peaceful solution to the Cambodian war. Even then, fighting among the political parties continued, as evidenced by the continuation of armed rebellion by the Khmer Rouge until 1998, violent attacks on rallies of the Buddhist Liberal Democratic Party (BLDP) and the violent overthrow in 1997 of First Prime Minister Norodom Ranariddh (FUNCINPEC) by his coalition partner, Second Prime Minister Hun Sen (CPP). Moreover, factionalism also grew deep within the political parties. The KPNLF, whose political party was the BLDP, fell victim to infighting, never recovered, and won no seats at all in the National Assembly after the 1998 national election. FUNCINPEC also fell apart because of internal fighting, and now hardly functions as a party. The traditional reverence for the monarch has diminished, especially after the death in 2012 of Norodom Sihanouk, who had been put back on the throne after the 1993 election. The Cambodian National Rescue Party (CNRP), made up of two parties united by their opposition to the CPP, was also far from united, and was banned in 2017 by the CPP government, whose aim was to monopolize power. The struggle for power within the CPP between the Chea Sim and the Hun Sen camps grew deeper until Chea died in 2015. The party emerged as the hegemonic party but still suffers from intra-party factionalism, despite Hun Sen's efforts at power consolidation.

Almost forty years after the disastrous socialist revolution, the people of Cambodia have yet to develop a deep sense of solidarity even though the largest majority of them share the same ethnic identity. They remain divided along partisan lines (pro- and anti-CPP), and maintain a deep sense of distrust among themselves and towards external powers.

The Khmer Rouge Revolution shaped Cambodian attitudes towards politics. For survivors of the Pol Pot regime, many aspects of Cambodian politics today can be made sense of only by referring to what happened during the 1970s. They see themselves as victims of the Khmer Rouge, and often ask: 'Why did Khmers kill Khmers?' They also believe that this explains why Cambodians have a hard time trusting each other. Survivors and those who did not live under the reign of terror engage in partisan politics: those who are anti-CPP tend to regard the ruling party as communist and pro-Vietnam or treasonous, but those who support the party tend to view it as the one that 'liberated' Cambodia from the 'genocidal' Khmer Rouge.

But for many of those who were born after 1979, what happened under the Khmer Rouge regime has become an almost unbelievable historical event, something not to think too much about. They tend to give more thought to their daily affairs, or to simply disengage from politics for various reasons – one of which is that it is too dangerous to even talk about politics. Moreover, one of the traditional pillars that used to bind most Cambodians together (based on the old myth that the kingdom cannot endure without a king) has now weakened. The current king has been regarded as politically unable to help bring about national reconciliation or unity. Because of strong economic growth in the last few decades, respect for tradition also appears to have given way to consumerism.

Things that still bring Cambodians together are their collective identity, their memory of a glorious past and their long-simmering distrust of the Thais and Vietnamese. They refer to themselves as 'Khmer Yeung' ('We Khmer'), whose ancestors built an empire and numerous religious structures. The most famous of these is Angkor Wat Temple, which has appeared on all national flags. Buddhism was revived after the Khmer Rouge was overthrown, and remains central to Cambodia's collective identity. For many, to be Khmer is to be Buddhist; however, religious tolerance has now become a social norm. Moreover, most Cambodians still see themselves as victims of Thai and Vietnamese attempts to dominate their country or take advantage of its weaknesses. The Hun Sen government's pro-China policy, which has been adopted in recent years, appears to have much to do with its search for security in the midst of a rising China seen as capable of protecting both the regime and the country, whose border disputes with Thailand and Vietnam remain unresolved. Meanwhile, growing dependence on China and the ongoing flow of Chinese people into Cambodia have given rise to a new sense of anxiety, fear and insecurity among many Cambodians.

The Khmer Rouge emerged initially as a tiny movement, but it quickly developed, succeeded and then self-destructed, leaving a bitter legacy that still haunts many Cambodian people today. Factional and personal politics had always been part of Cambodian history, but the civil war, the destruction of existing institutions and the mass murder in the 1970s left the country institutionally weak, undemocratic and prone to violence. The political struggle for security through power maximization among the factions, and even within them, remains endemic, although the CPP's consolidation of power through institutional control, coercive means and co-option has brought a fragile political stability. The ruling elite's politics of self-preservation remains nasty. In spite of these bitter revolutionary legacies, the Cambodians as a nation remain resilient because of their collective identity, their deep sense of pride rooted in their country's glorious past, and their perception of themselves as victims of foreign domination and influence. Any efforts to demonize, criminalize or punish one's alleged enemies are unlikely to lead to sustainable national reconciliation; such efforts will only perpetuate mutual distrust shaped by past violence, animosity and the absence of highly legitimate state institutions.

Norodom Sihanouk

Norodom Sihanouk (1922–2012) was a Cambodian king
(r. 1941–55, 1993–2004), prime minister (1945, 1950, 1952–3,
1954, 1955–6, 1956, 1957, 1958–60, 1961–2) and head of state/
president (1960–70, 1975–6, 1993). From 1954, after the French
withdrew from Indochina, Sihanouk adopted a policy of neutrality, tacitly supporting the Viet Cong fight against the United
States. Exiled by a US-inspired coup in 1970, he allied with the
Khmer Rouge against the new regime but was put under house
arrest upon his return to Kampuchea in 1975, and only released
in 1979. Some of his family members were killed. He denounced
both the Vietnamese invasion and the Khmer Rouge, but in 1981
was under pressure to lead an anti-Vietnam coalition including both the Khmer Rouge and the anti-communist KPNLF.
Following the 1993 election he resumed the throne, initially
with his son as prime minister. Sihanouk abdicated in 2004.
He was also known as a filmmaker and composer.

Pol Pot

Pol Pot (1925–98), Khmer Rouge leader and prime minister of Democratic Kampuchea 1976–9, was born into a prosperous family. He studied in Paris, where he first encountered radical politics, and joined the Cambodian communist movement on his return to the country in 1953. In 1963, his movement, now known as the Khmer Rouge, began a guerrilla insurgency against Prince Sihanouk's government. When Sihanouk was overthrown in 1970, Pol Pot led the Khmer Rouge against the new Lon Nol government, taking Phnom Penh in 1975. Acting as prime minister, he imposed extreme revolutionary and autarkic policies, leading to up to two million deaths. Following the Vietnamese invasion of 1978, Pol Pot moved to Thailand to continue the fight against the invaders. Though officially removed from the Khmer Rouge leadership in 1985, he continued to lead the guerrilla war into the 1990s. In 1997 he was removed in a Khmer Rouge 'coup', and then convicted of treason by the coup masterminds.

TIMELINE

1969   US bombing of Vietnamese bases in Cambodia begins

1970
18 March   Lon Nol stages successful US-backed coup against Prince
            Norodom Sihanouk

1975
17 April   Khmer Rouge seize Phnom Penh, completing their takeover of the
            country; city residents are forced to leave the capital

1977   Fighting breaks out between Vietnam and Cambodia

1979
January   People's Republic of Kampuchea set up, supported by Vietnam

7 January   Vietnamese take Phnom Penh; Khmer Rouge move west

August   Tribunal in Phnom Penh finds Pol Pot guilty of genocide

1981   Coalition government of Prince Sihanouk, the Khmer Rouge and
            Son Sann

1990   Vietnamese troops withdraw from Cambodia

1991
23 October Paris peace accord signed, planning a national election under
            the supervision of the United Nations Transitional Authority in
            Cambodia

1993
23–8 May   Norodom Ranariddh wins elections, but the Cambodian People's
            Party (CPP) seeks to share power; Hun Sen (CPP) and Ranariddh
            are appointed co-prime ministers

1994   Cambodian government outlaws the Khmer Rouge

1997   Norodom Ranariddh ousted in coup by his coalition partner Hun
            Sen; Pol Pot tried in absentia by Khmer Rouge officials for crimes
            committed after 1979

1998   Pol Pot dies

1999   Khmer Rouge remnants surrender

2003   UN and Cambodia agree to set up a tribunal to try former Khmer Rouge leaders

2007   Tribunal hearings begin

THE IRANIAN REVOLUTION, 1979

Homa Katouzian

The dramatic overthrow of the Shah through a vast popular uprising, and the institution of an Islamic republic, overturned decades of pro-Western policy and made Iran a pariah state. This was undoubtedly a major revolution. It was explicitly anti-imperialist, with an anti-capitalist side to it – but instead of a youthful vanguard party, aging conservative clerics led and directed the largely unarmed people to seize the state, while the army kept out of the way. The Marxist analysis integral to many 20th-century revolutions was relegated to the sidelines.

Although the collapse and overthrow of the old regime appeared sudden, it had complex roots in the history of the preceding fifty years, from the overthrow of the popular Mosaddeq regime in the early 1950s to the increasingly autocratic rule by the Pahlavi dynasty. The Shah's spendthrift approach to modernization and Westernization, combined with a long suppression of political opposition, created tensions that exploded in late 1978 and early 1979.

The revolution had immediate worldwide impact because of its strident anti-Americanism, which led to the taking of fifty-two Americans hostage in the embassy for more than a year, revealing the impotence of the world's leading superpower in the face of resurgent Islam. It initiated a period in which political Islam itself became a significant issue in global politics. The revolutionary government sought to export its revolution across the Middle East through surrogate organizations such as Hezbollah and Hamas (and the Syrian regime in Damascus), and supported non-Muslim revolutionary movements across the world. It secured its position as the pre-eminent military power in the region, despite years of war with Iraq and the imposition of devastating sanctions aimed at ending its development of nuclear capabilities.

It also transformed Iranian life and society according to strict sharia law. Nevertheless, decades of rule by the revolutionary religious elite have taken their toll on life in Iran. Whereas initially women were veiled, there has been successful resistance to this policy; and the regime has had to resort to repression – for example, against popular demonstrations after the 2009 elections led to an apparently fraudulent victory for the populist Mahmoud Ahmadinejad, and again in 2017. Like many other successful revolutions, it risks becoming a victim of its own success and running out of steam.   PF

I n August 1953, Britain and the United States organized and financed a coup d'état against Iran's elected prime minister, Mohammad Mosaddeq (1882–1967) by his conservative opposition. This restored the reign of Mohammad Reza Shah (1919–80), who had been Shah since 1941 but had gone into exile long after Mosaddeq nationalized the oil industry. In February 1979, a massive revolution overthrew the Shah's rule and established the Islamic Republic of Iran. It is sometimes believed that the latter event was essentially a consequence of the 1953 coup; however, many things might and might not have happened to avoid the 1979 Revolution. The regime that came into existence in 1953 was not essentially the same one that was overthrown by the revolution of 1979.

To explain this requires a brief digression into the history of the Iranian state and society. Until the early 20th century, Iran had been governed by arbitrary rule, a system of one-person rule without legal limits to the state's actions. Typically, when an arbitrary state was overthrown by domestic or foreign forces, a period of chaos ensued until a superior force could take over and restore the state. In pre-20th-century Iran, arbitrary rule was believed to be the natural system of government, though the shah, an arbitrary ruler, was still expected to rule justly. Injustice would have led to revolt, which might or might not have succeeded. However, from the mid-19th century, the experience of constitutional government in Europe showed educated Iranians that a government based in law was a genuine alternative to arbitrary rule. The upshot was the Constitutional Revolution of 1906–11, which established a democratic constitution following a series of large demonstrations involving merchants, Shi'ite clerics and Westernizers. This revolution, however, was followed not by democracy, but by chaos (the familiar consequence of the fall of the state). In 1921, a coup by the Iranian Cossack Colonel Reza Khan (1878–1944) began the process of restoring order. Soon Reza Khan became dictator. He then overthrew the feeble Qajar dynasty and crowned himself shah, founding the Pahlavi dynasty in 1925.

Before long, however, the dictatorship of Reza Shah, which was a government of the elite with a limited amount of freedom, consultation and participation, changed into a personal rule and a modern absolute and arbitrary government. This lasted until 1941, when his government was overthrown following the Allied invasion and occupation of the country, and he was forced to abdicate in favour of his son Mohammad Reza Shah. Despite the presence of the Allies in the country until 1946, Iran returned to a generally chaotic state, both at the centre and in the provinces.

Meanwhile, protests against the Anglo-Iranian Oil Company led to the nationalization of the Iranian oil industry and Mosaddeq's premiership in 1951. And although Mosaddeq was personally a democrat, his rule increasingly resembled chaos rather than democracy. The coup of 1953 strengthened Mohammad Reza Shah and the military, and led to great public resentment, especially given the involvement of Britain and the United States. However, the new regime was more a typical dictatorship than absolute and arbitrary rule. It also brought a growing involvement of the United Sates in the country's affairs.

By 1960 economic depression, strong Soviet hostility and the relative cooling of relations with John F. Kennedy's America – not to mention public discontent – led to three years of power struggle that ended in the Shah's dismissal of Ali Amini's reformist government. The Shah seized the moment and, in the absence of the parliament, put forward a six-point programme that was designated the White Revolution. Its main points were a land reform and women's franchise – a relatively positive change, even though elections were not free. In a public 'vote' in January 1963, inevitably the result was overwhelming public approval. The White Revolution inaugurated the Shah's phase of arbitrary rule. Not only landlords, but the entire political establishment, lost power. The Shah's old entourage and advisors, though still loyal, were set aside and dismissed, often with contempt.

The religious establishment, which had enjoyed close relations with the political establishment, was disenchanted by both the land reform and women's franchise; however, what angered them all most was the Shah's assumption of total power. Ayatollah Khomeini (1902–89), who at the time was not well known among the general public, led the protest from the holy city of Qom; troops were sent to that city and the arrest of Khomeini led to a massive revolt, especially in Tehran but also other main cities, that was ruthlessly suppressed. During this revolt of June 1963 the bazaar and the urban crowd played a far greater role than the land-owning class, even though land reform did not threaten their interests at all. The revolt greatly increased the Ayatollah's power and prestige among the public. This was further enhanced when his strong and daring protest against the highly unpopular granting of immunity from prosecution to American personnel and their families in Iran led to his exile – first to Turkey and then to Najaf, Iraq.

Politics was now completely abolished. Not a single member of parliament was freely elected. If in the first ten years of the Shah's rule communists were given military trials, it was now the turn of liberals and socialists. Even verbal dissent in private, if reported, was punished. The secret police (SAVAK) rapidly extended their power and presence and struck fear into the hearts of the public, regardless of income and station. Politics having ceased, two urban guerrilla movements, one Marxist–Leninist (Fada'ian) and one Islamic Marxist (Mojahedin), emerged from the mid-1960s onwards. The Shah benefited from the ending of the economic depression and steady growth in oil revenues as exports rose. From 1963 the economy began to grow rapidly as the increases in oil revenues were paid straight into the coffers of the state. Standards of living rose, albeit unevenly, benefiting the urban sector much more than the rural areas, and merchants, businessmen, the military and higher state officials considerably more than the urban crowd. This added to a discontent that was already widespread. The quadrupling of oil prices in 1973 looked like a great blessing, but the state's harmful decisions in response to it turned this potential blessing into a curse.

Apart from intensifying repression, the Shah's policy of spending far above the productive capacity of the country led to rising inflation and more discontent. Imports could not relieve the situation because port, storage and transport facilities were limited. The Shah blamed the high inflation rate on 'profiteering'. By attacking shopkeepers, merchants and businessmen he spread anger among these groups without reducing the anger of the public, who regarded them as mere scapegoats. In 1974, in the wake of the oil-price revolution, the Shah launched a one-party system: the entire populace was obliged to join the Resurgence Party. In a memorable speech, he said that the great majority of the people supported the state; a small number might be neutral, but 'should not expect anything from us'; and the still smaller number of dissidents should leave the country.

Discontent in the midst of growing standards of living was by no means only economic. The politics of elimination had a dialectical effect. While it removed conservatives, liberals and democrats from politics, it encouraged the development of its opposites: beliefs, ideologies and movements that, one way or the other, aimed at the overthrow of the regime and the elimination of the Shah himself. The new classes that emerged as standards of living rose were generally religious, and were alienated from the state to the extent of boycotting the output of Americanized Iranian television. The lack of alternatives pushed many

ABOVE 'Historic victory', Vietnamese poster celebrating the battle of Dien Bien Phu, 1954. (12)

ДА ЗДРАВСТВУЕТ ВЕЧНАЯ, НЕРУШИМАЯ ДРУЖБА И СОТРУДНИЧЕСТВО МЕЖДУ СОВЕТСКИМ И КУБИНСКИМ НАРОДАМИ !

ABOVE Red Army soldiers read from *Quotations of Chairman Mao Zedong*. China, 1969. (13)

BELOW Fidel Castro and Nikita Khrushchev celebrate Cuba's alliance with the USSR. Soviet poster, 1963. (14)

OPPOSITE ABOVE May 1968. Paris, France. (15)

OPPOSITE BELOW Khmer Rouge soldiers and supporters outside the French Embassy. Phnom Penh, Cambodia, 1975. (16)

ABOVE Viktor Yushchenko supporters at a pre-election rally. Kyiv, Ukraine, 2004. (23)

LEFT Nefertiti street art on Mohamed Mahmoud Street, Cairo, Egypt, painted by El Zeft during the Arab Spring. This location, near Tahrir Square, was the site of protests in November 2011. (24)

young people towards Marxism–Leninism of various denominations, both at home and among students in the West, while widespread leftist tendencies and revolts in the West itself had further impact in Iran. In response to rising Americanism there was an intellectual revolt against the West, describing Iran as 'Westoxicated' – a sentiment shared by virtually all classes of society, high and low, man and woman, religious and secular.

Thus, absolute and arbitrary rule, abolition of politics, the impact of the oil-price revolution and Americanism were the principal causes of the revolution of February 1979, when the Shah was driven into exile following more than a year of widespread protests. These had been facilitated by the election of US president Jimmy Carter, who expressed a strong concern for human rights. It was a revolt of the society against the state; the Shah was the object of hatred, and the charismatic Ayatollah Khomeini became the hero of the revolution. No social class and political party resisted or opposed it. Although it was subsequently described as the Islamic Revolution, this is not quite accurate; various ideas and ideologies, though mainly Islamism and Marxism–Leninism, were represented.

In March 1979, in a referendum that offered a choice between the return of the monarchy or an Islamic republic, the people massively voted for the latter – although many, if not most, were unclear about what it meant. Within a few weeks, power struggles began between various protagonists, setting the scene for the politics of elimination: first of the liberals, followed by the Mojahedin, and finally all the Marxist–Leninist organizations, including the Communist Party. Parallel to that, a constitution was put to vote that, significantly, included *velayat-e faqih* or guardianship of the jurist – thus making Ayatollah Khomeini supreme head of the state. While it included the separation of powers, in time this began to look more like the confrontation of powers. After fifty-two American diplomats were taken hostage in November 1979 (and held until January 1981) and Iraqi president Saddam Hussein attacked Iran in September 1980, the rule of the Islamists was considerably consolidated. Many civil servants were expelled, *hejab* was made compulsory and there was a ban on alcohol. Gradually, some of the revolutionaries began to regret their actions. A growing number of people, mainly from the educated middle classes, began to emigrate to Western and later to other countries, forming the Iranian diaspora which in 2018 was estimated to number over four million.

Shortly after the end of the eight-year war with Iraq, which had no winners, Ayatollah Khomeini died in 1989 and was succeeded by Ayatollah Khamenei (b. 1939), though not before two to three thousand leftists, mainly Mojahedin, had been massacred in prisons. The deputy leader, Ayatollah Montazeri, the most senior dissident in the regime to date, strongly protested against the massacre and was forced out of office. Amendments to the constitution created an executive presidency, to which Akbar Hashemi Rafsanjani (1934–2017) was elected. A moderate pragmatist, he slowly began to normalize the situation and reconstruct the badly battered economy. The consolidation of the regime had already led to the emergence of four distinct factions: fundamentalist, conservative, moderate and reformist. The first two eventually became known as 'principle-ists'; the latter two became close to each other, though they maintained their separate identities.

In 1997, the reformist Mohammad Khatami (b. 1943) won a landslide victory in the presidential election. It was followed by eight years of power struggle, with all the unelected forces – the judiciary, the Revolutionary Guard, the Council of Guardians of the Constitution and the state media – being opposed to the President. Khatami tried to reform both the domestic situation and Iran's regional and international relations, but at every turn he had to face obstacles created by the unelected bodies. Eventually, he even lost the support of an increasing number of reformists, though typically this changed when they saw what was to come.

After Khatami's two terms of presidency ended in 2005, Mahmoud Ahmadinejad (b. 1956), an anti-Western populist who had the goodwill of Khamenei, was elected president. In the four years of his first term, he managed to entirely alienate the middle classes as well as the Western powers that Khatami had tried to conciliate. Corruption increased, and the economy was in a semi-chaotic state. In 2009, there was much hope in the candidacy of Mir Hossein Mousavi (b. 1942), the war years' prime minister and a leading member of the reformist faction. He had the support of the middle classes, while Ahmadinejad depended on populist voters. However, when it was announced that Ahmadinejad had received twenty-four million votes compared with Mousavi's fourteen, the public cried foul. There was a revolt, which took some time to put down; many reformists, including members of Khatami's government, were arbitrarily arrested, and Mousavi, his wife and Mehdi Karrubi, the other reformist candidate, were put under house arrest, which continues to the present day.

In Ahmadinejad's second term (2009–13), the situation turned worse: there were hardliners running both the domestic and international shows. Many more people were arrested on slender pretexts, long sentences were given and socio-cultural freedoms were curtailed; the economy went from bad to worse, corruption became widespread, inflation rose to 40 per cent and the P5+1 group of nuclear powers applied comprehensive sanctions against Iran. This was due to the conflict over Iran's nuclear ambition – Iran claimed this to be motivated by peaceful goals, while the powers believed it aimed at weaponization.

The 2013 election resulted in victory for Hassan Rouhani (b. 1948), a moderate with strong support from the reformists. He soon discovered that his power to act was much more limited than was expected from his election promises, though what redeemed him in the eyes of most Iranians was his successful agreement in 2015 with the P5+1 powers (the UN Security Council's five permanent members, plus Germany) on the nuclear issue. This resulted in the removal of the crippling sanctions, and he was returned to office in 2017. However, the removal of the sanctions did not bring the fruits that had been hoped for, as many Western banks and companies still hesitated to engage with Iran for fear of future American reprisals.

People in Iran were already getting disenchanted when Donald Trump's election to the US presidency and his subsequent withdrawal from the 5+1 agreement with Iran put the seal on the deteriorating situation in Iran, as well as the public discontent. There were protests, some violent, in January 2018, and a rapid decline in the value of the Iranian rial. Government mishandling of the situation was to some extent to blame, but the main cause was panic buying of the US dollar and other hard currencies by well-to-do Iranians, to protect the value of their savings and be ready to leave the country the minute things got out of hand. This was especially likely because of Iran's isolation in the region: not only Israel, but also Saudi Arabia and the Arab countries of the Persian Gulf were its deadly enemies.

Iran has gone almost full circle in the forty years since the triumph of the revolution. No accurate statistics are available, but there can be little doubt that a large number of the then revolutionaries now wish it had not happened. Even the reformists have lost much of their lustre, as the people have become disappointed that they could not make a significant impact. The economy is in bad shape, poverty is widespread, the rate of inflation is high and so too unemployment – especially among young people, including university graduates.

On balance, therefore, the legacy of the revolution has not been positive. The Islamic Republic's regime is highly complex as it combines elements of arbitrary rule and dictatorship as well as democracy. The critics focus on the undemocratic elements – which are appreciably more powerful than the democratic ones. The supreme leader is chosen for life in a roundabout way, and wields a great deal of power. The judiciary and Revolutionary Guard are answerable to no one except, ultimately, the supreme leader. The same is true of state TV and radio. An unelected Guardianship Council vets candidates for presidency and parliamentary seats before they are allowed to join the race, eliminating 'undesirables' – of whom there are many. It is probably true that the majority of the Iranian people are now disappointed in the regime; however, the desire for regime change is not widespread.

Ruhollah Khomeini

Ruhollah Khomeini (1902–89), Shia scholar and cleric, was the supreme leader of the Iranian Revolution. Arrested in 1962 for his opposition in Qom to the Shah's reform programme as well as the grant of capitulatory rights to the Americans, he spent fifteen years in exile in the Middle East and finally Paris. While there, he became the most vocal opponent of the Shah's regime, encouraging strikes and demonstrations in the late 1970s by means of tape recordings clandestinely distributed. His return to Tehran in February 1979 was greeted with huge popular enthusiasm, and he encouraged the establishment of an Islamic republic, creating a theocracy, enforcing sharia law and vigorously attacking Western culture and influence (the United States in particular). He was the unchallenged supreme leader of Iran until his death in 1989.

Ali Khamenei

Ali Khamenei (b. 1939), Islamic scholar and cleric, has been supreme leader since 1989. Involved in opposition to the Shah's reforms in 1963, he was imprisoned several times and was close to Khomeini, joining the Revolutionary Council on the latter's return to Iran in 1979. A man of conservative views, he founded the Islamic Republican Party and was extremely mistrustful of the United States, believing the West to be inherently Islamophobic. He was elected to the mainly honorific post of president in 1981 and, despite not being a senior cleric, was appointed leader of the country on Khomeini's death in 1989. Maintaining complex relationships with a succession of prime ministers over the next thirty years, he eventually supported the agreement signed with the West on nuclear research in 2015.

TIMELINE

1953   US-backed coup brings down Prime Minister Mossadeq

1963   Shah issues 'White Revolution' programme of land and electoral reform; demonstrations against White Revolution led by Ayatollah Khomeini

1964
November   Ayatollah Khomeini forced into exile

1974   One-party state declared by the Shah

1978
September   Shah declares martial law after months of tension

October   Iraq deports Khomeini, who goes to Paris

December   Demonstrations across Iran in support of Khomeini; Shah appoints Shapour Bakhtiar as prime minister

1979
16 January Shah leaves Iran for 'vacation' in Egypt

1 February Khomeini returns from exile, appoints interim government a few days later

10 February Khomeini declares a national revolution; the army declares its neutrality the next day, and Bakhtiar flees the country

March   Referendum produces massive majority for an Islamic republic

August   National elections to 'Council of Experts' to draw up constitution; boycotted by leftists and nationalist groups

October   New constitution creates post of supreme leader

November   Fifty-two Americans taken hostage in American embassy (until January 1981)

December   Constitution approved in a referendum; Khomenei becomes supreme leader for life

1980

April   Attempted rescue of hostages fails

September   Iraq attacks Iran, beginning an eight-year war

1989

February   Khomeini issues *fatwa* against novelist Salman Rushdie

June   Khomeini dies, and is succeeded by Ayatollah Khamenei

NICARAGUA: THE SANDINISTA REVOLUTION, 1979

Mateo Cayetano Jarquín

In Latin America, revolutionary activity was a feature of everyday life during the Cold War period. Inspired by the Cuban Revolution of 1959, armed leftist groups sprang up in virtually every country in the region, pursuing guerrilla struggle in order to redistribute wealth and transform their societies. Most failed. But unlike their contemporaries, Nicaragua's Sandinista National Liberation Front (FSLN) actually succeeded in 1979.

The insurrection they led against the sclerotic, US-backed Somoza dynasty brought about the Nicaraguan Revolution – the last major socialist project of the 20th century. At the time, the Sandinistas electrified the global left and briefly led Soviet analysts to believe that the USSR was winning the battle of hearts and minds in the Third World. Even more remarkable was the Sandinistas' staying power. After taking power in 1979, the FSLN ruled Nicaragua for eleven years – despite the US government's determination to destabilize what it saw as an unacceptable threat in America's 'own backyard'. As the administration of Ronald Reagan (1911–2004) resorted to illegal means to undermine Nicaragua's revolutionary government, for a moment it seemed as if a motley crew of irreverent Central American guerrillas might bring about the impeachment of the president of the United States. After a ruinous civil war – one that proved the Cold War was 'hot' in the global south – the Sandinista revolution came to an end in 1990, when Nicaraguans voted the FSLN out of power in the country's first truly democratic elections.   PF

Nicaragua's Sandinista revolution can be understood through its many paradoxes. The first paradox is that, unlike most Third World national liberation movements, the Marxist Sandinista Front came to power on the back of a pluralistic, multi-class alliance that included liberals, the church and some sectors of the Nicaraguan bourgeoisie. Although they eventually tried to advance an orthodox socialist agenda, the Sandinistas initially promised to rule according to moderate principles, which infused Marxism with liberal sensibilities. Second, the Nicaraguan Revolution saw the United States – the greatest economic and military power in human history – try but fail to topple the government of one of the poorest countries in the western hemisphere. Third, the revolution left a paradoxical legacy. The Sandinistas failed to eliminate poverty and inequality, but became the first political movement to leave power via elections after having come to power via armed means. In other words, they failed to achieve social transformation but inadvertently succeeded in creating Nicaragua's first-ever transition to liberal democracy.

That democratic legacy soon became undone. In the mid-2000s, longtime FSLN leader Daniel Ortega (b. 1945) returned to power and quickly consolidated a new dynastic dictatorship. The Sandinista Front now underwent a stunning ideological transformation, abandoning the leftist agenda of the 1980s in favour of a socially conservative and business-friendly programme. 'What never should have happened is happening again in Nicaragua,' writes Gioconda Belli, an internationally recognized poet and former FSLN cadre. 'It is as if Anastasio Somoza [the country's previous dictator, toppled in 1979] has returned to Managua.'

Few saw revolution coming in Nicaragua; in fact, like Iran under the Shah, *somocista* Nicaragua was seen as an island of stability in a troubled region. Much like the Shah, the Somozas had been invested by a foreign power. In the early 1930s, following an intense period of direct occupations in the area, US Marines sought to create stability in the strategically important Caribbean and Central American isthmus by training professional, non-partisan 'National Guards' in Cuba, the Dominican Republic and Nicaragua.

Like Cuba's Fulgencio Batista and the Dominican Republic's Rafael Trujillo, Nicaragua's first National Guard chief, Anastasio 'Tacho' Somoza García (1896–1956), imposed the desired stability by building a personalist military dictatorship. US officials lamented Somoza's cruel methods but ultimately acquiesced to his repressive rule, because he converted Nicaragua into a loyal *gendarme* of Washington's foreign policy interests. In 1954 Nicaragua gave crucial logistical support to a CIA-backed coup against a leftist government in Guatemala. Later, the Somozas assisted the botched Bay of Pigs invasion in Cuba. An oft-cited quote by US president Franklin D. Roosevelt, though apocryphal, nonetheless captures the essence of the arrangement: '[Somoza] may be a son of a bitch, but he's our son of a bitch.'

However, the United States was not solely responsible; the regime was built on solid domestic foundations. Somoza García enjoyed popular support because he pacified the countryside and ended a decades-long period of civil wars and foreign interventions. Nicaragua's powerful economic elite (the country is one of the hemisphere's most unequal) learned to love him because his government implemented modernizing economic policies favourable to their interests. Although a younger generation of middle-class professionals and university students despised Somoza, popular opposition was relatively sparse. In 1956, a twenty-seven-year-old poet named Rigoberto López Pérez assassinated Somoza García. But the regime could simply regenerate: the dictator was succeeded by his sons, Luis and Anastasio Jr, who deepened their father's corporatist and repressive model.

There were pockets of resistance. In the early 1960s, Marxist revolutionaries led by Carlos Fonseca Amador (1936–76) emerged to challenge the dictatorship. They styled themselves after the Vietnamese and Algerian *fronts de libération nationales* (FLN), but with a nationalist twist – they added an S, after an early 20th-century nationalist guerrilla named Augusto César Sandino (1895–1934) who had opposed Dollar Diplomacy-era US occupations. At first, the Sandinista National Liberation Front sought to emulate the Cuban style of guerrilla warfare; but they failed to cultivate the type of rural support base that Fidel Castro and Che Guevara had developed in Cuba's Sierra Maestra. They fared little better in the cities. Though the Sandinistas began quietly penetrating universities, literary circles and social movements, they remained mostly absent from mainstream politics. One exception came in 1974, when a small FSLN team crashed an elegant Christmas party and held its guests – who included senior government officials and foreign dignitaries – hostage. The government was forced to release several Sandinista prisoners as a result. But just two years later, historic leaders Eduardo Contreras and founder Carlos Fonseca were killed in combat; the Sandinista Front broke into three factions and fell into internecine conflict. By 1976 it was broke, isolated and divided.

Around the same time, however, cracks began to appear in the Somoza dictatorship. First, the ruling family broke its pact with the capitalist class. The Somozas' wealth had grown to the point of encroaching upon the interests of the traditional aristocracy. Government corruption had reached surreal levels; after a 1972 earthquake flattened the capital Managua, the ruling family brazenly pilfered the reconstruction and relief aid that flowed into the country. As it gradually lost its elite pillars of legitimacy, the National Guard relied increasingly on brute force and repression. In 1978, hitmen associated with the regime gunned down a popular journalist and civil opposition leader named Pedro Joaquín Chamorro (1924–78). His assassination triggered a tidal wave of spontaneous popular rebellions and motivated the country's aristocracy – to which Chamorro belonged – to definitively break with the dictatorship.

The Sandinistas, who had thus far operated in the political wilderness, masterfully exploited the situation. Their success was down to unique qualities that set their organization apart from other leftist guerrilla movements in Latin America and elsewhere in the global south. To be sure, the FSLN's top leaders were devout Marxist–Leninists who forged links with communist parties around the world, from Chile to Palestine to Vietnam. But to topple Somoza, they built an alliance that included non-communist liberals and, most importantly, progressive elements of the private sector and bourgeoisie. Crucially, the Nicaraguan Revolution did not break down neatly along class lines; indeed, many Sandinista leaders hailed from some of the richest families in the country. Because Somoza had closed all political avenues for change, broad sectors of Nicaraguan society came to see the armed struggle as the only way out. Additionally, the Sandinistas cultivated major support from the church; Nicaragua's revolution intersected with the 'liberation theology' revolution that was transforming global Catholicism. Thus, the Sandinistas promised that once in power, they would not repeat the Cuban model but would govern according to three moderate principles: political pluralism, a mixed economy and non-alignment in international affairs.

This infusion of socialism with liberal democratic sensibilities is partly what made the Sandinistas so exciting to the global left, which saw in them the hope that a leftist revolution might not degenerate into the totalitarianism of the Soviet Union or the horrors of the Khmer Rouge in Cambodia. To many sympathizers, the Sandinistas' youth – few *comandantes guerrilleros* were over the age of thirty – embodied the symbolism of political renewal promised by the revolution, which had a humanistic image burnished by a generation of talented writers and artists (including Ernesto Cardenal (b. 1925), Claribel Alegría (1924–2018), Daisy Zamora (b. 1950) and the Mejía Godoy brothers) who flourished in the effervescence of national insurrection. More importantly, without this broad-based popular front, the FSLN stood no chance of defeating Somoza either politically or militarily.

Anastasio 'Tachito' Somoza Debayle (1925–80) – the third and last of his clan – responded to insurrection with all-out aggression. But the National Guard's attempts to quash popular rebellion only added fuel to the fire, further legitimizing the Sandinista Front's armed struggle. In August 1978, ahead of a major revolutionary offensive, Sandinista commandos proved the regime's weakness by storming the National

Assembly and taking the entire legislature hostage. This spectacular stunt preceded a period of full-scale armed conflict that would ultimately claim some 40,000 lives.

Though Nicaraguans paid for their revolution with blood, Somoza's fate was sealed abroad. The US president, Jimmy Carter (b. 1924), fretted over losing a staunch Cold War ally, but ultimately baulked at decisively backing the regime. In the White House, concerns over the Somozas' human rights record ultimately trumped fears of a 'second Cuba' in Central America. The Sandinistas' moderation and alliance-building had mitigated those fears and helped win support from governments in Panama, Venezuela, Costa Rica and Mexico. A network of regional governments and political movements isolated Somoza diplomatically and armed the first Sandinista forays. Castro's Cuba weighed in with decisive support in early 1979. By June, after months of carnage, most of the region's countries – including Latin America's anti-communist military dictatorships – decided that Somoza should step down, and recognized the Sandinista-led provisional government. Somoza finally resigned on 17 July; less than forty-eight hours later, his National Guard chaotically disbanded as Sandinista columns marched into Managua. On 19 July, Nicaragua became the only Latin American country since Cuba to witness a successful armed revolution.

A broad-based junta formally took power, although de facto control fell into the hands of the FSLN's nine-man National Directorate. After all, it had been Sandinista fighters, bearing the red-and-black flag of socialism and workers' rights, who had militarily defeated Somoza's National Guard. Emboldened by their victory and popular support, the Sandinista leadership quickly pushed the revolutionary programme in a more orthodox socialist direction. The moderate agenda they had crafted with their allies in 1978–9 was no longer *the* agenda; now, FSLN strategists claimed to be in the midst of a temporary 'phase of democratic transition', as one internal document put it, 'on the path toward the full transformation of the social relations of production'.

Some of the revolution's early policies were both successful and implemented by popular demand. The government massively expanded access to healthcare, and their 1980 literacy campaign dramatically reduced illiteracy in just a few months. Their allies in the church and the business sector had also condoned the expropriation of the vast Somoza estate, which was reinvested into state-led initiatives to redistribute the gains from economic growth. Finally, the revolutionary government used international aid to reconstruct the country and reassert state control. In the process, the Sandinistas won praise for avoiding the grisly executions and show trials of the Cuban and Iranian revolutions.

But the National Directorate's Leninist view of politics ultimately destroyed the coalition that brought them to power. Reneging on their promises, they refused to hold elections and gradually began censoring criticism of the regime. The Sandinistas enforced vertical decision-making within the party under the principle of 'democratic centralism', and understood party and state to be one and the same; Nicaragua's armed forces, for example, were branded the Sandinista Popular Army. In this context, sceptics saw the FSLN's efforts to mobilize popular participation in politics as little more than a totalitarian effort to control and surveil the population. And perhaps most importantly, the government's inclination towards central planning in economic policy provoked the ire of the private sector.

Although the government joined the Non-Aligned Movement, the Sandinista Front's Department of International Relations quietly cultivated support from Cuba, the Soviet Union and others in the socialist camp such as Bulgaria and East Germany. Nicaragua's new leaders felt that they were part of a 'revolution without borders' and supported guerrilla groups throughout Central America, which at the time was mostly governed by US-backed anti-communist military regimes. In neighbouring El Salvador, Marxist revolutionaries inspired by the Sandinistas' success pushed to overthrow their government under the unified flag of the Farabundo Martí National Liberation Front (FMLN), the leadership of which established its headquarters in Managua.

This audacious foreign policy set the stage for a dramatic confrontation with the Reagan administration, which saw Nicaraguan meddling in El Salvador as proof for its view that the Sandinista government was unacceptable *a priori*. From late 1981, Washington began funding and organizing a proxy army called the Contra – as in *contrarrevolucionarios*, or counter-revolutionaries. 'For our own security,' said Reagan, 'the United States must deny the Soviet Union a beachhead....Will we give the Nicaraguan democratic resistance the means to recapture their betrayed revolution, or will we turn our backs and ignore the malignancy in Managua until it spreads and becomes a mortal threat to the entire New World?' Some Latin American governments shared these fears. Thus, neighbouring countries such as Honduras and Costa Rica hosted the Contra and its CIA benefactors. FSLN strategists saw this multi-front intervention and insurgency as a sort of permanent 'Bay of Pigs' scenario. Combined with economic sanctions and direct sabotage by the CIA, the effect of US-led intervention was devastating: the resultant armed conflict drained the government's coffers and claimed roughly 30,000 lives, nearly as many as were claimed during the insurrectionary period. The concomitant prioritization of national defence effectively thwarted the Sandinistas' efforts to carry out the rest of their revolutionary agenda.

Inspired by the Sandinistas' quixotic efforts to benefit the poor, and repulsed by Reagan's use of force against a country of only three million people, tens of thousands of North Americans and Europeans travelled to Nicaragua in solidarity. Many of the United States' traditional Cold War allies in western Europe broke with Washington on this issue because they feared that Reagan's hostility would only exacerbate the violence and push the Sandinistas further into the arms of the Soviet Union. Moreover, US intervention came at the same time that South American countries were transitioning away from US-backed military dictatorships and towards liberal democratic regimes. Predictably, their governments opposed Reagan's interference in Central America; they channelled their opposition into the Contadora process, a multilateral peace initiative that demanded an end to US aid to the Contra. In 1986, the International Court of Justice found the United States guilty of illegal acts of war against Nicaragua. Nonetheless, while European, Latin American and multilateral efforts threw a wrench in US policy, they ultimately failed to end the carnage in Nicaragua.

Violence persisted, in part because of the war's local roots. Though much of the Contra leadership was composed of ex-National Guardsmen handpicked and directed by the CIA and National Security Council, it was mostly rural peasants who filled the rebel ranks. Well before Reagan took power, thousands of Nicaraguan farmers had taken up arms because of the Sandinistas' botched agrarian reform, which in an attempt to collectivize agricultural production had turned smallholding farmers into class enemies. The country's ethnic minorities likewise felt excluded by the Sandinistas' urban-facing socialist nationalism. The Sandinista Popular Army's brutal mistreatment of the country's Miskito population led much of the country's indigenous and Afro-indigenous population to join the Contra.

By mid-decade, the Sandinista high command deemed this war unwinnable. Cuban advisors and Soviet weapons had helped the FSLN prevent the Contra from seizing sufficient territory to declare a parallel government. Yet the insurgent threat had not been vanquished. The economy was in tatters, and the civil war had irreversibly poisoned the original optimism of 1979. And the Soviet Union was now eager to stop bankrolling the Nicaraguan government. A central theme of the Nicaraguan Revolution was the tension between the Sandinistas' Marxist–Leninist dreams and the tactical, liberalizing promises they made during their insurrectionary struggle; after several years in power, the bitter realities of governance defeated their ideological convictions.

As a result, the Sandinista National Directorate reasoned that the time had come to pursue a negotiated settlement. The possibility of peace talks also improved in 1986, when newspapers revealed an elaborate scheme in which the Reagan administration illegally sold weapons to Iran in order to free hostages held by Iranian proxies in Lebanon, and then used the profits illegally to finance the Contra. The Iran–Contra affair scandalized the Reagan administration, and helped end congressional support for US proxy intervention in Nicaragua. As a result, the Contra gave up its dreams of an all-out military victory.

Meanwhile, Central American leaders were taking matters into their own hands. In November 1987, Costa Rican president Óscar Arias (b. 1940) received the Nobel Peace Prize for his plan to end the civil wars in Central America by terminating US aid for the Contra and turning the region's countries into democracies. The 1987 Central American Peace Accords signed in Esquipulas, Guatemala, were straightforward. Each of the region's governments – the Marxist Sandinista government, along with the anti-communist military regimes of Honduras, Guatemala and El Salvador – agreed to stop receiving military aid from foreign powers, and to cease attempts to overthrow their neighbours. In order to forge stability within each country, the agreement also required governments to recognize its respective armed insurgencies and to hold free and fair elections.

On the one hand, this settlement was a major victory for the FSLN. Their propagandists could plausibly claim that 'David' had successfully stood up against the North American 'Goliath'. On the other hand, the political legitimacy they won came at a price; in a shock upset, Sandinista incumbent Daniel Ortega lost the 1990 elections his government agreed to hold as a part of the peace process. The revolution was over. In April 1990, Violeta Barrios de Chamorro (b. 1929) – the Sandinistas' former colleague on the 1979 junta, and widow of Pedro Joaquín Chamorro – became the country's first democratically elected president.

The revolution left a paradoxical legacy. The Sandinistas made significant efforts to improve Nicaraguans' access to basic social services, but they failed to achieve the economic redistribution and poverty reduction that was so central to their vision of social transformation. Thus, they left a country destroyed by war, but also largely unchanged in its basic social hierarchies. The revolution attracted interest abroad because women leaders played an indispensable role in the insurrection; but after Somoza's overthrow these women found that their military leadership and sacrifice did not translate into real political power, and that socialist revolution did not easily undo the country's traditionally patriarchal culture. Sergio Ramírez (b. 1942), a longtime FSLN conspirator who served on the 1979 junta and later as vice president, reflected on the revolution's balance sheet:

> The revolution did not bring justice for the oppressed as had been hoped; nor did it manage to create wealth and development. Instead, its greatest benefit was democracy, sealed in 1990 with the acknowledgment of electoral defeat. As a paradox of history, this is its most obvious legacy, although it was not its most passionate objective.

As it turned out, the democratic legacy of the Sandinista revolution was ephemeral. The 1990s saw a flourishing of civil society and improvements to the rule of law. Three successive elections produced peaceful transfers of power. But a political order designed to end the civil war left underlying social and economic problems untouched. The move towards electoral politics came packaged with structural adjustment policies that generated latent social discontent. Nicaraguan society became ripe for a return to *caudillismo*, or strongman politics.

In 2006, Daniel Ortega squeezed back into the presidency despite winning only 38 per cent of the vote. By that time, most well-known figures from the revolutionary government had abandoned the Sandinista Front. Deepening the authoritarianism that had characterized the organization during the 1980s, Ortega turned the electoral-era FSLN into a personal vehicle. Moreover, he zapped the party of its original leftist ideology. While portraying his presidency as a continuation of the revolution, the erstwhile Marxist rebranded the Sandinista Front as a pro-business, Christian-conservative party. In order to forge new alliances with his former 'counter-revolutionary' foes in the capitalist class, he preserved the neoliberal model implemented by right-wing governments in the 1990s. And in an act of faith to cement an alliance with the Catholic Church, his government supported the full criminalization of abortion under all circumstances. In this way, the Sandinista Front underwent perhaps the most radical ideological metamorphosis of any political movement in Latin American history.

Apparently mimicking the Somoza dictatorship they had once helped to overthrow, Ortega and his wife, Rosario Murillo (b. 1951), deftly began using power-sharing agreements, selective repression and business-friendly policies to consolidate control over all branches of government as well as the country's security forces. They eliminated constitutional barriers to re-election and indulged their children with state-funded pet projects and prominent advisory roles, ostensibly grooming them to succeed their parents in power. Despite these blatantly dynastic aspirations, most Nicaraguans accepted the situation in the name of stability and decent economic growth.

Like its 20th-century predecessor, the Ortega regime initially created stability, but eventually mired the country in violence and bloodshed. In April 2018, university students woke Nicaraguans from their political slumber and led the greatest wave of peaceful protests in the country's history. The regime's decision to respond with violence left hundreds dead, and led the Inter-American Commission on Human Rights (IACHR) to accuse the government of crimes against humanity.

The repression also put a final nail in the coffin of the democratic transition. The new dictatorship under Sandinista leader Daniel Ortega has revived popular interest in the memory and legacy of the revolutionary period. Many Nicaraguans who opposed Sandinista rule in the 1980s feel that the new dictatorship is a logical consequence of the 1979 revolution. Those who participated in the revolution hold a different view. Ernesto Cardenal (b. 1925), a liberation theologian and poet who served in the revolutionary government as minister of culture, titled his political memoir *La Revolución Perdida* (2005) – an apparent allusion to Leon Trotsky's *The Revolution Betrayed*. 'It was a beautiful revolution,' the nonagenarian poet maintains, 'but what happened is that it was betrayed...now what we have is a family dictatorship run by Daniel Ortega. That's not what we supported.'

Daniel Ortega

Daniel Ortega (b. 1945), Nicaraguan revolutionary and president (1985–90, 2007–), came from a provincial middle-class background and joined the Sandinista National Liberation Front (FSLN) in 1963. He was arrested in 1967 and imprisoned until 1974; at that point he was exiled to Cuba, where he was trained in guerrilla warfare. He returned to Central America in the late 1970s, when he became a member of the National Directorate that led the FSLN to victory in 1979. Once in power, the Sandinistas tapped Ortega to serve on the revolutionary junta and, later, as president. These positions, combined with his brother's role as chief of the Sandinista Popular Army, allowed Ortega to emerge as 'first among equals' in the collective leadership of the revolution. In the 1990s, Ortega brought the Sandinista Front under personal control; in 2006 he re-won the presidency. Despite leftist rhetoric and alliances with Venezuela's Hugo Chávez, Ortega implemented business- and church-friendly policies in his second and third terms.

Violeta Barrios de Chamorro

Violeta Barrios de Chamorro (b. 1929) was president of Nicaragua from 1990 until 1997. From a wealthy background, in 1950 she married anti-Somoza journalist and newspaper publisher Pedro Joaquín Chamorro Cardenal; they spent several years in exile in the 1950s. After her husband's assassination in 1978, she supported the FSLN insurgency and became a member of the ruling junta after the overthrow of the Somoza regime the following year. She soon broke with the regime, ostensibly over its radical policies and ties to the Soviet Union. Under her leadership, the family-owned newspaper La Prensa offered consistent criticism to the revolutionary government, which led the ruling FSLN to censor and eventually shut the paper (1986–7). She defeated Daniel Ortega in the 1990 elections – the first democratic contest in Nicaraguan history – thereby becoming the first democratically elected woman president in the history of the Americas. Her administration oversaw a successful peace and reconciliation process, implemented liberalizing political reforms and rolled back Sandinista-era social programmes as part of a strategy to privatize industry.

TIMELINE

1934   Anastasio Somoza García executes nationalist leader Augusto
          César Sandino, marking the rise of the *somocista* dictatorship

1956   President Anastasio Somoza García is assassinated and
          succeeded by his son, Luis Somoza Debayle

1961   US-sponsored rebels depart from Nicaragua to invade Cuba, but are
          defeated at the Bay of Pigs; Sandinista National Liberation Front
          (FSLN) is founded

1972   An earthquake strikes the capital city of Managua; Anastasio
          Somoza Debayle embezzles money from international relief funds

1978   Pedro Joaquín Chamorro, editor of anti-Somoza newspaper
          La Prensa, is assassinated; Sandinista-led guerrillas begin a
          national uprising

1979   On 17 July Somoza resigns and flees; Sandinista forces enter
          Managua two days later

1980   Somoza is assassinated in Paraguay; Sandinista-led junta expands
          access to social services; Violeta Chamorro and Alfonso Robelo
          resign from the junta

1981   Sandinistas assist a failed rebel offensive in El Salvador; the
          government announces a socialist land reform law; US government
          begins organizing a proxy army to destabilize the regime

1982   The first Contra attacks mark the beginning of the Nicaraguan
          Civil War

1983   The Contadora process attempts to broker a settlement to end civil
          wars in Central America

1985   FSLN candidate Daniel Ortega becomes president; US imposes
          an embargo on Nicaragua, which declares a state of emergency,
          suspending civil rights

1986 The Iran–Contra Affair is revealed: US officials indicted for illegally channelling funds to the Contra; International Court of Justice rules in favour of Nicaragua over CIA operations

1987 The Central American Peace Accords commit Central American governments to democratization and peacebuilding; hyperinflation in Nicaragua

1988 Temporary truce is reached between FSLN and Contra

1990 UNO candidate Violeta Chamorro is elected president of Nicaragua

1991 Chamorro rolls back socialist programmes and improves diplomatic relations with the US

1996 Conservative Arnoldo Alemán Lacayo is elected president

2006 Ortega, having turned the FSLN into a Christian pro-business party, is re-elected

2011 Ignoring constitutional term limits, Ortega is re-elected and ramps up authoritarian consolidation

2018 University students lead wave of protest against Ortega and his wife, Rosario Murillo; the regime responds violently

POLAND: SOLIDARITY, 1980

Anita Prażmowska

Since the mid-19th century, the concept of revolution has often been inextricably associated with the socialist movement and trade unionism. It is therefore ironic that the iconic revolution in which the emergence of a massive trade union was not only able successfully to challenge the state, but eventually proved decisive to its overthrow, was one where the overthrown state was not a capitalist one but communist. And that Solidarity, the union in question, focused on bread-and-butter issues and questions of freedom, with its leadership taking care not to offer a direct political challenge to the state itself.

It may be true that the collapse of the communist Polish state in 1989 owed at least as much to the defeat of the Soviet Union in the Cold War, and to Moscow's overt withdrawal from involvement in the internal affairs of its eastern European satellites, as to agitation by Solidarity. Nevertheless, for ten years Solidarity had visibly focused Polish discontent and fatally undermined the state's last vestiges of legitimacy. Only a small faction within it sought to adopt truly revolutionary policies. Yet, in a broader sense, it did achieve a peaceful revolution that inspired many across both eastern and western Europe and proved one of the more successful of the second half of the 20th century – even if its aims and leaders were quickly transcended in the new democratic Poland that it did so much to bring about.

Internationally, Solidarity was seen as a benign revolution, both among those on the right for its contribution to the defeat of the Soviet system, and on the left for the power of the trade union – which boasted a membership of a quarter of the total population of the country – successfully to assert 'people power'.   PF

On 14 August 1980, an occupation strike took place in Poland's Gdańsk dockyard. The unique feature of this – as opposed to the numerous other strikes that overwhelmed Polish enterprises during the summer of that year – was the fact that the workers presented political demands. Of the twenty-one points put to the authorities by the strike committee, the first three would have the most important impact on future developments: the right to establish free and independent trade unions, the right to strike, and a guarantee that the government would respect constitutional clauses guaranteeing freedom of expression and freedom to disseminate information.

This was not the first time that Poland's communist government was confronted with workers' anger. In December 1970, after the government had tried to raise prices for basic foods, Polish workers had responded with strikes. In a confrontation with the armed police and soldiers, forty-one strikers in Gdańsk were killed. A political crisis developed, and during the following months the new Communist Party secretary Edward Gierek (1913–2001) sought to conciliate the workers. Economic reforms were implemented, and the government managed to raise living standards by obtaining foreign loans and entering bilateral trading relations with Western companies. Unfortunately, by the mid-1970s the economy was stalling, and once more the prices of essential goods had to be raised. This led to further strikes in the industrial town of Radom and the Warsaw suburb of Ursus; once more the regime responded with repression, but the perilous state of the economy was a matter that could not be resolved. Shortages of essential goods became the norm. Poland was unable to repay its debts, which spiralled out of control. The world economic recession caused by the oil embargo imposed by OPEC, the oil-producing countries of the Middle East, meant that western European banks were recalling their loans. Since the late 1960s the Soviet Union had become less willing to underwrite the economies of the countries of the socialist bloc; on the one hand this meant the loosening of restrictions on Polish trade with the West, but it also signalled that the Soviet Union was reluctant to step in and help when economic problems appeared.

One consequence of the spontaneous strikes of the second half of the 1970s was the maturing of political awareness on the part of the workers. Initially, anger had been focused on economic difficulties. Distrust of the Party and anger about low pay and shortages in shops dominated. In the case of Radom, the angry workers attacked Party headquarters and threatened to lynch the Party secretary. The regime responded by punishing the strikers with exemplary severity.

Separately, since the mid-1960s, disparate intellectual groups had formed discussion circles. These included left-wing academics such as Leszek Kołakowski (1927–2009), Jacek Kuroń (1934–2004) and Adam Michnik (b. 1946) as well as members of the Club of Catholic Intellectuals, of whom Tadeusz Mazowiecki (1927–2013) was one of the most prominent. After the 1976 strikes, the intellectuals came together to form the Committee for the Defence of the Workers (KOR). An alliance between the intellectuals and the workers was forged, on the basis that the former would help and advise the workers who had been put on trial for striking. The two groups remained respectful of each other's distinct aims.

In October 1978, Cardinal Karol Wojtyła (1920–2005), the archbishop of Kraków, was chosen to become the next Pope, as John Paul II. His elevation, and the fact that he laid stress on the need to respect human rights and dignity, emboldened the dissident and workers' organizations. In Poland, the Catholic Church was the only independent organization outside the state structures.

When strikes overwhelmed Poland in the summer months of 1980, it was obvious that the government was not able to resolve the economic difficulties. This in turn exposed the weakness of the Communist Party, which had been in power in Poland since the end of the Second World War.

But economic stagnation raised questions about the Party's ability to rule, because it rejected all calls for more democratization and accountability. In the summer of 1980 the strike leaders understood that they needed to move beyond economic demands, but they had to ensure that they had their own organizations, separate from the ruling political structures.

On 14 August 1980, a strike was called in the Gdańsk shipyard. The strikers not only demanded improved wages, but demanded that two prominent activists, Anna Walentynowicz (1929–2010) and Lech Wałęsa (b. 1943), both of whom had been active in the formation of an illegal independent trade union in 1978 and had been recently dismissed, should be re-employed. The strike was organized by the workers, and the demands put to the dockyard authorities were formulated by them without direct input from other outside organizations.

Initially the authorities were confident that they would be able to defuse this crisis by well-tried means, arresting the leaders and granting some concessions. Indeed, by 16 August these tactics seemed to have worked, and the striking workers started leaving. They were prevented from doing so by a group of four women, among them Walentynowicz, who called the men to go back and to continue negotiating. Wałęsa, who in the meantime had entered the dockyard by climbing the wall, was elected as leader of the strike committee. Other enterprises in Gdańsk now voted to strike in solidarity. By 18 August, Gdynia and Szczecin, the other two major Polish ports, declared that they too were on strike. All three ports coordinated their activities, and they jointly announced a list of twenty-one demands.

In all major industrial towns, production came to a halt; but the focus was firmly on events unfolding in Gdańsk. The workers occupied the dockyard and determined who was to enter. A local parish priest, Father Jankowski (1936–2010), joined them to take confession and to conduct masses; the strike thereby acquired a national, religious character. Then the leaders of various intellectual dissident movements in Warsaw defied the authorities' blockade of the town and travelled to Gdańsk to offer their support and advice. Tadeusz Mazowiecki and Bronisław Geremek (1932–2008), a prominent critic of the regime, were among those allowed by the strikers to enter the docks. Foreign media descended in great numbers on Gdańsk, making nonsense of the state-imposed news blackout. Poles could find out the full details of the strikers' demands from Radio Free Europe or the BBC World Service. The government was forced to the negotiating table, and a delegation headed by Deputy Prime Minister Mieczysław Jagielski (1924–97) arrived in Gdańsk on 21 August. The strikers' boldness in challenging the authorities, their organizational skills and ability to appeal to the foreign media resulted in an outpouring of support from European trade unions and progressive European communities. This meant that the strikers received moral support and, critically, material and financial support. The negotiations between the strike committee and the government were led by Wałęsa. Talks stalled several times. The key issue on which the government appeared unwilling to compromise was the demand for an independent trade union; but by 30 August Jagielski capitulated. The independent Polish trade union movement, which took the name Solidarność (Solidarity), came into being.

One of the striking features of the way the Solidarity movement emerged was the degree of spontaneity. Since the 1970s, Polish workers had grown in confidence and had learned the power of collective action. Although the regime had long allowed for trade unions and workers' committees to function in workplaces, they were not allowed to genuinely represent the interests of the employees. They acted as no more than transmission lines between the management and the workers. Even elections to trade union posts were determined in advance and in line with the needs of the management and the Party. They rarely, if ever, took up issues of safety in workplaces, wages, corruption or mismanagement. Each act of outrage on the part of the workers had its consequences; arrests and repression inevitably followed every strike or protest. After the 1976 riots in Radom and strikes in Ursus, the dissident movement KOR reached out to the victims of repression, indicating to them a need for better organization. The events played out in Gdańsk in August 1980 showed that the workers had understood it was necessary to make sure that a strike secured tangible results. The twenty-one demands, when finally formulated and put on the table as the basis of negotiations with the government team, were a truly eclectic mix of predictable workplace grievances and a politically critical demand for true workers' representation.

The strikers could not have anticipated the collapse of communism in Poland and across eastern Europe less than a decade later – so, however bold their demands may appear, their actions cannot be seen as an attempt to topple or even weaken the political system itself. What they sought was representation, and protection from the arbitrariness of the state. Nor could they or their advisors have predicted the momentous implications of what had been achieved: namely, the formation of a movement that became an alternative authority, one which would reluctantly – but inevitably – become an organization challenging the state. In the future months, when Solidarność was registered as a legal entity, the leaders decided not to go for a centralized structure, preferring a federated movement. In this way, Solidarność could embrace a variety of ideas and evolve over time, until it represented over ten million members – a quarter of Poland's population.

Wałęsa in many ways symbolized the movement's origins and character. His ability to articulate the workers' grievances and to carry the crowd made him the natural leader of the emerging movement. In his down-to-earth style he represented what the workers believed to be the essence of the protest; anger at workplace mismanagement, corruption and lack of proper reward. In August he was appointed leader of the Gdańsk strike committee, but others were equally important in formulating the list of demands. Andrzej Gwiazda (b. 1935), his wife Joanna Gwiazda (b. 1939) and Bogdan Lis (b. 1952) were prominent among the team of workers. The advisors who came to the docks played a crucial back-room role in guiding the course of negotiations to a successful outcome. In addition to Mazowiecki and Geremek they included Bohdan Cywiński, Tadeusz Kowalik, Waldemar Kuczyński and Andrzej Wielowieyski. These men had a clearer idea than the workers themselves of the pitfalls that they needed to avoid. They spoke to them of the need to create a truly democratic and representative movement.

In Poland, the implications of the creation of a genuinely independent workers' movement could not be underestimated. Following the Gdańsk agreement, strike committees in other coastal enterprises proceeded to register with the courts the creation of regional Solidarity organizations. Once united in a federated structure, they formed a powerful challenge to the communist monopoly of power. This was immediately apparent during the following months, when the government struggled to deal with the ongoing economic problems. Even though Solidarity tried to avoid being drawn into state matters, it became to all intents and purposes an opposition party. This in turn exposed conflicts within the movement where, increasingly, Wałęsa came to represent the moderate group, determined to negotiate with the government over living conditions and workplace grievances but resisting the urge to become a political party. In this he was strongly supported by the Catholic Church. At the same time, more radical groups emerged that formulated demands beyond those agreed in August 1980. Jan Rulewski (b. 1944), the leader of the Bydgoszcz Solidarity trade union, who had been savagely beaten by the police in March 1981, came to represent an opposing view to Wałęsa's, calling for Solidarity to bring down the regime.

Internationally, the emergence of Solidarity was a source of inspiration. Trade unions in the West had long campaigned for the workers in communist countries to be given genuine rights, in line with international commitments signed by those countries. During the formative period, and after the regime declared a state of martial law in December 1981, foreign support came to be of immense importance. All western European trade unions and progressive organizations became involved in supporting the Polish trade unionists in all ways possible: with funds, material aid, organizational support and backup, and help for the families of those who were victims of repression. The British prime minister Margaret Thatcher (1925–2013) and the US president Ronald Reagan (1911–2004) warned the Soviet Union not to interfere in Polish affairs, and offered words of encouragement to the Solidarity members.

In September 1981 Solidarity issued a proclamation to the people of eastern Europe, calling for a joint struggle for the establishment of free representative organizations. Each dissident and protest movement in those countries at that time was evolving as a result of the particular difficulties experienced by the people there, which makes it impossible directly to relate what happened in Poland to the course of developments in other countries of the socialist bloc. The common threat would be the impact of the decision of Soviet general secretary Mikhail Gorbachev (b. 1931), formulated in 1986, not to interfere in the internal affairs of these countries. The weakening of Soviet control had implications for the local communist parties in eastern European states, and this in turn emboldened dissident movements. Each one evolved differently, depending on its past experiences and policies.

Poland found that the road from a communist state to a liberal democratic political system and a free-market economic model was not a smooth one; nor was this transition something that the Solidarity activists had aimed to achieve. Their hopes did not extend that far. In December 1981, during the period of martial law, the ruling Military Council for the Defence of the Nation delegalized Solidarity. Members of the Solidarity movement were interned (including Wałęsa himself, for almost a year), and those who escaped had to remain in hiding. They – namely Zbigniew Bujak, Bogdan Lis, Władysław Frasyniuk and Władysław Hardek – formed an underground Solidarity organization. Not until 1986, mainly due to international condemnation, changing Soviet policies under the leadership of Gorbachev and internal disintegration, did the regime accept that it had to negotiate with the Solidarity leadership. This led to round table talks in February 1989, resulting in the final agreement two months later – which can be described as ending the communist period in Poland, ending the domination of the Communist Party and creating a new office of president. In December 1988 Wałęsa had founded the Solidarity Citizens' Committee, which was effectively a political party, and in June 1989 it swept the board in parliamentary elections.

During the period of martial law, Wałęsa was interned separately from other activists. The leadership of the underground Solidarity took over. Wałęsa, with strong support from the Catholic Episcopate, was instrumental in the negotiations that led to the ending of martial law. In 1983 he was awarded the Nobel Prize for Peace. He played a key role in the round table talks, but he himself did not cope well with the post-communist transformation. His period as president is remembered for his failure to adapt to the new role. New, younger members of Solidarity came to dominate the political life of Poland, even though Wałęsa continued to express his views on many issues.

Wałęsa's detractors, including some of his colleagues, subsequently accused him of being a paid agent of the secret service during the 1970s. He always denied that this was the case, but in 2016 evidence was leaked to the press, and it proved difficult to refute. These were secret service files that showed he had briefly been recruited after the 1970 strikes in Gdańsk. From these documents, it was evident that under pressure Wałęsa had agreed to inform on the mood of the workers in the dockyards. They also show that he quickly came to regret this decision, and that he had not provided the secret service with any information of consequence. The fact that during the communist period many people were coerced and blackmailed to do the same made no difference: in their campaign, which was largely driven by disappointment about the consequences of the rapid post-communist transformation, Wałęsa's critics were merciless in their determination to destroy his reputation,

Solidarity, formed out of the trade union movement that boldly hit the headlines in August 1980, has since undergone several transformations, atomizing, splintering and reforming. Several parties in present-day Poland claim Solidarity's mantle. In the 2010s the ruling PiS (Law and Justice) party – nationalist and conservative – embarked on rewriting history to diminish the achievements of the Solidarity veterans and to enhance the credentials of the Kaczyński twins – Lech (1949–2010), who died in the Smolensk air crash while president of Poland, and Jarosław, who is a highly influential figure in Poland and chairman of the ruling PiS. So persuasive has this recasting the recent past been that by the late 2010s few people recalled the achievements, let alone the names, of those who negotiated the right for the workers to form independent trade unions – and thereby to challenge the communist regime's claim to rule on behalf of the workers.

Tadeusz Mazowiecki

Tadeusz Mazowiecki (1927–2013) was a journalist, politician and prime minister of Poland (1989–91). A liberal Catholic journalist in the 1950s, Mazowiecki defended anti-communist labour activists in the 1970s, and in 1980 he assisted the Gdańsk strikers and mobilized wider support. In 1981 be became editor of Solidarity's newspaper, and worked closely with Wałęsa. Active in the round table talks in 1989, he was appointed prime minister following Solidarity's victory in the June elections. He introduced free-market reforms, but the resulting unemployment meant he was unsuccessful in the presidential elections of 1990.

Lech Wałęsa

Lech Wałęsa (b. 1943), Solidarity leader (1980–90) and president of Poland (1990–95), worked as an electrician in the Gdańsk shipyards. In August 1980, despite having recently lost his job, he climbed the fence to join shipyard strikers and came to lead the strike committee. When the free trade union, Solidarity, was established soon afterwards, Wałęsa became its chairman and chief spokesperson. He was kept under house arrest for a year under martial law, and was subsequently awarded the 1983 Nobel Peace Prize. In 1989 he led the negotiations for elections to the upper house, but refused to serve as premier in the coalition government. He was elected president in 1990, and oversaw the introduction of a market economy; he failed to be re-elected in 1995 and 2000. In the 2000s, accusations that he had acted as an informer for the secret services throughout the period 1970–76 badly eroded his reputation.

TIMELINE

1947   Poland becomes a Communist People's Republic

1955   Poland joins the Soviet-run Warsaw Pact military alliance

1970   Food price riots in Gdańsk are suppressed, with forty-one killed;
          Edward Gierek becomes party leader

1978   Karol Wojtyła, cardinal of Kraków, is elected Pope John Paul II

1979   Pope John Paul II visits Poland

1980
14 August Disturbances at the shipyard in Gdańsk

18 August Posts of Gdynia and Szczecin join strike

30 August Government accepts Solidarność (Solidarity) as an independent
          trade union

1981   Martial law imposed; 10,000 people are arrested; Wałęsa and other
          Solidarity leaders are imprisoned

1983   Martial law is lifted

1989
February   Round table talks begin between Solidarity, the Communist Party
          and the church

June   Solidarity wins a landslide election victory and helps form coalition
          government

August   Tadeusz Mazowiecki becomes prime minister

1990   Wałęsa elected president of Poland; market reforms, including
          large-scale privatization, are launched

1993   Reformed communists enter coalition government

1995   Former communist Aleksander Kwaśniewski beats Lech Wałęsa in
          presidential election

EASTERN EUROPE, 1989

Vladimir Tismaneanu and Andres Garcia

The year 1989, like 1848 and 1968, was a fast-moving time of tumultuous and often confusing liberal change driven by mass protests across many countries – in this case, countries of central and eastern Europe, former members of the Soviet bloc. General Secretary Mikhail Gorbachev's policies of *perestroika* (restructuring) and *glasnost* (openness) accelerated the waning of the Soviet Union's ability to intervene in the internal affairs of its satellites. Unlike Budapest in 1956 or Prague in 1968, where the Warsaw Pact demonstrated its commitment to crush opposition, the absence of Soviet tanks lined up on their borders empowered occupied countries to take matters in their own hands for the first time since the 1940s.

In 1989 itself, Poland, East Germany, Hungary, Czechoslovakia and Romania all underwent revolution and saw the fall of their communist regimes, unexpectedly and with minimal violence, and in most cases minimal planning or leadership. In addition, revolution had begun in Bulgaria and Albania; the breakup of Yugoslavia had started (and was soon to bring war to Europe on a scale not seen since 1945); while over the next two years, the Soviet Union was to collapse, bringing independence to fourteen nation states while the Russian Federation emerged as a multi-party democracy and moved to a market system.

Leadership was often in the hands of intellectuals who had suffered at the hands of the old regime, but did not see themselves as political actors: thus in Czechoslovakia, the

playwright Václev Havel, a broadly non-political figure, found
himself as the figurehead of the movement to set his country
on a new course.   PF

I n 2019, we commemorated thirty years since what Pope John Paul II
(r. 1978–2005) called '*annus mirabilis*': a year of extraordinary political
events that led to the demise of the ideologically driven communist
experiments in east-central Europe.

No single factor can fully explain the collapse of Leninism in a region
where it appeared to be quite stable, and we should recognize the tremen-
dous complexity of the revolutionary upheavals of 1989. Nevertheless,
we can focus on three themes: the deep-seated meanings of the collapse
of state socialist regimes in east-central Europe; the nature of the revolutions at the end of the 20th century; and the role of civil society and
public intellectuals in politics. We should also note some disconcerting
developments, such as the marginalization of the first post-communist
liberal elites, the conversion of many former communists and their
return to leading positions in government, and the rampant cynicism
that seemed to plague all these societies, thirty years on.

The communist regimes in east-central Europe were not just any
type of autocracy; they were what American sociologist Daniel Chirot
calls 'tyrannies of certitude', which derived their legitimacy from the
ideological and teleological claim that they represented the vanguard of
the working class and were consequently the sole carriers of a universal
emancipatory mission. These Leninist regimes derived their claim to
legitimacy from the Marxist–Leninist 'holy writ', with its firm belief that
history was on their side, and once this ideological mystique ceased to
function the whole edifice started to falter. In a way, the revolutions of
1989 were an ironical vindication of Lenin's famous definition of a revolutionary situation: those at the top cannot rule in old ways, and those
at the bottom do not want to accept these ways anymore. They were
more than simple revolts, because they attacked the very foundations of
the existing systems and proposed a complete reorganization of society.

Once ideology ceased to be an inspiring force and influential members of the ruling socialist party lost their commitment to the Marxist idea, the foundations of the Leninist promise were doomed. Here we see the role of what has been called the Gorbachev effect. The international climate was turned upside down by the shockwaves of the policies of *glasnost* (openness) and *perestroika* (restructuring), initiated by Mikhail Gorbachev (b. 1931) after his election in March 1985 as general secretary of the Central Committee of the Communist Party of the Soviet Union – policies that allowed for an incredible amount of open dissent and political mobilization in eastern and central Europe. Until 1987, Gorbachev's strategy towards eastern Europe had been one of moderate intra-systemic changes, with no possibility of the communist parties losing their privileged positions; however, after 1988 things started to change considerably. It was Gorbachev's denunciation of the ideological perspective in international politics (de-ideologization) and the abandoning of the 'class struggle' perspective that changed the rules of Soviet eastern European nations.

The Gorbachev factor was itself a consequence of the loss of self-confidence among communist elites. However, Gorbachev was not the liberator of eastern Europe, and even less was he the conscious and deliberative grave-digger of Sovietism. Initially he used his power to repair rather than ruin the system. Much of what happened as a result of his reforms was spontaneous and unpredictable, and a reflection of the immense gap between the Soviet leader's neo-Leninist illusions and the practical conditions of these societies. By 1988 Gorbachev acknowledged that, without the use of force, the Leninist system could not be preserved in the countries of the former Warsaw Pact. But unlike his predecessors, he refused to resort to tanks as the ultimate political argument and rejected the Leninist position that might creates right. In doing so, Gorbachev fundamentally changed the rules of the game. Thanks to the 'new foreign policy thinking' advocated by Gorbachev and his close associates, chief ideologue Aleksandr Yakovlev (1923–2005) and Foreign Minister Eduard Shevardnadze (1928–2014), the possibilities for political experimentation in east and central Europe expanded dramatically.

The revolutions of 1989 started in Poland with the overwhelming triumph of Solidarity in the June parliamentary elections and round table agreements in Poland and Hungary that allowed these countries to move towards a multi-party constitutional democracy. These were followed by the fall of the Berlin Wall on 9 November, and the Velvet Revolution in Czechoslovakia (November–December); and they culminated on 25 December with the execution of the Romanian dictator Nicolae Ceauşescu (1918–89) and his wife Elena (1916–89). These breathtaking events represented the triumph of civic dignity and political morality over ideological monism, bureaucratic cynicism and police dictatorship. Rooted in an individualistic concept of freedom and inherently sceptical of all ideological recipes for social engineering, these revolutions were fundamentally civil, liberal and non-utopian. Unlike traditional revolutions, they were primarily non-violent, did not originate in a millenarian vision of the perfect society and rejected the role of any self-appointed illuminated vanguard group in directing the activities of the masses. No political party headed their spontaneous activities, and in their early stages they even insisted on the need to create new political forms of action that were different from the traditional and rigid ideological party differentiations that had defined the political arena. To be sure, the road to 1989–91 was prepared by the less visible, often marginal but critically important workings of what we now call civil society (the Solidarity trade union in Poland, the Charter 77 petition in Czechoslovakia, unofficial peace, environmental and human rights groups in the GDR, the Democratic Opposition movement in Hungary). Importantly, the *modus operandi* of these dissent movements did not seek an open confrontation with the governing regimes. On the contrary, their strategy was non-violent and geared towards the gradual recovery of the public sphere as an alternative to the totalitarian presence of the ideological party state. In this way, 'anti-politics' came to be understood as a non-Machiavellian experience of authenticity, transparency, civility and good faith.

Nowadays we take the end of the Soviet system for granted, but during those fateful years it was only a slim possibility, not even a very likely one. True, some dissident thinkers like Ferenc Fehér, Agnes Heller, Václav Havel, Adam Michnik, Václav Benda and Jacek Kuroń thought that the system was slowly decaying and had no future, but even they were not considering the collapse an immediate possibility. What is more, the upheaval in the East, and primarily in the central European core countries, represented a series of political revolutions that led to the decisive and irreversible transformation of the existing order. Instead of autocratic, one-party systems, pluralist societies emerged which allowed citizens of the former despotic Leninist regimes to recover their main human and civic rights and to engage in the building of open societies. Instead of centrally planned command economies, they embarked on creating market economies. In their efforts to meet the triple challenge of creating political pluralism, a market economy and a vibrant civil society, some succeeded better than others. Although not all these societies have become well- or fully functioning liberal democracies, Leninist systems based on ideological uniformity, political coercion, dictatorship over human needs and suppression of civic rights have been dismantled in all of them.

It is important to note that while the structural causes of communism's collapse were similar, the dynamics, rhythm and orientation of these revolutions depended largely on the local conditions of each country. The strength or weakness of the reformist trends inside the national communist parties before 1989, as well as oppositional traditions, together explain the striking distinctions between these events in different countries. In Poland and Hungary, the revolutions were gradual and peaceful and the radical changes resulted from negotiations between enlightened exponents of the ruling elites and moderate representatives of the opposition. In Czechoslovakia and the GDR, on the other hand, the disappearance of the Soviet protective shield led to complete disarray at the top and the crumbling of the party machines. The existence of unofficial civic initiatives and the strategic vision of Czechoslovak playwright and opposition leader Vaclav Havel (1936–2011) and his fellow Charter 77 activists explain the 'velvetiness' of the November revolution in Prague and Bratislava. In contrast, Romania's dictator Nicolae Ceaușescu used the military and secret police to suppress anti-communist demonstrations in Timișoara and Bucharest. Any form of collective endeavour to challenge Ceaușescu's uniquely personalistic autocracy had been long stifled by the Securitate (secret police). Alienated from his own party bureaucracy, internationally isolated by both East and West and outraged by Gorbachev's reforms (which he publicly denounced as a treason to socialism), Ceaușescu was an increasingly erratic despot; and his wife, Elena, had become the regime's number two person. Thus, on 22 December 1989, mass upheaval in Bucharest and other major cities succeeded in getting rid of the Ceaușescus. Their successors, however, were not anti-communist civic democrats or pro-Western liberals, but exponents of the second echelon of Party and government bureaucracies. They immediately formed a National Salvation Front as the country's new political leadership and did their utmost to contain the rise of civic and liberal political movements and parties committed to fulfilling the liberal ideals that fuelled their revolutionary expectations. The widening chasm between those who hoped that Romania would finally break with its communist past and the authoritarian, restorative policies of Ceaușescu's successors led to a climate of continuous strife, suspicion and confrontation in Romanian politics.

The meanings of those events, the role of dissidents in the resurrection of civic societies and the decline of the communist parties' hegemony have generated an enormous interpretative literature. Initially, the general temptation was to acclaim the role of dissidents in the breakdown of Soviet-style regimes and the rise of civic initiatives from below. Euphoric accounts of the revolutionary wave flourished, often comparing these events to the 1848 'Spring of Nations'; British academic Timothy Garton Ash described them eloquently in his gripping contributions to the *New York Review of Books*, collected in the volume *The Magic Lantern* (1990). The dominant view was to regard these revolutions as part of a universal democratic wave, the confirmation of the ultimate triumph of liberal democratic values over collectivist-Jacobin attempts to control human fate. However, caught up in the romance of the revolutionary excitement, most observers glossed over the diversity of these anti-communist movements. Crucially, very few analysts insisted on the less visible, but nonetheless persistent, illiberal and neo-authoritarian components of the anti-communist upheaval in the East. Not everyone who rejected Leninism did so because he or she was dreaming of an open society founded on liberal values. As it turned out, among the revolutionaries were populist fundamentalists, religious fanatics and those who longed for the return of the undemocratic pro-communist regimes. In the early 1990s, it became unmistakably clear that the post-communist era was fraught with all manners of threats, as much of the region – most notably the states of the former Yugoslavia, whose breakup in 1991–2 derived from and extended the revolutions of 1989 – descended into bloody ethnic conflict and social unrest, with the infectious rise of old and new kinds of populism and ethnic tribalism. This type of politics was not ideological, as it was neither left nor right. Rather, policies were adopted only in accord with the needs and whims of the power-holders. Elites deployed nationalistic and manipulative political slogans with utter disregard for their long-term consequences. The popularity and manifestation of this genre of government (identifiable to varying degrees in such countries as Croatia, Estonia, Hungary, Romania and Slovakia) in the first decade of post-communism seemed to confirm the fears expressed by political scientist Ralf Dahrendorf following the events of 1989:

> The greatest risk is probably of another kind altogether. I hesitate to use the word, but it is hard to banish from one's thoughts: fascism. By that I mean the combination of a nostalgic ideology of community which draws harsh boundaries between those who belong and those who do not, with a new political monopoly of a man or a movement and a strong emphasis on organization and mobilization rather than freedom of choice. (*Reflections on the Revolution in Europe*, 1990)

Another significant factor in the political dynamics of the post-communist years was the perception that the civic and moral stage of the revolution is over, and that the kleptocratic, often authoritarian bureaucracy was intent on consolidating its power. Critical intellectuals seemed to have lost much of their moral authority, and were often attacked as the embodiment of futility or incorrigible daydreamers. This was also partially true in Romania, where the media, controlled by oligarch trusts with strong connections to the communist regime and its anti-pluralist successor, viciously defamed pro-Western, liberal, anti-totalitarian intellectuals. Their status was extremely precarious precisely because they symbolized the principle of pluralism that neo-authoritarian politics tried to suppress. In this context of widespread political apathy, trusted intellectuals were desperately needed, their voices crucial to social and political moderation. They were among the few who could call upon their fellow citizens to avoid mass hysteria, to recognize the need for constitutional consensus and to foster a culture of predictable political procedures.

Since most countries in the region experienced both forms of totalitarianism, namely fascism and communism, they had to overcome not only the absence of democratic traditions but also the memory of the traumatic events of the 20th century. Regardless of the civic initiatives and scholarly articles that have emphasized and documented in detail the criminality of communist regimes, we are still a long way from full domestic and international recognition of the abuses and atrocities perpetrated under Leninist rule. It can be argued that after 1989, an uncanny amnesia buried the lessons of the totalitarian past from the present. The unmastered past of the 20th century in central and eastern Europe prevents these countries from acknowledging the logical connection between violent totalitarianism, memory and democracy. Joachim Gauck (b. 1940), federal commissioner for the archives of the Stasi (East German secret police) and later president of a united Germany, has argued that 'reconciliation with the traumatic past...can be achieved not simply through grief, but also through discussion and dialogue'. This view stresses the importance of true reconciliation, understood as a process of reckoning or 'working through the past', without which the field of memory is left open to dangerous, ideologically motivated alternative interpretations of historical events.

Given these circumstances, it is necessary to recognize that a new identity can be based upon negative contrasts, whereby both are characterized by a repudiated totalitarian past and with anti-democratic forces in the present. Therefore, the recollection of the past by new regimes must have as its foundation an ethical framework determined by both the knowledge of historical truth and the official acknowledgement of that history. Such a framework would invalidate the destructive power of silence and festering guilt. Given the events that have flourished in east-central Europe in the last few years, it has become painfully clear that only on the basis of a moral consensus about the shared past can democracy become truly possible in these societies. Indeed, the more vague and nebulous the past upon which post-communist polities have been founded, the more aggressive, feverish and intolerant the proponents of neo-romantic, populist mythologies have become.

The discomfort with democratic challenges and the pluralist constitutional model is linked not only to the Leninist past but also to a larger problem of legitimizing the new state in the face of competing visions of the common good and rival symbols of collective identity. At the same time, the post-communist countries have benefited from the example of western Europe, where sustainable democratic post-war societies emerged and transnational bonds were forged after the region came to terms with its traumatic past. Although difficult histories sometimes impart negative legacies, they can also serve as motivation to build and preserve democratic rule. Thus the memory of both Auschwitz and the Gulag, if acknowledged and taught in the post-communist region, can help to entrench the societal values and political culture that were lost under the 20th-century totalitarianisms. The acceptance of most of the revolutionary countries of east-central Europe into the European Union in the early 2000s became a major catalyst and incentive for the liberal parties and associations. Political demagogues became accountable to a transnational community of states committed to the observance and the defence of human right. The same can be said about the expansion of NATO into the region, an affirmation of what Havel once called a civilizational, not only a military and political, alliance.

To conclude, the revolutions of 1989 fundamentally changed the political, economic and cultural maps of the world. Resulting from the widespread dissatisfaction with Leninist ideological domination, they allowed for a rediscovery of democratic participation and civic activism. After decades of state aggression against the public sphere, these revolutions reinstituted the distinction between what belongs to the government and what is the territory of the individual. Emphasizing the importance of political and civil rights, they created a space for the exercise of liberal democratic values. In some countries these values have become the constitutional foundation on which the institutions of an open society can be safely built. In others, the reference to pluralism remains somewhat superficial only. Yet even in the less successful cases of democratic transitions, as in the Balkans, the old order, based on suspicion, fear and mass hopelessness, is irrevocably defunct. In other words, while the ultimate result of these transitions is not clear, the revolutions have succeeded in their most important task: disbanding the Leninist regimes and permitting the citizens of these countries to autonomously engage in the shaping of their own destinies.

Václav Havel

Václav Havel (1936–2011), Czech playwright and president of Czechoslovakia (1989–92) and the Czech republic (1993–2003), was a long-standing opponent of the communist regime, as well as a world-renowned writer. He was active in the Prague Spring of 1968 – after which his plays were banned – and with the Charter 77 initiative, which led to four years in prison (1979–83). In 1989, he helped to establish and then led the Civic Forum coalition of dissidents aiming to overthrow the regime. When the regime collapsed in November, following ten days of public protest, Havel was the natural, if reluctant, choice for president, taking the state into the elections of 1990. One of his earliest acts was to pardon a large number of prisoners jailed by the previous regime. In 1992 he resigned when Slovakia sought its independence (the 'velvet divorce'), but he was re-elected president with a largely formal role. He was active in ending the Warsaw Pact, and took his country into NATO.

József Antall

József Antall (1932–93) was a former history teacher and museum director who served as Hungarian prime minister (1990–93). Antall became involved in the Hungarian Democratic Forum (MDF) in the mid-1980s, and led its delegation in talks for a transition to democracy. In 1990 he led the MDF to victory in the first free parliamentary elections and became prime minister, adopting a conservative centre-right position, valuing political stability and cultural continuity, but selling state enterprises to foreign investors. During his term in office, questions arose over his attitude to anti-Semitism. He died before the term was complete.

TIMELINE

1988

7 December   Gorbachev announces withdrawal of Soviet troops from eastern Europe

1989

3 February   Soviet troop withdrawals from Czechoslovakia begin

6 February   Solidarity and Polish government begin round table talks

25 April   Soviet forces begin leaving Hungary

2 May   Hungary lifts 'iron curtain' border fence with Austria

4 June   Solidarity wins landslide in Polish election; on the same day, more than 1,000 pro-democracy demonstrators are massacred in Tiananmen Square, Beijing

7 July   Gorbachev tells Warsaw Pact leaders they can choose their own road to socialism

23 August   'Human chain' of two million people in Estonia, Latvia and Lithuania

24 August   First non-communist government in eastern Europe since 1948 takes power in Poland

September   Almost 20,000 East Germans flee to Austria via Czechoslovakia and Poland

10 September Hungary opens border with Austria, allowing East Germans to flee

7 October   Hungarian Communist Party becomes a socialist party

4 November   Huge demonstrations in East Berlin

9 November   Berlin Wall opens

10 November   Todor Zhivkov ousted in Bulgaria

17 November	Peaceful demonstration in Prague is put down forcibly; Velvet Revolution begins
19 November	Václav Havel forms Civic Forum in Czechoslovakia
25 November	800,000 attend Civic Forum rally in Czechoslovakia
24 November	Czechoslovak Politburo resigns
3 December	East German government resigns
10 December	Non-communist government appointed in Czechoslovakia
17 December	Violence sweeps Romania, following crackdown by army and police
25 December	Nicolae Ceaușescu and his wife Elena executed in Romania
29 December	Václav Havel becomes first democratic president of Czechoslovakia

1990

| 3 October | Reunification of Germany |
| 9 December | Lech Wałęsa elected president of Poland |

1991

| June | Croatia and Slovenia declare independence from Yugoslavia and war breaks out |
| December | Soviet Union abolished |

SOUTH AFRICA: THE END OF APARTHEID, 1990–1994

Thula Simpson

The South African revolution of the late 1980s and early 1990s saw the dismantling of the uniquely unjust and racist apartheid system that had been in force for more than forty years, and its replacement with a fully democratic South Africa that became known as the 'rainbow nation' for its racial inclusivity. This process was known as the National Democratic Revolution, its aims set out in the Freedom Charter of 1955. That the revolution eventually proved relatively peaceful, and the many prophesies of widespread violence unfounded, was down to a careful process of negotiation and talking agreed by both main parties.

Although in 2004 the African National Congress (ANC) declared itself a social democratic party, it had previously been avowedly revolutionary in the sense of having a military wing – Umkhonto we Sizwe, founded in 1961 – that did not renounce violence until very late in the day. It was also closely associated with the Communist Party, whose vision of transcending capitalism through the public ownership of the means of production, and eventually introducing communism, was at the heart of the National Democratic Revolution programme.

The task that Nelson Mandela faced on his release from prison in 1990 was to balance the expectations of the various wings of the ANC, as well as manage the international situation. While apartheid in South Africa had long been considered a bastion of Western interests against Soviet expansion in the region since the Second World War, the end of the Cold War and collapse of the Soviet Union rendered this redundant, and made it impossible for the state to resist majority rule indefinitely, as F. W. de Klerk clearly understood.

Achieving a successfully negotiated revolution, however, was precarious, complex and involved careful choreography. It was, however, no less revolutionary for that. **PF**

The National Party's (NP) triumph in South Africa's 1948 elections on a platform of 'apartheid' heralded a dramatic escalation of political conflict in the country. The following years saw the rigid enforcement by statute of many forms of racial segregation hitherto upheld by custom, and this was accompanied by ever more stringent security legislation. A multi-racial alliance headed by the African National Congress (ANC, originally formed in 1912) led the resistance to the apartheid onslaught. The alliance's 'Defiance Campaign against Unjust Laws' in 1952 was met with legislation the following year providing for the imposition of martial law and the prosecution of activists involved in civil disobedience. These prohibitive measures induced the ANC to retreat from mass protest and make its next campaign a nationwide effort to gather demands for a manifesto outlining the shape of a post-apartheid South Africa. The Freedom Charter agreed at the Congress of the People in June 1955 articulated demands for political, social, economic and cultural equality under ten broad headings. The state responded in December 1956 by arresting 141 activists on charges of conspiracy to overthrow the government and establish a communist society based on the Freedom Charter.

By the time the charges against the last of the accused in the 'Treason Trial' were dropped in March 1961 (the evidence for the charges proved too flimsy), a number of activists within the alliance had ironically begun planning an armed struggle. The turning point came with the Sharpeville Massacre of 21 March 1960, followed by the imposition of a state of emergency and the prohibition of the ANC and the Pan Africanist Congress (PAC, formed in 1959, which organized the march against the pass laws that led to the killings at Sharpeville). The state of emergency ended in August 1960, but during its course the first serious discussions occurred within the alliance about forming a military wing. These discussions led to the launch of Umkhonto we Sizwe (MK) in December 1961, with Nelson Mandela (1918–2013) as its first commander-in-chief.

In an interview in June 1994, the former chief of the South African Defence Force (SADF) Constand Viljoen (b. 1933) recalled that in the 1970s and 1980s he had explored 'virtually every case study of Revolutionary War in Africa' from Mau Mau in Kenya to the revolts against settler and colonial rule in Rhodesia and the Portuguese Empire. The study led him to conclude that the South African conflict would 'never be a military war alone', and that these other non-military factors would ultimately be decisive. He accordingly advised his superiors that a 'long drawn-out war from the military point of view is completely possible but from the country's psychological point of view it is not possible'.

F. W. de Klerk (b. 1936) was elected president of South Africa in September 1989. During his speech marking the opening of South Africa's Parliament on 2 February 1990, he drew attention to the psychological dimension of the war when referring to the toll exacted on South Africans by having been 'embroiled in conflict, tension and violent struggle for decades'. The 'silent majority' was, he claimed, yearning to 'break out of the cycle of violence and break through to peace and reconciliation'. Recalling that during his inauguration he had committed government to 'give attention to the most important obstacles in the way of negotiation', de Klerk said he was able to announce a number of important steps in that regard, the most important of which was that 'the prohibition of the African National Congress, the Pan Africanist Congress, the South

African Communist Party [SACP] and a number of subsidiary organiza-tions is being rescinded'. This step would 'normalize the political process in South Africa without jeopardizing the maintenance of good order'. He pointed to the collapse of communism in eastern Europe in 1989 as a factor that had further weakened the organizations concerned, to the point where the South African police felt able to contain them without requiring outright proscription. Declaring 'the agenda is open' for constitutional negotiations, he added: 'Nelson Mandela could play an important part,' and he emphasized that 'the Government has taken a firm decision to release Mr Mandela unconditionally'.

Although de Klerk insisted that his reform package meant there was 'no longer any reasonable excuse for the continuation of violence' by the unbanned movements, when Mandela was released on 11 February after twenty-seven years in prison, he used his first public address at Cape Town's Grand Parade that evening to say that the reforms did not go far enough. Mandela argued that the factors that had necessitated the establishment of MK in 1961 'still exist today'. Specifically, he mentioned the 'Harare Declaration', a document drafted by the ANC in 1989 setting out a hardline position on negotiations, and called on the government to undertake 'the immediate ending of the State of Emergency, and the freeing of all – and not only some – political prisoners'.

Progress towards constitutional negotiations would be frustrated by the need to reconcile these positions amidst the persistence of various forms of conflict inherited from the past. Political violence in South Africa in 1990 took three main forms: conflict between the state and ANC-supporting communities; the ANC's armed struggle; and violence between the ANC and the Inkatha Freedom Party (IFP). The continuation of these conflicts would lead to the separation of peace talks from constitutional negotiations, delaying the onset of the latter by almost two years.

The first direct meeting between the ANC and the government occurred at the Groote Schuur mansion in Cape Town in May. The resulting 'Groote Schuur Minute' involved both sides undertaking to combat the 'existing climate of violence and intimidation from whatever quarter as well as a commitment to stability and to a peaceful process of negotiations'.

From the government's perspective, the ANC's armed struggle was a key obstacle to the creation of a climate suitable for negotiations. The issue was brought to a head with the arrest of two operatives of the ANC underground in Durban in July. This led to the uncovering of 'Operation Vula', an ANC mission launched in 1986 to establish underground politico-military command structures in South Africa. By 1990, Ronnie Kasrils, Mac Maharaj and Siphiwe Nyanda had been deployed to the country as Vula's internal commanders.

Only a declaration by Mandela that the ANC still abided by the Groote Schuur Minute enabled talks to proceed on 6–7 August. The 'Pretoria Minute' issued at the close of the meeting saw the ANC make an important concession, in that it deviated from the Harare Declaration by consenting to suspend 'armed actions and all related matters' in return for the government merely committing to 'consider' lifting the state of emergency in Natal (emergency rule had been lifted in the country's three other provinces in June), and undertaking a 'further release' of political prisoners beginning in September.

The continued state of emergency in Natal was a consequence of a conflict between the ANC and IFP in that province that dated from the mid-1980s and by 1990 had already caused over 5,000 deaths. The days before the Pretoria meeting saw a dramatic enlargement of the scope of the conflict when an IFP rally in Sebokeng on 22 July led to violent clashes with local ANC-supporting township residents. This brought the ANC–IFP clash to the Transvaal. Then, just days after the Pretoria meeting, the violence migrated on the Transvaal from the Vaal Triangle to the Rand when clashes erupted in Thokoza.

A working group established under the Pretoria Minute was supposed to clarify by September what the suspension of armed struggle would entail; however, amidst the recriminations caused by the violence in the Transvaal, it was not until February 1991 that the D. F. Malan Accord clarified that the suspension meant an end to all attacks, infiltrations, creation of new underground structures and military training inside South Africa. President de Klerk proclaimed that this accord would herald the start of formal constitutional talks. Political violence would, however, again dash these hopes.

In May 1991 the ANC withdrew from talks with the government over the issue of violence, and it called in the process for church mediation to resolve the ongoing conflict. This led in September to a National Peace Accord brokered by church and business, whereby twenty-seven political organizations agreed a code of conduct aimed at limiting political violence. Violence surged again following its signing, but the accord did enable constitutional negotiations to commence on 20–21 December, with the inaugural sitting of the Convention for a Democratic South Africa (CODESA).

The decision to push on with constitutional talks despite the fact that the issue of political violence was far from resolved reflected the fact that for all their differences, the two main protagonists in the negotiations (i.e. the ANC and the National Party, who between them could claim the allegiance of a vast majority of the population) were each committed for their own reasons to the success of the process initiated by de Klerk in 1990. With the end of de Klerk's five-year term approaching in 1994, it was essential for the negotiations for a new South Africa to commence.

Ten by-elections between de Klerk's inauguration and the beginning of 1992 had produced a 7 per cent shift to the opposition Conservative Party (CP), which rejected the government's policy of negotiation. A further CP victory in a by-election in Potchefstroom (Transvaal) in February 1992 led de Klerk to call a whites-only referendum for 17 March that year, with the question: 'Do you support continuation of the reform process which the State President began on February 2nd, 1990, and which is aimed at a new constitution through negotiation?' The outcome was a resounding 68.6 per cent 'yes'.

Five working groups had been established at the December 1991 CODESA talks to report on matters likely to impede progress when negotiations resumed in mid-1992. All reported ahead of the scheduled resumption on 15 May, except for Working Group Two, which was deadlocked on the issue of the majority needed to pass the constitution: the ANC was calling for a two-thirds majority, and the National Party three-quarters.

The CODESA II talks broke down on this issue. Following their failure, the ANC and its allies adopted 'Operation Exit', a plan of mass action aimed at driving the National Party to accede to the liberation movement's demands.

Operation Exit was quickly overshadowed by incidents in the Vaal Triangle township of Boipatong on the following evening, when IFP-supporting hostel workers killed over forty township residents. Boipatong highlighted the fact that the issue of violence had remained unresolved amidst the shift to constitutional talks. Mandela announced a few days later that the ANC was withdrawing from the negotiations. In the process he called for United Nations (UN) intervention. This proved to be a turning point, because within days the government invited the UN secretary general Boutros Boutros-Ghali (1922–2016) to visit South Africa. This led to the passage on 16 July of UN Security Council Resolution 765, which called on the Secretary General to appoint a special representative to visit South Africa prior to recommending measures to 'assist in bringing an effective end to violence and in creating conditions for negotiations'.

Cyrus Vance (1917–2002) was Boutros-Ghali's chosen envoy. After arriving in South Africa on 21 July, he engineered ANC–government talks about the release of the final batch of political prisoners (this most sensitive category involved those responsible for incidents that had led to the death of unarmed civilians). This was the first contact between the groups since CODESA II, and it paved the way for the commencement of direct discussions between the ANC's secretary general Cyril Ramaphosa (b. 1952) and the government's constitutional development minister Roelf Meyer (b. 1947) about removing obstacles to the resumption of formal constitutional talks.

These talks led to a meeting between de Klerk and Mandela on 26 September at which they signed a 'Record of Understanding' reaffirming the need for an interim government and parliament, while committing government to release the remaining ANC prisoners, to fence off migrant-worker hostels implicated in violence and to ban all dangerous weapons at marches.

While this Record of Understanding was necessary for constitutional talks to resume, those talks had stalled earlier in 1992, and would do so again without movement from the protagonists. In October 1992, SACP leader Joe Slovo (1926–95) published an article in which he suggested that in order to secure a stable transition, the ANC would need to consider offering guarantees for the *post*-election period, including power sharing, job security for civil servants and security force members, and an amnesty for political offences. This was important because previously the ANC had been preponderantly hostile to the perpetuation of apartheid personnel and structures beyond the democratic elections.

Slovo's ideas were eventually incorporated in a document approved by the ANC's National Executive Committee on 25 November.

Bilateral talks between the ANC and the National Party about the resumption of multi-party negotiations commenced in December 1992. They culminated on 12 February 1993 with an agreement to hold elections in April 1994, and to establish a power-sharing government of national unity lasting five years thereafter. This brought the two most important parties in the negotiations into accord.

This agreement preceded the resumption of multi-party negotiations on 1 April 1993. The renewed negotiations would be marked by desperate attempts by white right-wing paramilitaries to scupper them. On 10 April, the leading ANC and SACP member Chris Hani (1942–93) was killed outside his Boksburg home by Janusz Waluś, a member of the Conservative Party and the Afrikaner Weerstandsbeweging (AWB). The talks continued. On 25 June, the day negotiators had set to decide the election date, AWB paramilitaries stormed the World Trade Centre, where the negotiations were taking place. Again the talks proceeded, with 27 April 1994 eventually being agreed as the election date. In September, agreement was reached for a Transitional Executive Council (TEC) to lead South Africa up to the elections. This was followed in November by agreement on a transitional constitution to take South Africa past the elections and to agreement of a final constitution. When the TEC sat for the first time on 7 December 1993, the negotiations per se ended; South Africa entered fully into the transition to majority rule.

The Record of Understanding of 26 September 1992 was, therefore, a major turning point. It was seen to be at the time. Days later, the Concerned South Africans Group (COSAG) was established, bringing together Lucas Mangope (1923–2018), Oupa Gqozo (b. 1952) and Mangosuthu Buthelezi (b. 1928), the leaders of the three nominally independent homelands of Bophuthatswana, Ciskei and KwaZulu respectively. They were joined by the white right-wing Conservative Party and the Afrikaner Volksfront. COSAG was bound by a commitment to a 'federalism' that would permit the continued existence of the black homelands and the creation of a white one. In October 1993, COSAG's members reconstituted themselves as the 'Freedom Alliance' in opposition to the constitutional agreements.

The early months of 1994 would see the Alliance's components collapse like dominoes. The first to fall was Bophuthatswana. When the homeland's cabinet announced that it would not participate in the elections, civil service protests emerged in its major cities, Mmabatho and Mafikeng. On 10 March Lucas Mangope called on the Afrikaner Volksfront – led by the former SADF Chief Constand Viljoen – to muster military reinforcements. The less disciplined AWB also deployed, however, and in the early hours of the next day its members shot at looters and even pedestrians in Mmabatho. This caused the Bophuthatswana army and police to rally in order to drive them out. Television footage of the execution of three AWB stragglers offered a powerful symbol of the military rout of the white right. Viljoen announced on the 12th that he would participate in the elections, while he blasted the AWB for leaving him in the lurch.

The following week in the Ciskei, Oupa Gqozo resigned after protests developed among civil servants and soldiers who were worried about the security of their pensions. This left KwaZulu and Inkatha. International attempts at mediation ostensibly failed on 14 April, when the ANC and IFP failed to agree terms of reference and most of the diplomats, including Henry Kissinger and Britain's Lord Carrington, left. One diplomat, the Kenyan Washington Okumu (1936–2016), stayed, and on the 15th he met Mangosuthu Buthelezi. Okumu offered his old friend nothing but straight talk, telling the IFP leader that time was not on his side, because after the 27th the ANC would rejoin the fight bolstered by the full power of the South African state. The argument registered. Buthelezi flew back to the KwaZulu capital Ulundi to consult with other members of the IFP. On 19 April an agreement was signed by Buthelezi, Mandela and de Klerk providing for Inkatha's participation in the election, in exchange for post-election international mediation on the issues of federalism and the Zulu king's constitutional status.

The first ever elections to give a vote to all South African citizens got underway with special voting on 26 April, before the main voting the following day. The ANC received 62.65 per cent of the vote; the National Party 20.3 per cent; and Inkatha 10.5 per cent, with no other party garnering over 2.5 per cent. On 9 May the new members of the National Assembly were sworn in, and on the following day, Nelson Mandela was inaugurated South African president before 45 heads of state and over 140 official delegations.

Ultimately, it was the conclusion of the negotiations in 1993 that enabled the resolution of the interlocked issues of political violence. Above all, the negotiations established a fixed date for the elections, and the approach of the 27 April 1994 deadline had a catalytic effect that overwhelmed the resistance of the last of the holdouts against the settlement. The prospect of being left out of the elections triggered the People's Power revolution in Bophuthatswana, while a failed attempt to prop up Mangope caused the white right to split on the issue of participation in the vote. Uncertainty over pensions also stirred civil servants in the Ciskei into action. Finally, the resistance of the IFP, the most powerful component of the Freedom Alliance, was overcome by both its growing isolation and the dawning realization that it would soon have to treat with an ANC equipped with the full might of the South African state.

The transition of power in South Africa was not a revolution in the sense that the ANC had come to define that term during the liberation struggle. In 1992 Slovo emphasized the fact that since neither side won the power struggle, neither could be expected to surrender at the negotiating table – hence compromise was inevitable. The concessions made by the ANC in 1992–3 to facilitate the negotiated settlement came to be known as its 'historic compromises'.

In the initial post-1994 years, those who regretted the fact that the struggle in South Africa had not culminated in a revolutionary seizure of power had to reckon with the palpable, widespread relief among many citizens of all races that the country had managed to avoid a civil war fought along racial and tribal lines. Euphoria over the 'miracle' of the South African transition would not last, however, and questions about the merits of the compromises would emerge. But among these criticisms, there was a notable absence. The issue of 'federalism' had formed the basis for much of the resistance to the prospect of a negotiated settlement. The transition would serve to weaken these centrifugal forces. Majority rule would put an end, once and for all, to white right-wing political control of the rural platteland, while the IFP's share of the national vote would gradually erode. Within a decade of the transition, there was simply no longer opposition of any significance to the idea of South Africa as a unitary non-racial state. The democratic state therefore quickly achieved a political legitimacy among a majority of South Africans that the apartheid system never possessed.

Criticism of the compromises instead came to focus on social and economic issues, particularly the continued plight of the poor, and the ways in which the settlement and the accompanying focus on reconciliation served to close off certain possibilities for the kinds of radical change envisaged in the Freedom Charter. This critique originated from the political left rather than the right.

The post-transition period was accompanied by signs of the growing enfeeblement of the democratic state. The 2004 elections were followed by the emergence of 'service delivery' protests, involving communities taking to the streets demanding access to water, electricity, housing and the like. These protests led to violent clashes with the police in scenes resembling those of the late apartheid era. The election of Jacob Zuma

(b. 1942) as president in 2009 would lead to another term being added to the South African political lexicon, namely 'state capture'. Throughout it all, however, the ANC continued to win elections with commanding majorities.

One of the ubiquitous phrases of the left critique of the transition was that post-apartheid South Africa was sitting on a 'ticking time bomb'. Whether accumulated frustrations over poverty, inequality, delivery and corruption will serve to strip the democratic state of its legitimacy to the point where constitutional questions might again be broached is one of the key issues facing post-apartheid South Africa in the next phase of its development.

Nelson Mandela

Nelson Mandela (1918–2013), first president of democratic multi-racial South Africa (1994–9), was the son of a chieftain of the Madiba clan of the Tembu people. After studying law, he joined the ANC in 1944. In 1952, with Oliver Tambo, he created the first black law practice in South Africa, campaigning against the pass laws; in 1955 he contributed to the draft of the Freedom Charter calling for democracy. He was charged with treason in 1956, but eventually acquitted. Abandoning non-violence after the Sharpeville massacre of 1960, he advocated acts of sabotage and founded Umkhonto we Sizwe, the ANC's military wing. In 1963 he was tried and sentenced to life imprisonment. He became an international focus for anti-apartheid feeling, and in the late 1980s was involved in preliminary negotiations with the government. He was released in February 1990 and became the ANC's president in 1991, meeting President de Klerk and leading negotiations for the transition to a multi-racial democracy. The two men were jointly awarded the Nobel Peace Prize in 1993, and as national president after the elections of 1994 Mandela oversaw the dismantling of the apartheid state.

Joe Slovo

Joe Slovo (1926–95), Lithuanian-born lawyer and general secretary of the South African Communist Party (1984–91), was the first white member of the ANC National Executive Committee (1985). A friend of Nelson Mandela from university, he worked with the banned Communist Party in the 1950s, helped draft the Freedom Charter and supported the foundation of Umkhonto we Sizwe. He lived in exile in 1963–90, returning after Mandela was released from prison, after which he contributed to the negotiations and served in the first multi-racial government.

TIMELINE

1948   Afrikaner National Party wins national elections, leading to the
introduction of apartheid legislation (1949–53)

1949   Oliver Tambo, Walter Sisulu and Nelson Mandela take leadership
positions in the ANC

1955   ANC, SAIC and other organizations form the Congress of the
People and adopt the Freedom Charter

1960   The Pan Africanist Congress launches campaign against pass
laws; crowds destroy their passes in an effort to get arrested and
clog
the system

21 March   Police fire on a crowd at the Sharpeville police station near
Johannesburg, killing sixty-nine people; PAC and ANC are banned;
Mandela and other leaders arrested

1961–3   ANC and PAC authorize violent resistance, including bomb
attacks and sabotage

1964   Mandela and Sisulu convicted of treason and sentenced to life
imprisonment on Robben Island

1973   UN General Assembly declares apartheid a crime against humanity

1983   The United Democratic Front is founded to coordinate internal
resistance to apartheid by 600 different groups of all races;
it endorses the 1955 Freedom Charter

1986   South Africa invades Zimbabwe, Zambia and Botswana to attack
ANC bases; US Congress imposes economic sanctions

1989   F. W. de Klerk becomes prime minister; he releases Sisulu
from prison

1990
11 February   Mandela is freed from jail

1991   Talks begin on the creation of a new constitution
             (CODESA – Convention for a Democratic South Africa)

1992   The ANC unilaterally suspends its armed struggle; white voters
             choose reform by 2–1 margin in referendum

1993   Mandela and de Klerk share the Nobel Peace Prize

1994
26–9 April South Africa's first multi-racial elections take place, and Mandela
            becomes president

1995   Parliament creates a 'Truth and Reconciliation Commission'

1996   New constitution approved

UKRAINE: THE ORANGE REVOLUTION, 2004–2014

Yaroslav Hrytsak

The late 20th and early 21st century saw the emergence of a new kind of revolution, often branded as colour revolutions, named for the colours or plants adopted as symbols by the usually peaceful protestors. Three in particular – the Rose Revolution in Georgia (2003), the Tulip Revolution in Kyrgyzstan (2005) and – perhaps most significant – the Orange Revolution in Ukraine, occurred in former Soviet republics. While each succeeded in overthrowing an established regime by popular pressure, some have questioned the extent to which these were genuine revolutions or led to significant social change.

The fact that there is little in common between these events – which are apparently seeking to enhance democracy by direct popular action – and the Marxist revolutions that responded to structural inequalities in places such as Russia, Cuba and China, has led some commentators to seek a new explanation for revolution. This is been found in an analysis that sees them as typically occurring in formerly backward countries as a result of sudden modernization, as affluence spreads and liberal values emerge; the younger and educated middle classes are then drawn into conflict with the old, established and possibly corrupt elites, which are seen as failing in their role as promoters of the modernization they are seeking to represent. The first such event is said to be the attempted student revolutions of 1968, but the changes in eastern Europe after 1989 made them almost commonplace.

Ukraine, an ancient cultural entity with a national identity that proved troublesome to its Russian and Soviet rulers throughout the 20th century, may have exemplified this pattern – although its history has been rendered more complex by national and nationalist passions, by cultural and political divisions between different regions and by its position as a frontline state in the emerging geopolitical and ideological tensions between the European Union and Putin's Russia.

PF

In late 2004, elections were held for the Ukrainian presidency in which the prime minister Viktor Yanukovych (b. 1950), who had the support of the outgoing president Leonid Kuchma (b. 1938), narrowly defeated his pro-Western opponent Viktor Yushchenko (b. 1954). In response, the capital city Kyiv was paralysed by weeks of demonstrations and strikes involving protestors alleging widespread corruption and electoral fraud. The elections were eventually declared null by Ukraine's Supreme Court, and Yushchenko easily won the rerun in December 2004. This peaceful revolution was characterized by the orange favours worn by Yushchenko's supporters, leading it to be designated the Orange Revolution.

In 2010, Yanukovych at last won the presidency, and after an association agreement with the European Union (EU) was suspended in favour of a closer relationship with Russia, a new wave of demonstrations broke out in November 2013, with demonstrators demanding the President's resignation and an end to government corruption and human rights abuses. In February 2014, riot police used violence to end the protests and more than 100 protestors lost their lives. Following the signing of a peace accord, Yanukovych fled to Russia. The incoming government took a strongly pro-EU line, and the revolution was rejected as a coup by many, especially in the east of the country. The country descended into war, with Russian involvement that led to the Russian annexation of the Crimea in March 2014.

There were striking similarities between the events of 2004 and the protests of 2013–14, known as the Euromaidan. Both started in late November, took place in Kyiv's Maidan Nezhalezhnosti ('Independence Square', colloquially called Maidan) and had the same anti-hero, Viktor Yanukovych. In both cases the core of the protest was made up of young people and the middle class, most of whom came from Kyiv and Western Ukraine.

The Orange Revolution had been entirely peaceful, whereas some 100 protestors lost their lives on 18–20 February 2014, in the Euromaidan protest. Even so, both protests were relatively free of bloodshed. Violence was triggered only by the anti-protest laws of 16 January 2014 that were passed in the parliament. These laws criminalized civil protest, and led to security forces opening fire.

These similarities can be extended backwards in time to previous protests such as the 1990 student hunger strike that had sought the resignation of the chairman of the Council of Ministers of the Ukrainian SSR. This was organized by young people from Kyiv and Lviv (the main city of Western Ukraine), and likewise took place on the Maidan (known at the time under its Soviet name as the Square of the October Revolution). The hunger strike was called the Revolution on Granite. And in a sense, it *was* a revolution: it was the first instance in the history of the USSR of a high-ranking official being compelled to resign under pressure of mass protests. Most of the 1990 strike organizers were later involved in the Orange Revolution and the Euromaidan, too.

Yet none of these events led to systemic political change, and doubts have been raised as to whether they could be called revolutions at all. US analyst Paul Quinn-Judge, for example, claims that the Euromaidan:

> was no revolution, unfortunately. Euromaidan was a heroic and stubborn act of mass defiance in the face of ruthless and

well-armed government forces. It was most certainly not a
revolution as defined by standard Ukrainian, Russian, or Polish
dictionaries, all of whose definitions emphasize fundamental change and the creation of a new system. In the case of
Ukraine, the protestors sliced off the top layer of the regime
but left most of the structure intact.

I believe, to the contrary, that the Euromaidan was a revolution – very
much like the Orange Revolution. It was, however, a different type of
revolution from 1917, but one that became the new norm by the late 20th
century, and for which the early 21st century provides many examples.

I first heard about Ukraine's Orange Revolution three years before
it started, on 12 September 2001, when Ukrainian sociologist Yevhen
Holovakha, who had long been surveying Ukrainian public opinion,
gave a presentation on the most recent tendency his team spotted by the
late 1990s. If one asked Ukrainians about their economic situation and
how it had changed compared to the previous year, the standard reply
was that it was getting worse. However, if one asked whether during
the previous year they had bought a computer, a car, gone on vacation
or privatized their apartment, more often than not the answer was 'yes'.
Both responses were sincere, but a computer, a car or a vacation were
no longer seen as extraordinary: instead they were taken for granted.
These answers pointed to the emergence of a new middle class whose
basic needs were already met, and who now had their sights set on higher
things. Once such a class has emerged, concluded Holovakha, we must
be prepared for radical political change – even, possibly, for revolution.

At the time I was sceptical. A few months earlier, Ukraine had
witnessed mass protests against the authoritarian and corrupt regime
of President Leonid Kuchma, but these protests had come to nothing.
There was a sense of defeat. New protests, much less a revolution, seemed
unlikely. Still, in a year's time, a new wave of mass protests emerged,
known as 'Ukraine, rise!' Three years later, the Orange Revolution began.

Holovakha's arguments resembled those of Ronald Inglehart
(b. 1934), a US sociologist who went to Paris in 1968 to investigate the

student protests and strikes that had paralysed France in May of that year. The fact that the strikers used Marxist slogans made him think the protests were manifestations of a class conflict. Yet in elections held a month later, much of the working class voted for the ruling Gaullist party. It was mainly middle-class voters who supported the protesters. Inglehart interviewed both groups. Working-class respondents overwhelmingly mentioned materialist interests; above all, salaries. Middle-class respondents said they wanted a freer, less impersonal society. Based on his interviews, Inglehart hypothesized that the 1968 Paris events were a values-driven conflict. Once basic needs are satisfied, people, especially young ones, strive for self-expression. They protest against restrictions imposed by the establishment, usually represented by older generations.

To test his hypothesis, Inglehart organized larger surveys, initially covering western European countries and later worldwide. With the collapse of communism, his investigation was extended to former communist countries including Russia and Ukraine. His World Values Survey revealed a global shift among young people from materialist (survival) to post-materialist (self-expression) values. The shift started in the 1960s in the West as a result of local economic miracles. It was also related to a transition from industrial to post-industrial (service) economics. Inglehart called these changes a 'Silent Revolution'. Once it starts, one may expect increasingly strong demands for democracy (where it does not already exist), or for more responsive democracy (where it does exist).

The Orange Revolution and, even more so, the Euromaidan reflected this trend. They involved younger people and the middle classes, and started when the economic situation was improving. Indeed, in 2004 Yanukovych asked indignantly about the Orange Revolution: what kind of revolution is this? He could see no reason for revolutionary protests, since the economic situation was visibly improving.

Inglehart had also concluded that a shift to post-materialist values requires at least a minimum of democracy. This again reflects the Ukrainian situation. Since the early 1990s, power in Ukraine had been regularly changing through relatively democratic elections. It was an imperfect democracy, but it was working, and it was based on a tacit consensus that after an election victory the winners do not repress the losers, because they can find the tables turned at the next elections.

There were two attempts to break this scheme. The first was by President Leonid Kuchma, who, at the end of his term in 2004, tried to promote Prime Minister Viktor Yanukovych as his successor. In this, Kuchma was emulating Russia when in 1999 Yeltsin appointed Putin as the next Russian leader. The second attempt to derail democracy was made by Yanukovych, who, after his victory in the 2010 presidential elections, imprisoned his main rival Yulia Tymoshenko. Each time the Ukrainian power elites tried to embark on this authoritarian scenario, they were 'punished' – by the revolutions of 2004 and 2013–14.

Ukraine had been less Sovietized than some other former Soviet republics, as its western part had only been annexed to the Soviet Union at the start of the Second World War. Unlike the heavily industrialized, Russian-speaking Eastern Ukraine, the largely agrarian Western Ukraine preserved the Ukrainian language as well as the distinctive memory of previous non-Russian/Soviet (Austrian, Hungarian, Polish, Czechoslovak) rule. There was also an anti-Soviet nationalistic guerrilla resistance in 1944–9.

The west–east divide is a persistent factor of Ukrainian politics and creates a variety of problems, but the regionalism at least prevents the country succumbing to authoritarianism. Until 2010, each of the four presidents was backed either by the Ukrainian West (Kravchuk, Yushchenko) or the East (Kuchma, Yanukovych). None, however, could run the country single-handedly, without a risk of strong protests from the other part.

In the 2000s there emerged a third, central, Ukraine. It is neither so nationalistic as Western Ukraine nor as pro-Russian as Eastern. It was also neither agrarian nor industrial, but based on the service sector, which since the 2000s has been driving the Ukrainian GDP and is largely responsible for the emergence of a new middle class. This new Ukraine is also bilingual. It is epitomized by the capital city of Kyiv. This third Ukraine complicated the political landscape and made an authoritarian scenario less and less plausible.

History mattered in another way. Ukrainian historians argue the basic differences between Russia and Ukraine are not to be found in economics, language or culture, but in different political traditions of the relationship between state and society. These stem from the fact that until the establishment of Russian rule in the 18th century, most Ukrainian territories were linked to Catholic Europe and participated in Europe's social and cultural processes.

Ukrainian history is rich in revolutions. In 1648–56, there had been a large-scale Ukrainian Cossack revolution that reshaped the political landscape of east-central Europe. And Austrian Galicia (later Western Ukraine) was directly affected by the 1848 revolutions; it was the furthest east that the 'Spring of Nations' reached.

In 1917–20, Ukrainian lands were swept by national and peasant revolutions that were particularly unnerving for the Bolsheviks. And in 1930, the Soviet Ukraine was covered by mass peasant uprisings against the Stalin collectivization, which were a distant echo of the revolutionary events of 1917–20.

After 1945, Soviet Ukraine seemed to be a tamed country. This was, however, a superficial vision. Within the Soviet Union, Ukraine remained a weak link. The nationalist guerrilla campaign of 1944–9 in Western Ukraine was the largest anti-communist resistance in east-central Europe prior to the 1956 Budapest uprising. And when the Prague Spring arose in Czechoslovakia in 1968, Soviet leaders feared that unless that revolution was squashed, they might lose control over Ukraine as well.

All of these Ukrainian revolutions emerged in a shadow of large European crises – and the closer to the western border, the stronger were the protests. This was seen in the 1848 and 1968 revolutions, the uprisings of 1930 and the 1940s. The same occurred during the collapse of communism. In 1990, Western Ukraine elected the anti-communist opposition in the first relatively free Soviet elections.

Within this long history of revolutions, 1989–91 was the first with a non-ideological and non-violent character. Unlike in neighbouring Poland, anti-communist opposition failed to mobilize large masses and could not win power.

Even so, the events of 1989–91 shared some features with those of 1968. Back then, there were two regions that raised special concerns for the Soviet authorities: Western Ukraine, and the industrial Donbass in East Ukraine. Twenty years later, both regions were again centres of anti-Soviet opposition. Beyond these regions, in 1968 there was a third factor: a small nationwide group of young intellectuals. Like their counterparts in the West, they were called the 'sixties generation' (*shestydesyatnyky*) and strove for self-realization – in their case, for self-realization beyond the limits of Soviet ideology and culture. Twenty years later, these same intellectuals became leaders of the Rukh – the largest oppositional organization in Soviet Ukraine in 1989–91. In 1968, Western Ukraine, Donbass and *shestydesyatnyky* had been unable to cooperate – but twenty years later they could. Their alliance was not strong enough to remove the communist elites from power, and after the proclamation of independence in 1991 they fell apart, with former allies – Western Ukraine and Donbass – turning into bitter enemies. Nevertheless, in 1991 their union smoothed the transition to independence.

The way the events of 1989–91 evolved became a decisive argument in a debate on the role of revolution in Ukraine's future. This was held in the Ukrainian diaspora of North America and western Europe (given the stifling ideological conditions in the Soviet Union, such a discussion could not occur in Ukraine itself). There were two schools of thought. One group comprised Ukrainian nationalists, who thought that independence would come as a result of mass national uprising against Soviet power in the centre. Ukrainian nationalists were especially inspired by the example of 1917–20 mass revolution, and the post-war nationalist guerrilla uprising in Western Ukraine. They believed that these experiences could be repeated, given an opportunity. The nationalist leader of the 1940s, Stepan Bandera (1909–59), put the position succinctly: 'National revolution, not anti-regime resistance'. Anything less was not worthy of consideration.

The other group comprised liberal intellectuals. They were much less numerous, but more sophisticated in their analysis. They believed that independent Ukraine would emerge not from a national revolution, but from a general evolution of the Soviet system, which they thought was doomed to collapse. And then Ukraine would proclaim its independence.

The events of 1989–91 proved the liberals right. However, in independent Ukraine, part of the opposition considered that this independence was not genuine since it had not been won in a struggle or coloured by blood. They referred to the example of the first (2004) Maidan, and saw its failure, with the return of Yanukovych in 2010, as proof that a revolution without blood is worth little.

In this sense, the Euromaidan was different. It was marked by violence, and so the Ukrainian nationalists saw it as a real national revolution. Ironically, many leftists and left-wing liberals in the West shared the same perspective. In their understanding, supporters of Bandera and other Ukrainian nationalists played a leading role in the Euromaidan – so this was a nationalist revolution. Russian propaganda extended this point to an extreme, presenting the Euromaidan as a coup carried out by fascist-like nationalists and supported by the West.

The national dimension of the Euromaidan cannot be denied, nor the role of nationalistic organizations. Still, this is a half-truth only. While the Euromaidan needed nationalists for success, nationalists alone could not have won the Euromaidan. During parliamentary elections a few months later, they could manage only 1 per cent support. Even in Lviv, where before 2014 they had had a majority in the municipal power, afterwards they failed almost completely.

Nationalism is a potent force in mobilizing opinion, and revolutions with a national dimension seem to have a better chance of success than those without. Euromaidan protestors saw Yanukovych as a stooge of the Kremlin; therefore they were fighting against the Russian regime of Putin, too. But the Euromaidan was also a revolution of a new middle class, and in this sense it resembled protest movements such as Occupy Wall Street (2011), the Arab Spring (2011), Bolotnaya Square in Moscow (2011–13) and Taksim Square in Istanbul (2013). The difference was that the Euromaidan succeeded while others failed.

The supporters and opponents of Euromaidan on social networks can be mapped through the crucial days of the end of February and the beginning of March 2014. Supporters dominated in all regions, both Ukrainian- and Russian-speaking, except for the Crimea and Donbass. At the time, most users of social networks were young people with university education, so this can be taken as an indicator of mass support of Euromaidan by the younger generation.

The first Maidan had a strict hierarchy topped by Yushchenko: without his charismatic leadership, the Orange Revolution would hardly have happened. By contrast the Euromaidan had no strong hierarchy, and its leaders played a secondary role. This difference reflects the egalitarian ethos characteristic of many segments of post-industrial society, especially the young.

In 2019, Ukraine underwent another political hurricane. Presidential and parliamentary elections swept away the old Ukrainian political elites and the middle-aged generation raised under Kuchma. Both Yushchenko and Yanukovych, the hero and anti-hero of the Orange Revolution, had long gone. Yulia Tymoshenko did not make the second round of presidential elections, as she had done in 2010 and 2014, and her party is a minority in the parliament. Petro Poroshenko (b. 1965), who had become president after the Euromaidan and won a landslide victory in 2014, suffered a humiliating defeat in 2019.

The victors were forty-one-year-old Volodymyr Zelensky (b. 1978), the new president, and his party 'Servant of the People'. Like Poroshenko in 2014, Zelensky enjoyed a landslide – but with even more impressive results. More than half the new MPs are under forty-five years old. The new intake also included a record number of journalists, sportsmen, celebrities and the like. These results seemed to confirm preliminary conclusions about the new middle class and the Third Ukraine.

The 2019 results have been called the 'electoral Maidan'. They took place against the backdrop of an improving economic situation. There are, of course, voices that deny the revolutionary character of these changes, but these are nothing new. Doubts regarding Ukrainian revolution reflect the type of narrative that questions any revolution at all. It would be fairer to say that we are now facing a 'revolution in revolution' – that is, a revolution in our understanding of what revolution actually is.

Viktor Yushchenko

Viktor Yushchenko (b. 1954), president of Ukraine (2005–10), was governor of the country's national bank from 1993 and oversaw the creation of its national currency. Appointed prime minister in 1999, he initiated financial reforms, but his rising popularity led to his dismissal by President Kuchma in 2001. He established an opposition coalition, Our Ukraine, which adopted the colour orange as its symbol. Though he was defeated in the first presidential election of 2004, mass demonstrations against alleged electoral fraud led to the vote being annulled, and Yushchenko won the rerun in December 2004. His time as president was difficult and after his opponent, Yanukovych, became prime minister in 2006, Yushchenko was forced to transfer considerable powers from the presidency to the prime minister.

Yulia Tymoshenko

Yulia Tymoshenko (b. 1960), Ukrainian businesswoman and prime minister (2005, 2007–10), built her fortune in a gas company in the early 1990s. She became a minister under Prime Minister Yushchenko in 1999 and later joined his Our Ukraine party and was prominent in the Orange Revolution. Yushchenko named her prime minister in 2005, but she was forced to resign after a corruption scandal. In 2007 she was again appointed prime minister and directly challenged Yushchenko's authority, taking a more pro-Russian line. She lost the 2010 presidential election to Yanukovych, and was immediately dismissed by the incoming president. In 2011 she was charged with abusing her power and sentenced to seven years in prison, but she was released during the Euromaidan Revolution of 2014.

TIMELINE

1921   Ukrainian Soviet Socialist Republic is established as the Russian Red Army conquers two-thirds of Ukraine; the western third becomes part of independent Poland

1932-3   Stalin imposes terror and famine on Ukraine; millions die in the famine

1941   German army enters Ukraine

1942   Ukrainian Insurgent Army, or UPA, is created and battles both Soviet and Nazi forces

1943   Soviet forces reconquer Kyiv

1945   Soviet annexation of western Ukraine

1954   Soviet leader Nikita Khrushchev transfers the Crimean peninsula to Ukraine

1988   Prominent writers and intellectuals set up Ukrainian People's Movement for Restructuring (Rukh)

1990   Student protests and hunger strikes bring down government of Vitaliy Masol

1991   Ukraine declares independence from USSR

1996
28 June   President Leonid Kuchma pushes new constitution through parliament

1999   Viktor Yushchenko becomes prime minister, and reverses the country's economic decline

2000   Yushchenko wins approval for a plan to cut state bureaucracy, deregulate business, open up privatization efforts, create a private land market, lower taxes and improve tax collection

2001   Half a million protesters call for the resignation of Kuchma

2002   Kuchma appoints Viktor Yanukovych prime minister

2004
November   Official count indicates presidential election victory for Yanukovych;
              observers report widespread vote rigging; defeated candidate
              Yushchenko launches campaign of street protest and civil
              disobedience

December   Yushchenko tops poll in election rerun; parliament adopts electoral
              and constitutional changes to defuse political crisis

2005   NATO pledges to help Ukraine push through military reforms

2006   Parties behind the Orange Revolution form a coalition government;
              Yanukovych is named as prime minister and suspends a bid to join
              NATO

2010   Yanukovych wins presidential election

2013   Mass protests in Kyiv and other cities at the government's decision
              to abandon an association agreement with the EU

2014
January   Yanukovych drives a law through parliament to curb anti-
              government protests, sparking outcry from the opposition

February   70,000 pro-Western Ukrainians throng Kyiv, vowing to oust
              Yanukovych for his alliance with Russia

              Yanukovych accuses opposition leaders of trying to seize power
              by force; protesters seize control of Kyiv's central post office;
              opponents of the President declare autonomy in the major western
              city of Lviv

              Security forces kill c. 100 protestors in Kyiv; Yanukovych flees to
              Russia, opposition takes control; Russia refuses to recognize
              takeover

March   Russian forces help separatists seize power in Crimea, which
              Russia then annexes; US and its European allies impose sanctions
              on Russia

17 July
A passenger aircraft, Malaysian Airlines Flight 17, comes down in rebel-held territory, killing all 298 people on board

August
Russia sends unauthorized aid convoy to besieged rebel-held cities; Ukraine declares it has been invaded

October
Pro-Russian insurgents assault Donetsk Airport; Ukraine's president approves legislation to purge government bodies of officials linked to Yanukovych

THE ARAB SPRING: EGYPT, 2011

Yasser Thabet

The Arab Spring of 2011 saw attempted revolutions in several countries of the Middle East. These were spontaneous outpourings of popular anger at many years of government repression and mistreatment of the people, and assumed the form of massive daily demonstrations which took the authorities by surprise. They were both coordinated and publicized worldwide by means of social media tools which could not, at the time, be subjected to the usual censorship (though the people of some countries had better access to social media than others). Beginning with protests in Tunisia following the self-immolation of a Benghazi fruit-seller in despair at harassment by officialdom, the revolutions had some real successes. Regime change took place in Tunisia (where the long-standing president was driven out and a new constitution introduced), Libya (where Muammar Gaddafi was ousted by a rebel alliance assisted by a Western bombing campaign), Yemen and Egypt, serious unrest or insurgency broke out in Bahrain and Syria, while demonstrations took place in many other countries.

The massive demonstrations in Tahrir Square, Cairo, drew the most attention, and resulted in the overthrow of long-standing president Mubarak. However, the spontaneous nature of the revolution meant that its supporters were both disorganized and had contradictory objectives for the future. As a result, the army, long-term arbiter of the country's political settlement, stepped in once again.

Beyond the immediate desire to seek regime change, the broader objective of many demonsrators was to break the power of existing political elites, but this has not proved possible anywhere. Instead, the optimism of 2011 has been lost, either in devastating civil wars (Syria or Yemen), a rise of Islamism and sectarianism, or a return to repression.   PF

On 25 January 2011, Egyptians initiated massive demonstrations in Cairo's Tahrir Square and elsewhere. The factors that initially mobilized people included poverty, rampant unemployment, government corruption and autocratic governance. Soon, however, the focus shifted to overthrow the regime of President Hosni Mubarak (1928–2020), who had governed the country since 1981 following the assassination of Anwar Sadat by Islamists.

Anger at Mubarak's rule had built up over the previous decade. Even when he began his second term, in 1987, he had refused to reform the constitution, extended the state of emergency, promulgated laws to exclude opposition parties from local councils and tightened the grip of the ruling National Democratic Party (NDP) over parliament. He denounced opposition groups for criticizing his policies, and started to threaten them.

From 1990, Mubarak became increasingly anti-democratic, and he used the campaign against Islamic extremism to prolong the state of emergency that had followed Sadat's assassination. The opposition was suppressed, newspapers were censored and freedom of expression and human rights were violated. Although there were constitutional amendments in 2005 and 2007 to allow pluralism in presidential elections, these seemed to be nothing more than a kind of cosmetic surgery to keep Mubarak in power.

The regime established a security state, where the country was controlled by security reports for everything: the appointment of ministers, governors, mayors, deputy mayors and heads of universities. Moreover, security forces arrested and harassed any individuals, activists or union officials who challenged the 'official' discourse or expressed dissenting opinions.

In 2006 the regime allowed judges to be assaulted for demanding the independence of the judiciary, and turned a blind eye to similar attacks on university professors. Many of those who dared to oppose the government were sent to military courts, where they were subjected to harsh rulings with no right of appeal.

In 2010 the human rights organization Amnesty International concluded that torture was 'systematic in police stations, prisons and SSI [State Security Investigations] detention centers and, for the most part, committed with impunity....[Security and plainclothes police assault people] openly and in public as if unconcerned about possible consequences.'

The regime never allowed political parties to discuss or oppose the state's decisions. The president had the power to appoint and remove the prime minister and government, dissolve parliament and veto laws. Civil and political rights and freedoms of the citizen were confiscated; authoritarian decisions were common, as were the intervention and violence of security institutions, while power was concentrated in the executive branch of the government.

The authorities ignored democracy and the rule of law, apart from formal changes offering restricted political pluralism and some electoral processes. There was very little renewal of the blood of the ruling elite.

The opposition parties, unable to direct the state, monitor its actions or control its conduct or to hold the president to public account, were effectively paralysed. The ruling NDP controlled at least three-quarters of the seats in the People's Assembly – except for in 1995 and 2010, when it won 94 per cent and 97 per cent of the seats respectively. Further, its dominance in the local elections encouraged widespread corruption among local government officials.

To sweep the 2010 general election, the NDP engineered a plan to exclude opposition candidates from running or winning seats.

Meanwhile, there were systematic crackdowns on the media and university life. The government closed down nineteen TV channels and put on pressure to silence outspoken critics and talk-show hosts. The Association for Freedom of Thought and Expression (AFTE) concluded: 'The Ministry of Mass Media and Communication has tightened its fist over all media channels to markedly reduce the space for freedom of expression, especially [during and] after the last parliamentary elections.'

Despite this, opposition escalated, from journalists' and lawyers' syndicates to new movements demanding better wages or political rights, such as 'Doctors without Rights' and 'Youth for Change'. Opposition groups were led by the Egyptian Movement for Change (*Kefaya*/Enough), the March 9th Movement, and the April 6th Youth Movement. In a country where almost 60 per cent of the population is under thirty, youngsters were the leading force in such movements.

Public opinion became outraged after the murder of blogger Khaled Said, who was beaten to death in Alexandria on 6 June 2010. This murder became a symbol of the power of the police to brutalize citizens with impunity. One of the social media sites that helped organize the protests of 25 January 2011 was a Facebook page called 'We Are All Khaled Said.'

Other factors, including low rates of growth, rising unemployment, poverty, lack of satisfaction of needs, absence of social responsibility and the spread of slums, all contributed to the unrest.

The 'inheritance' of jobs and positions within state institutions, handed down from parents to children or grandchildren, is the most striking example of the systematic corruption of the middle class. This resulted in the creation of networks of interests benefiting from the situation, and rejecting any change that would affect their significant unwritten social privileges.

Mubarak's younger son Gamal (b. 1963) was expected to succeed his father as the next president of Egypt. Gamal began receiving attention from the media, since there were apparently no other heirs to the presidency. He wielded increasing power as NDP deputy secretary general and chair of the party's policy committee. Analysts described Mubarak's last decade in power as 'the age of Gamal Mubarak'.

After Mubarak's 2005 re-election, several political groups (primarily unofficial) had expressed their opposition to the inheritance of power; they demanded reforms, and asked for a multi-candidate election. In 2006, with opposition increasing, *Daily News Egypt* reported an online campaign initiative (the National Initiative against Power Inheritance) demanding that Gamal reduce his power. The campaign said, 'President Mubarak and his son constantly denied even the possibility of [succession]. However, in reality they did the opposite, including amending the constitution to make sure that Gamal will be the only unchallenged candidate.'

The Egyptian people broke through the barrier of fear on 25 January 2011. Motivated by the success of the revolution in Tunisia earlier in the year, protesters from different economic, religious and cultural backgrounds poured into the streets to defy the regime and protest police brutality, injustice and the inheritance of power.

It was the first time for thirty years that hundreds of thousands had taken to the streets in protest against the regime in this manner. Marches organized through social media began in Cairo, Alexandria and Suez, only to be joined by others from other major cities across the nation. Protests started to attract millions of Egyptians, including liberals, Islamists, anti-capitalists and other activists. As the security forces clashed with protesters, the confrontations resulted in at least 846 people being killed and over 6,000 injured. Protesters retaliated by burning more than ninety police stations across the country. Strikes by labour unions added to the pressure on government officials. The protestors' demands soon grew to include the ousting of Mubarak and the end of emergency law.

Mubarak dissolved his government, appointing the former head of the General Intelligence Directorate, Omar Suleiman, vice president in an attempt to quell dissent. Mubarak asked Ahmed Shafik (b. 1941), a former chief of Egypt's air force, to form a new government. Mohamed El Baradei became a major opposition figure, with all major opposition groups supporting his role as negotiator for a transitional unity government. In response to mounting pressure, Mubarak announced that he did not intend to seek re-election in September.

Finally, the Supreme Council of the Armed Forces (SCAF) forced Mubarak's hand. The generals compelled the newly appointed Vice President to inform the President that if he didn't step down, he would face charges of high treason.

Suddenly on Friday 11 February – as millions of people surged angrily through the streets – Mubarak vanished.

The Vice President announced that Mubarak would resign as president, turning power over to SCAF. Then the military junta, headed by Mohamed Hussein Tantawi (b. 1935), announced on 13 February that the constitution would be suspended and both houses of parliament dissolved. The military would rule for six months, until elections could be held. The existing cabinet would serve as a caretaker government until a new one was formed.

Prime Minister Shafik, seen by the masses as another Mubarak figure, resigned a day before planned protests to force him to step down. Mubarak was ordered to stand trial on charges of premeditated murder of peaceful protesters and, if convicted, could have faced the death penalty. On 2 June 2012, Mubarak was found guilty of complicity in the murder of protesters and sentenced to life imprisonment, but the sentence was overturned on appeal and a retrial ordered. A number of protesters, upset that others tried alongside Mubarak (including his two sons) had been acquitted, took to the streets. Again, Mubarak was eventually cleared of all charges.

International reaction to all of this varied, with most Western nations condoning peaceful protests but expressing concern about the stability of Egypt and the region. The simultaneous Egyptian and Tunisian revolutions influenced demonstrations in other Arab countries, including Yemen, Bahrain, Jordan, Syria and Libya, in the so-called Arab Spring.

After Mubarak's resignation, Egypt went through a transition via military rule to Islamist rule. The Islamist Muslim Brotherhood (MB) took power in Egypt through a series of popular elections, with Egyptians electing Mohamed Morsi (1951–2019) to the presidency in June 2012. However, the failure of the Muslim Brotherhood to manage the country in such a critical period, when people's expectations were extraordinarily high, led to mass dissatisfaction and another call for change. MB had neither the governing experience nor the capacity to implement meaningful political and economic reforms; nor did it control Egypt's coercive apparatus, or have rigid support from foreign actors that could assist in holding power.

Morsi's government encountered fierce opposition to his attempt to pass an Islamic-leaning constitution. A presidential decree that raised his decisions over judicial review to enable the passing of the constitution sparked general outrage from secularists and members of the military, and mass protests broke out against his rule on 28 June 2013.

On 3 July 2013, Morsi was himself deposed by a coup d'état led by the minister of defence, General Abdel Fattah el-Sisi (b. 1954), as millions of Egyptians again took to the streets in support of early elections. In the following six months, estimates suggest that more than 2,500 Egyptians were killed, 17,000 wounded and 18,000 arrested. The press described this as a necessary 'war on terror'.

Sisi went on to become Egypt's president by popular election in 2014 (he was re-elected in 2018). He faced no serious challenger after a string of potentially strong candidates withdrew under pressure or were arrested.

The military's performance after Mubarak's resignation has defined the nature of Egypt's further development. Although SCAF was initially viewed as the revolution's protector, many started to see it as an agent of counter-revolution as it held all power for a year after the 2011 uprising, maintaining tight control over the executive, legislative and judiciary branches and altering Egypt's path towards democracy.

The governing regime did not change much after January 2011. The regime personified by Hosni Mubarak was not deposed, and its institutions were not significantly affected.

One might argue that the Egyptian revolution of January 2011 failed to change the fundamental political structure of the country, which ended up under military rule. Several essential conditions for a successful revolution and transition to democracy did not occur. There was no change in the country's elite or reformation of state institutions, and the revolutionary masses failed to establish a broad, lasting coalition. Several Egyptian peculiarities contributed to this failure, including the strong military, the inability of the revolution's initiators to develop their success and the lasting support from international networks of the existing elites.

Egypt was undergoing a difficult transition in searching for ways to bring back stability and move towards building a more democratic society. Meanwhile, the Gulf States remained fearful of another wave of unrests as the number of Islamists in the region continued to grow.

In 2013 the media, controlled by the regime, started to demonize 25 January, and Sisi has warned repeatedly that he would not allow another similar popular protest. In 2018 he said that what happened on 25 January was 'a wrong treatment, for a wrong diagnosis'.

In the years after Egyptians took to the streets in the boisterous demonstrations that helped oust Mubarak, a quiet cynicism has replaced optimism. The democratic, anti-Mubarak common ground rapidly eroded, allowing the return of the politics of ideological polarization, less concerned with making promises than with mobilizing fear, whether of Islamists or the military.

Officials, politicians and activists from the post-Morsi era frequently describe Egypt as being in a state of war, and the failing states and the rise of terror organizations across the region underpin this argument. Fear of chaos is equally palpable. As the academic Gerard Padró i Miquel puts it, 'Fear of falling under an equally inefficient and venal ruler that favours another group is enough to discipline supporters.'

However, a younger generation still aspired to democracy and a real civil rule and ruler. Despite the widespread arrests in Egypt against opposition groups and youth, some refused to believe it was all over, and speculated that there would be another episode similar to January 2011 in the near future.

Owing to the tight grip of security and the military in Egypt, social media, particularly Facebook, continues to play a central role in providing a platform and opportunities for protesting and even criticizing Sisi's regime, in a way that traditional methods cannot.

Mohamed Morsi

Mohamed Morsi (1951–2019), engineer and academic, was a Muslim Brotherhood politician and president of Egypt (2012–13). First elected to the People's Assembly in 2000, he urged political reform and social conservatism. He was imprisoned in 2006–7 for campaigning for reforms to the judiciary, and again during the Arab Spring risings of 2011. In April 2012 he was made the Muslim Brotherhood candidate for the presidency, which he won in June. He faced immediate opposition from the interim military government, but was quickly accused of authoritarianism. His draft Islamist constitution was opposed by Christians, liberals and others in huge demonstrations, but approved in a referendum. Further demonstrations against worsening economic conditions led the army head, Sisi (whom Morsi had appointed minister of defence) to remove him from office in July 2013; in April 2015 he was sentenced to death. However, the sentence was later overturned, and he remained in prison. He died during a courtroom hearing in 2019.

TIMELINE

2010

6 June   Blogger Khaled Said is beaten to death in Alexandria

November–December   Egypt's ruling NPD party wins 97 per cent of seats in
                     general election

17 December   Tunisia: Mohamed Bouazizi sets himself on fire outside a
                     local government office; street protests begin throughout
                     the country

2011

14 January   Tunisian president Zine El Abidine Ben Ali resigns and flees
                     to Saudi Arabia

25 January   The first coordinated mass protests are held in Tahrir
                     Square in Cairo

11 February   Egypt's president, Hosni Mubarak, steps down

15 March   Pro-democracy protests begin in Syria

22 May   Police beat thousands of pro-democracy protesters in
                     Morocco

20 August   Rebels in Libya launch battle to take control of Tripoli

23 September   Yemenis hold a 'Million Man March' pro-democracy protest

23 October   Tunisia holds first democratic parliamentary elections

28 November   Egypt holds democratic elections

2012   Mohamed Morsi is elected president; Mubarak is sentenced
                     to life imprisonment

2013   Morsi is removed by coup following protests against his rule

2014   General Abdel Fattah el-Sisi becomes president

2017   Mubarak is cleared of all charges

FURTHER READING

GENERAL

Armitage, D. and S. Subrahmanyan. 2010. *The Age of Revolution in Global Context*. Basingstoke

Davidson, N. 2012. *How Revolutionary Were the Bourgeois Revolutions?* Chicago

Goldstone, J. 2011. *Revolutions and Rebellion in the Early Modern World: Population Change and State Breakdown*. Abingdon

Halliday, F. 1999. *Revolution and World Politics*. London

Hobsbawm, E. 1962. *The Age of Revolution*. Ilford

Katz, M. 1997. *Revolutions and Revolutionary Waves*. New York

Lawson, G. 2004. *Negotiated Revolutions*. London

—— 2019. *Anatomies of Revolution*. Cambridge

Lenin, V. I. 1918. *The State and Revolution*. St Petersburg

Losurdo, D. 2015. *War and Revolution*. London

Malia, M. 2006. *History's Locomotives: Revolutions and the Making of the Modern World*. New Haven

Mishra, P. 2012. *From the Ruins of Empire: The Revolt against the West and the Remaking of Asia*. London

Mitchell, L. 2012. *The Color Revolutions*. Philadelphia

Nepstad, S. 2011. *Nonviolent Revolution*. Oxford

Polasky, J. 2015. *Revolutions Without Borders: The Call to Liberty in the Atlantic World*. New Haven

Sanderson, S. 2005. *Revolutions: A Worldwide Introduction to Political and Social Change*. Abingdon

Skocpol, T. 1979. *States and Social Revolutions*. Cambridge

1848

Evans, R. J. W. and P. von Strandmann (eds.) 2002. *The Revolutions in Europe 1848–1849*. Oxford

Körner, A. 2003. *1848 – A European Revolution? International Ideas and National Memories of 1848*. London

Moggach, D. and G. Stedman Jones (eds.) 2018. *The 1848 Revolutions and European Political Thought*. Cambridge

Rapport, M. 2008. *1848: Year of Revolution*. London

1968

Elbaum, M. 2018. *Revolution in the Air: Sixties Radicals turn to Lenin, Mao and Che*. London

Gassert, P. and M. Klimke. 2018. *1968: On the Edge of World Revolution*. Montreal

Gildea, R., J. Mark and A. Warring. 2013. *Europe's 1968: Voices of Revolt*. Oxford

Vinen, R. 2016. *The Long '68: Radical Protest and its Enemies*. London

1989

Garton Ash, T. 1990. *The Magic Lantern: The Revolution of 1989*. London

Katsiaficas, G. (ed.) 2001. *After the Fall: 1989 and the Future of Freedom*. Abingdon

Kotkin, S. and J. Gross. 2009. *Uncivil Society: 1989 and the Implosion of the Communist Establishment*. New York

Tismaneanu, V. and M. Stan. 2018. *Romania Confronts its Communist Past: Democracy, Memory, and Moral Justice*. Cambridge

AMERICA

Klooster, W. 2018. *Revolutions in the Atlantic World: A Comparative History*. New York

Middlekauf, R. 2007. *The Glorious Cause: The American Revolution 1763–1789*. Oxford

Raphael, R. 2014. *Founding Myths: Stories that Hide our Patriotic Past*. New York

Taylor, A. 2017. *American Revolutions: A Continental History 1750–1804*. New York

CAMBODIA

Brinkley, J. 2012. *Cambodia's Curse: The Hidden History of a Troubled Land*. New York

Kiernan, B. 2008. *The Pol Pot Regime: Race, Power and Genocide in Cambodia under the Khmer Rouge 1972–79*. New Haven

Peou, S. 2000. *Cambodia: Change and Continuity in Contemporary Politics*. Abingdon

Strangio, S. 2014. *Hen Sen's Cambodia*. New Haven

CHINA

Gao, M. 2018. *Constructing China: Clashing Views of the People's Republic*. London

Dikotter, F. 2016. *The Cultural Revolution: A People's History, 1962–1976*. London

Lovell, J. 2019. *Maoism: A Global History*. London

CUBA

Anderson, J. 1997. *Che Guevara: A Revolutionary Life*. London

Brown, J. 2017. *Cuba's Revolutionary World*. Cambridge, MA

Gott, R. 2004. *Cuba: A New History*. New Haven

Perez-Stable, M. 2012. *The Cuban Revolution: Origin, Causes, and Legacy*. Oxford

ENGLAND

Israel, J. 1991. *The Anglo-Dutch Moment: Essays on the Glorious Revolution and its World Impact*. Cambridge

Harris, T. 2006. *Revolution: The Great Crisis of the British Monarchy, 1685–1720*. London

Hill, C. 1975. *The World Turned Upside Down: Radical Ideas During the English Revolution*. London

Pincus, S. 2011. *1688: The First Modern Revolution.* New Haven

EGYPT
Bayat, A. 2017. *Revolution without Revolutionaries: Making Sense of the Arab Spring.* Redwood City

Brownlee, J., T. Masoud and A. Reynolds. 2013. *The Arab Spring: the Politics of Transformation in North Africa and the Middle East.* Oxford

Danahar, P. 2013. *The New Middle East: The World after the Arab Spring.* London

Ketchley, N. 2017. *Egypt in a Time of Revolution.* Cambridge

FRANCE
Furet, F. 1981. *Interpreting the French Revolution.* Cambridge

Palmer, R. R. 2017. *Twelve Who Ruled: The Year of Terror in the French Revolution.* Princeton

Stone, B. 2002. *Reinterpreting the French Revolution: A Global Historical Perspective.* Cambridge

Wahnich, S. 2016. *In Defence of the Terror: Liberty or Death in the French Revolution.* London

HAITI
Bello, B. 2019. *Sheroes of the Haitian Revolution.* Washington, D. C.

Dubois, L. 2005. *Avengers of the New World: The Story of the Haitian Revolution.* Cambridge, MA

Geggus, D. 2001. *The Impact of the Haitian Revolution on the Atlantic World.* Columbia, SC

James, C. L. R. 1938. *The Black Jacobins.* London

INDIA
Bose, M. 2017. *From Midnight to Glorious Morning: India since Independence.* London

French, P. 2011. *Liberty or Death: India's Journey to Independence and Division.* London

Guha, R. 2018. *Gandhi: The Years that Changed the World 1914–1947.* London

Khan, Y. 2017. *The Great Partition: The Making of India and Pakistan.* New Haven

IRAN
Axworthy, M. 2013. *Revolutionary Iran: A History of the Islamic Republic.* London

Katouzian, H. 2018. *Khalil Maleki: The Human Face of Iranian Socialism.* London

Keddie, N. 2003. *Modern Iran: Roots and Results of Revolution.* New Haven

Kurzman, C. 2005. *The Unthinkable Revolution in Iran.* Cambridge, MA

IRELAND
Fanning, R. 2013. *Fatal Path: British Government and Irish Revolution 1910–19.* London

Ferriter, D. 2015. *A Nation and Not a Rabble: The Irish Revolution 1913–1923.* New York

Townshend, C. 2014. *The Republic: The Fight for Irish Independence.* London

Walsh, M. 2016. *Bitter Freedom: Ireland in a Revolutionary World.* London

JAPAN
Hellyer, R. and H. Fuess (eds.) 2020. *The Meiji Restoration: Japan as a Global Nation.* Cambridge

Jansen, M. 2000. *The Making of Modern Japan.* Cambridge, MA

Ravina, M. 2017. *To Stand with the Nations of the World: Japan's Meiji Restoration in World History.* Oxford

MEXICO
Benjamin, T. 2000. *La Revolución: Mexico's Great Revolution as Memory, Myth, and History.* Austin

Buchenau, J. 2011. *The Last Caudillo: Alvaro Obregón and the Mexican Revolution.* Oxford

Escalante-Gonzalbo, F., J. Garciadiego et al. 2013. *A New Compact History of Mexico.* Mexico City

Gonzales, M. 2002. *The Mexican Revolution 1910–1940.* Albuquerque

NICARAGUA
Belli, G. 2003. *The Country Under My Skin: A Memoir of Love and War.* New York

Kinzer, S. 2007. *Blood of Brothers: Life and War in Nicaragua.* Cambridge, MA

Ramírez, S. 2011. *Adiós Muchachos: A Memoir of the Sandinista Revolution.* Durham, NC

Zimmerman, M. 2001. *Sandinista: Carlos Fonseca and the Nicaraguan Revolution.* Durham, NC

POLAND
Garton Ash, T. 1999. *The Polish Revolution: Solidarity.* London

Kowanik, T. and E. Lewandowska. 2011. *From Solidarity to Sellout: The Restoration of Capitalism in Poland.* New York

Ost, D. 2011. *The Defeat of Solidarity: Anger and Politics in Postcommunist Europe.* Ithaca, NY

Paczkowski, A. 2015. *Revolution and Counterrevolution in Poland 1980–1989.* Rochester, NY

PORTUGAL
Maxwell, K. 1995. *The Making of Portuguese Democracy.* Cambridge

de Meneses, F. R. and R. McNamara. 2018. *The White Redoubt, the Great Powers and the Struggle for Southern Africa, 1960–1980.* London

Pinto, P. R. 2013. *Lisbon Rising: Urban Social Movements in the Portuguese Revolution, 1974–75.* Manchester

McQueen, N. 1997. *The Decolonization of Portuguese Africa: Metropolitan Revolution and the Dissolution of Empire.* London

RUSSIA
Engelstein, L. 2017. *Russia in Flames: War, Revolution, Civil War 1914–1921.* Oxford.

Figes, O. 1997. *A People's Tragedy: The Russian Revolution 1891–1924*. New York
McMeekin, S. 2018. *The Russian Revolution: A New History*. London
Smith, S. A. 2017. *Russia in Revolution: An Empire in Crisis 1870–1928*. Oxford

SOUTH AFRICA
Davis, S. 2018. *The ANC's War against Apartheid: Umkhonto we Sizwe and the Liberation of South Africa*. Bloomington
Gleijeses, P. 2013. *Visions of Freedom: Havana, Washington, Pretoria and the Struggle for Southern Africa 1976–1991*. Durham, NC
Simpson, T. 2016. *Umkhonto we Sizwe: The ANC's Armed Struggle*. London
Van Vuren, H. 2017. *Apartheid, Guns and Money*. London

TURKEY
Hanioğlu, M. 2001. *Preparation for a Revolution: The Young Turks, 1902–1908*. Oxford
Levy-Aksu, N. and F. Georgeon. *The Young Turk Revolution and the Ottoman Empire: The Aftermath of 1908*. London

Sohrabi, N. 2011. *Revolution and Constitutionalism in the Ottoman Empire and Iran*. Cambridge
McMeekin, S. 2015. *The Ottoman Endgame: War, Revolution and the Making of the Modern Middle East 1908–1925*. London

UKRAINE
Hrytsak, Y. 2009. *New Ukraine, New Interpretations*. Lviv
Krushelnyky, A. 2006. *An Orange Revolution*. London
Kadygrob, V., K. Taylor, *et al.* 2014. *Euromaidan: History in the Making*. Kyiv
Sakwa, R. 2016. *Frontline Ukraine: Crisis in the Borderlands*. London

VIETNAM
Brocheux, P. 2011. *Ho Chi Minh: A Biography*. Cambridge
Goscha, C. 2016. *The Penguin History of Modern Vietnam*. London
Marr, D. 2013. *Vietnam: State, War, and Revolution 1945–1946*. Berkeley
Morris, V. and C. Hills. 2018. *Ho Chi Minh's Blueprint for Revolution: In the Words of Vietnamese Strategists and Operatives*. Jefferson, NC

CONTRIBUTORS

Stephen Barnes has made a lifelong study of the revolutions of 1968 and their cultural impact. He is currently writing about the hidden mechanics of markets.

Bayyinah Bello is Professor of History at the State University of Haiti, and founder of Fondation Marie-Claire Heureuse Félicité Bonheur Dessalines, or Fondasyon Félicité (FF), an organization dedicated to humanitarian, social and educational work to aid the people of Haiti.

Mihir Bose is a British Indian journalist and historian, who has been a sports reporter for the *Daily Telegraph* and sports editor for the BBC. He is not related to Chandra Bose.

Diarmaid Ferriter is Professor of Modern Irish History at University College Dublin and author of *The Border: The Legacy of a Century of Anglo-Irish Politics* (2019).

Mobo Gao is a Chinese-born historian whose research interests include rural China, contemporary Chinese politics and culture, and Chinese migration to Australia.

Andres Garcia is a doctoral student at the University of Maryland, researching truth commissions in Chile and Romania.

Javier Garciadiego is a Mexican historian who has served as President of El Colegio de México and Director-general of the National Institute of Historical Studies on the Mexican Revolutions (INEHRM).

Mehmed Şükrü Hanioğlu is Professor of Near Eastern Studies at Princeton University. He has done extensive research on the history of the CUP from its foundation to the Young Turk Revolution.

Yaroslav Hrytsak is Director of the Institute for Historical Research at Lviv National University. He is Professor of History at the Ukrainian Catholic University and at Lviv National University,

Mateo Jarquin is Assistant Professor of History at Chapman University, California; his research explores how 20th-century revolutions in the 'Third World' have framed debates about development, democratization, and international relations.

Simon Jenkins is a British historian and columnist for *The Guardian*. His many books include *A Short History of England* (2011) and *A Short History of Europe* (2018).

Homa Katouzian is the Iran Heritage Foundation Research Fellow at St Antony's College, University of Oxford, and author of many books on Iranian politics.

Shin Kawashima is Professor of International Relations at the University of Tokyo and a senior researcher at the Institute for International Policy Studies.

Dina Khapaeva is Professor of Russian at Georgia Institute of Technology. Her interests lie on the intersection of cultural studies, post-Soviet memory studies, neomedievalism, and death studies.

Axel Körner is Professor of History at University College London and Director of the UCL Centre for Transnational History. His main fields of research are the intellectual and cultural history of Europe between the eighteenth and twentieth centuries.

Luis Martínez-Fernández is Professor of History at the University of Central Florida and author of *Key to the New World: A History of Early Colonial Cuba* (2019).

Sorpong Peou is Professor of Politics and Public Administration at Ryerson University, Canada. He specializes in global peace and security studies, particularly in the Asia–Pacific region.

Anita Prażmowska is Professor of International History at the London School of Economics; her research interests lie in the Cold War, communism,

fascism, and Poland. Her published work includes *Władysław Gomułka: A Biography* (2015).

Ray Raphael is an American historian and author of many books including *Mr. President: How and Why the Founders Created a Chief Executive* (2012).

Filipe Ribeiro de Meneses is a Portuguese historian based at Maynooth University, Ireland. He is the author of *Salazar: A Political Biography* (2009).

Thula Simpson is Professor of History at the University of Pretoria. He has published extensively on the ANC's armed struggle and the organization's relationship with popular protest movements in South Africa.

Yasser Thabet is an Egyptian journalist and co-founder of the daily newspaper *Al-Dostour*. He has written many books on Egyptian politics and culture.

Vladimir Tismaneanu is Professor of Politics at the University of Maryland and author of numerous books including *The Devil in History: Communism, Fascism, and Some Lessons of the Twentieth Century* (2012).

Stein Tønnesson is a Norwegian historian and former director of the Peace Research Institute, Oslo. His research focuses are revolution, conflict, and peace in East Asia.

Sophie Wahnich is a French historian and Director of Research at the Centre Nationale de la Recherche Scientifique (CNRS) in Paris. Her interests focus on the role of emotions in the creation of social bonds.

SOURCES OF ILLUSTRATIONS

1 Caird Collection, National Maritime Museum, Greenwich, London; 2 Gift of John Stewart Kennedy, 1897, Metropolitan Museum of Art, New York; 3 Abraham Giraudet, *Fusilade au Fauxbourg St. Antoine*. Sammlung Archiv für Kunst und Geschichte, Berlin. akg-images; 4 World History Archive/Alamy Stock Photos; 5 akg-images; 6 Photo John Stevenson/Corbis Historical via Getty Images; 7 UtCon Collection/Alamy Stock Photo; 8 Jalisco State Legislature, Guadalajara. Photo Schalkwijk/Art Resource/Scala, Florence; 9 Dmitry Moor, *Death to World Imperialism*, 1919; 10 Windmill/Robert Hunt Library/UIG/Bridgeman Images; 11 Pictures from History/Bridgeman Images; 12 Photo SeM Studio/Fototeca/Universal Images Group via Getty Images; 13 Photo Rolls Press/Popperfoto via Getty Images; 14 Private Collection. Photo © Fine Art Images/Bridgeman Images; 15 Photo Gérard-Aimé/Gamma-Rapho via Getty Images; 16 Photo Roland Neveu/Light Rocket via Getty Images; 17 Photo Hervé Gloaguen/Gamma-Rapho via Getty Images; 18 Photo AFP via Getty Images; 19 Photo Cindy Karp/The LIFE Images Collection via Getty Images; 20 Photo Jean-Louis Atlan/Sygma via Getty Images; 21 Photo Walter Dhladhla/AFP via Getty Images; 22 Photo Alain Nogues/Sygma via Getty Images; 23 Photo Sergei Supinsky/AFP via Getty Images; 24 © Amnesty International/artist: El Zeft.

INDEX

Colour plates (numbered **pl.1–24***)*
are listed at the end of relevant
entries.

1848, Year of Revolutions 70–85,
291, 296, 325, **pl.5**
1905 Revolution (Russia) 139, 149
1968 Student Revolution 14,
213–23, 291, **pl.15**
1989 Revolutions 291–303, **pl.22**
26th of July Movement (Cuba)
194, 195, 208, 209

Abdulhamid II, Sultan 97, 104,
107–8
Abe, Shinzo 91
Act of Union 124, 134
Africa, Africans 56, 57, 59, 60
African Americans 37
Ahmadinejad, Mahmood 253,
258, 259
Albania, Albanians 101, 102, 291
Alexander II, Tsar 149
Alexandria 336, 337, 147–50
All-India Muslim League 155
Alonso, Alicia 204
Ambedkar, Bhimrao 160
American Civil War 35, 36
American Constitution 7, 11, 31,
34, 37, 38, 40
American Revolution 7, 29–40,
41, 42, 52, 59, 99, 166, 170, **pl.2**
Amini, Ali 255
Amnesty International 335
Amritsar massacre 153
Anakaona, Kaisikess 60, 64
ANC (African National Congress)
11, 304–8, 311, 313–16, 317,
318, **pl.23**
Angka 242
Anglo-Iranian Oil Company 254
Anglo-Irish Treaty 124, 127, 133,
135, 154
Angola 199, 206, 211, 228, 233,
235, 237
Antall, József 301
anti-semitism 143, 301
apartheid 304–18
Apollo 8 222
Arab Spring 327, 333–42, **pl.24**
Arabs 101
Ararás, Raúl Martínez 204
Arawak people 56, 58–60
Arias, Óscar 273
Armstrong, Neil 226
Aromanians 101
Assembly of Notables 43

Atatürk, Mustafa Kemal 102–4
Attlee, Clement 154, 157
Auchinleck, Claude 156
August Revolution 167, 168, 171
Aunt Tòya (Victoria Montou) 64
Auschwitz 299
Austria 75, 76, 84
AWB (Afrikaner
Weerstandsbeweging) 311, 312
Ayiti *see* Haiti
Azores 233

Bahrain 333, 338
Bakhtiar, Shapour 262
Balfour, Arthur 152
Balkan Wars 106, 108
Bamberger, Ludwig 77
Bandera, Stepan 326
Bangladesh 158, 165
Bao Dai, Emperor 167, 171, 177
Bastille 7, 41, 43, 44, 46
Batista, Fulgencio 193, 194, 196,
203, 206, 208, 210, 266
Bay of Pigs invasion 197, 203, 204,
210, 266, 271, 278
Bazile, Marie Sainte Dédée 64
Beat Generation 220
Bedeus, Joseph 73
Belli, Gioconda 265
Ben Ali, Zine el Abidine 342
Bentinck, Hans Willem 20
Berlin Wall 173, 294, 302, **pl.22**
Bharatiya Janata Party (BJP) 165
Bill of Rights (England) 7, 23,
27, 28
Bill of Rights (US) 34, 37, 38
Black Panthers 225
Bloody Sunday (Russia) 149
Bohemia 75
Bois Caiman 60
Bolívar, Simón 62
Bolivia 209
Bolotnaya Square 327
Bolsheviks, Bolshevism 12, 98,
104–6, 123, 136, 138, 139–44,
pl.9
Bophuthatswana 312, 313
Bose, Subhas Chandra 155, 164,
165
Boston Tea Party 30, 40
Bouazizi, Mohamed 342
bourgeoisie 141
Boutros-Ghali, Boutros 310
Boxer Rising 178, 191
Boyne, Battle of the 16, 25, 28
Brest-Litovsk, Treaty of 150
Brezhnev, Leonid 219

Budapest 49
Buddhist Liberal Democratic
Party 245
Bulgaria 270, 291
Burke, Edmund 10, 15
Buthelezi, Mangosuthu 312, 313

Caetano, Marcelo 228–30, 236,
237
Cahiers de doléances 45, 46
Cairo 24, 334, 337
Cambodia 10, 16, 238–51
Cambodia People's Party (CPP)
243, 250
Carbonari 82
Cardenal, Ernesto 275
Cárdenas, Lázaro 117
Carnation Revolution 17, 227–39
Carranza, Venustiano 113–16,
120–2
Carrington, Lord 313
Carson, Rachel 219, 220, 225
Carter, Jimmy 257, 269
caste system 159
Castro, Fidel 193–6, 199–204,
208, 210–12, 267, 269, **pl.14**
Castro, Raúl 195, 196, 198–202,
204, 208, 210, 212
Catholicism, Catholic Church
18, 19, 44, 58, 60, 62, 118, 265,
286, 287
CCP (Chinese Communist Party)
179, 180–2, 184, 186–92
Ceaușescu, Elena 294, 296
Ceaușescu, Nicolae 294, 295,
296, 303
Central American Peace Accords
273, 279
Chamber of Deputies (Ottoman)
98, 99, 107
Chamorro, Pedro Joaquín 267,
273, 277, 278
Chamorro, Violeta 273, 277–9
Charles I of England 9, 15, 18, 27
Charles II of England 9, 15, 19, 27
Charles Albert, King of Piedmont-
Sardinia 83
charter 77 294, 295, 301
Chartism 79, 83
Chávez, Hugo 276
Chea Sim 243, 245
Chiang Kai-shek 90, 170, 180,
182, 189
Chihuahua 112, 114, 119
Chile 268
China 12, 30, 87, 88, 89, 90, 91,
95, 246, 319

Chinese Communist Revolution 178–94, **pl.13**
Chittagong 155
Churchill, John, Duke of Marlborough 21, 22
Churchill, Winston 153
CIA 266, 271, 272
Ciskei 312
Civic Forum (Czechoslovakia) 224, 301, 303
Civil Rights Act 225
Club of Rome 220
Code Noir 63
CODESA (Convention for a Democratic South Africa) 309, 310, 318
Cohn-Bendit, Daniel 216
Coke, Edward 18
Cold War 233, 240, 244, 265, 289, 305
Collins, Michael 126, 127, 130, 133, 135
Colour Revolutions 319
Comintern 150
Committee of Progress and Union (Ottoman) 97, 99, 101, 106, 107
Committee of Public Safety (France) 51, 53
Committee of Union and Progress (Ottoman) 96, 97, 99, 100, 101, 104, 107
Communism 137, 140
Communist Manifesto 8, 70, 78, 79, 83
Communist Party (Cuba) 199, 201, 211
Communist Party (Czechoslovakia) 224
Communist Party (France) 49, 168, 169
Communist Party (Iran) 257
Communist Party (Poland) 280–3, 285–7
Communist Party (South Africa) 304, 306–7, 311, 316
Communist Party (USSR) 137, 138, 143, 145, 148, 150, 293
Congress of Berlin 107
Congress Party (India) 156, 157, 158, 162, 163
Congress of the Peoples of the East 106
Conservative Party (South Africa) 309
Constantinople Conference 107
Constitutional Convention (America) 39, 40
Constitutional Revolution (Iran) 254
Constitutionalists (Mexico) 114, 115
Contadora process 271, 278
Continental Army 39

Continental Congress 39, 40
Contra 271, 272, 279
Contreras, Eduardo 267
conventionists, Mexican 114, 116, 118
Cornwallis, Lord 40
Cossacks 325
Costa Gomes, Francisco 230, 231
Costa Rica 271
Council for Mutual Economic Assistance (CMEA) 199, 211
Creole language 63
Crête-à-Pierrot 61, 67, 68
Crimea 145, 146, 321, 331
Crimean War 107
Cripps, Stafford 164
Croatia 297, 303
Croke Park 134
Cromwell, Oliver 16, 18, 27
Cuba 118, 269, 270, 272, 278, 319
Cuban Missile Crisis 197, 203, 211
Cuban Revolution 193–214, 264, 266, **pl.14**
Cultural Revolution 178, 179, 184–90
Curzon, Lord 152
Czechoslovakia 198, 214, 226, 291, 294, 295, 302
Czechs 75, 78

d'Alembert, Jean le Rond 44
Dahrendorf, Ralf 297
Daley, Richard 218
Dalits 159, 160
Danton, Georges 10, 48
Dashnaktsutiun (Armenian Revolutionary Federation) 98
Davis, Jefferson 36
de Gaulle, Charles 217
de Klerk, F. W. 305–10, 316, 317, 318
de Valera, Éamon 126, 127, 130, 133–5
Declaration of Independence (US) 29, 36, 39, 40
Declaration of the Rights of Man and the Citizen 48, 49, 51, 52
Democratic Republic of Vietnam 167, 171
Deng Xiaoping 185, 187, 190
Descourtilz, Michel 58
Dessalines, Jean-Jacques 58, 61, 64, 67, 68, 69
dialectical materialism 181
Díaz, Porfirio 109–14, 117, 120, 121
Díaz Ordaz, Gustavo 216
Díaz-Canel, Miguel 201, 202, 212
dictatorship of the proletariat 140, 141, 142
Diderot, Denis 44
Diem, Ngo Dinh 171, 177

Dien Bien Phu 171, 172, 175, 177, **pl.12**
divine right of kings 7, 18, 42, 44
División del Norte 112, 113, 115
Dominican Republic 266
Donbass 326
Douglass, Frederick 34
Dual Monarchy 81
Dubček, Alexander 214, 218, 219, 224
Dugin, Alexander 146
Duma 99
Dutty, Boukman 60
Dyer, Reginald 153

Eanes, António Ramalho 235
East Germany 270, 291, 294, 295, 298
East Timor 235
Easter Rising, Dublin 123, 125, 126, 134, 155, **pl.10**
Edirne 106
Edo 85, 93, 94
EEC (European Economic Community) 132, 234, 236
Egypt 333–42, **pl.24**
Eisenstein, Sergei 10
El Baradei, Mohamed 337
El Salvador 273
Emancipation Proclamation (US) 35
Engels, Friedrich 8, 70, 79, 141
English Revolution 15–27, **pl.1**
Enlightenment 7, 28, 44, 72
Enver Pasha 103, 104, 106
Environmental Protection Act 222
Estado Novo (New State) 227, 231, 232, 234, 237
Estates General 42, 43, 46, 51, 52
Estonia 297
EU (European Union) 132, 299, 320, 321
Euromaidan 321, 322, 327, 328, 329

Facebook 340
Fada'ian 256
Family Code (Cuba) 199, 211
February Revolution (Russia) 138, 147, 149
Federalists, American 33
Félicité, Empress of Hayti 61, 64
Ferdinand I, Emperor of Austria 74, 84
Fianna Fáil 130, 133, 135
Fine Gael 130
First World War 124, 125, 129, 131, 143, 145, 147, 149, 152, 164
FMLN (Farabundo Martí National Liberation Front) 270
Fonseca Amador, Carlos 266
Fort Knox 56
Foucault, Michel 49

Four Modernizations 192
France 13, 78, 79
Franco, Francisco 227
Frankfurt 77
Franqui, Carlos 204
Frederick, Rebecca 59
Freedom Alliance 312, 313
Freedom Charter 304, 305, 314, 316–18
Freedom Riders 225
FRELIMO (Mozambique Liberation Front) 228, 235
French and Indian War 40
French Revolution 7, 13, 41–55, 72, 99, 166, **pl.3**
Friedan, Betty 219, 225
Friends of the Earth 222
FSLN (Sandinista National Liberation Front) 264–9, 272, 273, 276–8
Furet, François 49

Gaddafi, Muammar 333
Gaidar, Yegor 143
Gandhi, Indira 165
Gandhi, Mohandas 'Mahatma' 151, 153–60, 162, 163, 164, 165, **pl.11**
Gang of Four 185
Garibaldi, Giuseppe 76, 82
Gauck, Joachim 298
Gdańsk 281, 283, 284, 289, 285, 288, 290
GDR see East Germany 294
Gdynia 283, 290
George I of Great Britain 24
George III of Great Britain 10
Georgia 319
Geremek, Bronisław 283, 285
Germany 77
Gettysburg Address 35
Giap, Vo Nguyen 172
Gierek, Edward 281
Gioberti, Vincenzo 76
glasnost 291, 293
Glorious Revolution 7, 17, 30, **pl.1**
GNR (Portuguese Republican National Guard) 229
Gonçalves, Vasco 232, 236
González, Elián 206, 211
Gorbachev, Mikhail 200, 287, 291, 296, 302
Gorky, Maxim 141
Government of India Act 164
Government of Ireland Act 127, 134
Gqozo, Oupa 312
Granma 195, 204
Great Debate (Cuba) 197, 198
Great Leap Forward 179, 183–4, 186, 189, 192
Great Rebellion (England) 9
Greene, Nathaniel 32

Greenpeace 222
Grégoire, Henri 47, 48
Grenada 199
Griffiths, Arthur 127, 133, 134
Groote Schuur Minute 307, 308
Grosvenor Square, London 216
Guatemala 266, 273
Guevara, Ernesto 'Che' 193, 195, 196, 197, 209, 267
Gulag 299
Gwiazda, Andrzej and Joanna 285

Haiti 33, 55–70, **pl.4**
Hamas 253
Hampden, John 15, 24
Hani, Chris 311
Habsburg Empire 78, 81, 83
Harare Declaration 307, 308
Harley, Robert 23
Havana 195, 210
Havel, Václav 224, 292, 295, 299, 301, 303
Hayti see Haiti
Heavenly Kingdom of Harmony 180
Henry Christophe (Henry I of Hayti) 61, 67, 69
Hezbollah 253
Hindus 157, 158, 159, 162
Hindutva 160, 161
hippies 220, 225
Hispaniola 60, 68
Hitler, Adolf 137, 227
Ho Chi Minh 166–75, 177
Hoffman, Abbie 218, 226
Holland 18, 19, 20
Holovakha, Yevhen 322
Home Rule (Ireland) 124, 134
Honduras 271, 273
Hong Xiuquan 180
House Un-American Activities Committee 224
Huerta, Victoriano 113, 115, 119
Humphrey, Hubert 218
Hun Sen 243, 245, 246, 250
Hungarian Democratic Forum (MDF) 301
Hungary 73–5, 81, 84, 291, 294–7, 301, 302

ICA (Irish Citizen Army) 125
IFP (Inkatha Freedom Party) 307, 308, 313, 314
INA (Indian National Army) 155, 156, 165
India, Indian Revolution 8, 151–66, **pl.11**
Indian Army 155, 156
Indian National Congress 153, 164
Indochina 166, 177, 240
Indochina War 170, 177
Indochinese Communist Party 167, 170, 174–6, 240

Inglehart, Ronald 322
Inter-American Commission on Human Rights 275
Internal Macedonia-Adrianopolitan Revolutionary Organization 98
International Court of Justice 271, 279
IPP (Irish Parliamentary Party) 124, 125, 126
IRA (Irish Republican Army) 124, 126–9, 131, 133–5
Iran-Contra Affair 272, 279
Iranian Revolution 9, 104, 252–63, **pl.18**
IRB (Irish Republican Brotherhood) 125
Irish Civil War 127, 133
Irish Free State 127, 128, 130, 135
Irish Revolution 123–36, **pl.10**
Irish Volunteers 124, 126, 133
Iron Curtain 302
Irwin, Lord 154
Islamic Revolution 257
Israel 260
Italy 76, 77, 82
IVF (Irish Volunteer Force) 124, 125

Jacques I, Emperor of Hayti see Dessalines, Jean-Jacques
Jagielski, Mieczysław 284
James I of England 18
James II of England 7, 9, 15, 16, 17, 20–2, 27, 28
Jamestown, Virginia 40
Jankowski, Father 283
Japan 85–96, **pl.6**
Jefferson, Thomas 29, 30, 31, 36, 39, 62
Jiang Qing 185
Jinnah, Muhammad Ali 155, 156, 157, 165
John Paul II, Pope 282, 290, 292
Johnson, Lyndon B. 214
Jordan 338
July monarchy 71

Kaczyński, Lech and Jarosław 288
Kanagawa, Treaty of 94
Kashmir 158
Kemal, Mustafa see Atatürk
Kennedy, John F. 225, 255
Kennedy, Robert 218, 226
Kerensky, Alexander 149
Khamenei, Ayatollah Ali 258, 261, 263
Khatami, Mohammad 258, 259
Khmer People's Revolutionary Party 243, 268
Khmer Rouge Revolution 16, 238–251

Khmer Yeung 246
Khomeini, Ayatollah Ruhollah 18,
  255, 257, 258, 261–3
Khrushchev, Nikita 330
King, Martin Luther 151, 217, 226
Kissinger, Henry 233, 313
Kołakowski, Leszek 282
KOR (Committee for the Defence
  of the Workers) 282, 284
Korea 87, 95
Korean War 182
Kossuth, Lajos 73, 78, 81, 83, 84
Kuchma, Leonid 320, 322, 324,
  329, 330, 331
Kuomintang (KMT) 178, 180–2,
  191
Kuroń, Jacek 282
Kwaśniewski, Aleksander 290
KwaZulu 312, 313
Kyiv 320, 321, 324, 330, 331
Kyoto 86
Kyrgyzstan 319

La Prensa 277
Lao Dong (Vietnam Workers'
  Party) 172, 176
Le Duan 172, 176
Lebanon 272
Legislative Assembly (France) 53
Lenin, Vladimir Ilyich 11, 12, 136,
  139–50, 241, 242
Leninism see Marxism
Libya 333, 338, 342
Lincoln, Abraham 35
Linlithgow, Lord 152, 156, 157
Lis, Bogdan 285, 287
Little Red Book (Quotations from
  Chairman Mao Zedong) 186,
  189, 192, pl.13
Liu Shaoqi 185
Lloyd George, David 134
Locke, John 15, 22, 25, 28
Lockhart, Rob 156
Lombardy 76, 82
Lon Nol 240, 249, 250
Long March 176, 181, 189, 190,
  191
Louis XIV of France 7, 10, 19, 20,
  21, 23, 27, 42
Louis XVI of France 41, 43, 51,
  52, 53
Louis-Napoleon (Napoleon III)
  71, 79, 84
Louis-Philippe of France 70,
  71, 83
Louisiana Purchase 39
Louverture, Toussaint 56, 58,
  60, 67–9
Loyalists, American 31, 32

Macaulay, Thomas Babington 17
McCarthy, Eugene 218
Macedonia 106, 107

Machado, Gerardo 203, 210
Machel, Samora 235
Madero, Francesco 111–15,
  120, 121
Maduro, Nicolás 186
Magna Carta 17, 18, 30
Magón, Ricardo Flores 116
Magyars 73, 81
Maidan Nezhalezhnosti
  (Independence Square) 321,
  327, 328
Maidan revolution 145
Malan, D. F. 308
Malcolm X 225
Malevich, Kazimir 10
Managua 267, 271, 278
Mandela, Nelson 11, 305–10, 313,
  316–19, pl.21
Mangope, Lucas 312, 313
Mann, Thomas 79
Mao Zedong 12, 105, 169, 176–9,
  183–9, 192, 238, 241, 249, pl.13
Mariel exodus 199
Martínez, Raúl 203
Marx, Karl 8, 11, 70, 79, 83, 109,
  136, 139, 141, 241
Marxism, Marxism-Leninism 8,
  9, 138–141, 146, 163, 166, 167,
  181, 182, 194, 219, 239, 243,
  252, 256, 257, 265, 268, 270–3,
  292, 295, 297–300, 319, 323
Mary II of England 7, 15–17, 19,
  20, 22, 23, 25–8
Massachusetts 31, 40
Matsukata Masayoshi 90
Matviyenko, Valentina 144
Mau Mau 306
May Fourth Movement (China)
  189, 191
Maytorena, José María 115
Mazowiecki, Tadeusz 282, 283,
  285, 289, 290
Mazzini, Giuseppe 76, 82
Mehmet V, Sultan 108
Meiji Emperor 93, 94
Meiji Restoration 85–96, pl.6
Metternich, Klemens von 70, 83
Mexican Revolution 109–23,
  pl.8
Mexico 10, 11, 30, 148, 269
Meyer, Roelf 310
MFA (Armed Forces Movement)
  228–31, 234
Michnik, Adam 282, 295
Milan 77
Mirabeau, Comte de 51
Miranda, Francisco de 62
Mitani Horoshi 88, 89
Modi, Narendra 160, 161
Mohammad Reza Shah 253, 254,
  255, 256, 262
Mojahedin 256, 257, 258
Monastir 97, 106

Moncada garrison 194, 204,
  296, 210
Monmouth's Rebellion 19
Montazeri, Ayatollah 258
MORENA (National Regeneration
  Movement), Mexico 119
Morocco 342
Morsi, Mohamed 338, 339, 341,
  342
Mosaddeq, Mohammad 252, 253,
  254, 262
Mountbatten, Louis 157
Mousavi, Mir Hossein 259
Mozambique 228, 235, 237
MPLA (People's Movement for the
  Liberation of Angola) 228, 233
Mubarak, Gamal 336, 337
Mubarak, Hosni 333, 334, 336–42
Mudros, Armistice of 102
Muslim Brotherhood (MB) 338,
  339, 341
Muslim League 156, 157, 164
Muslims 101, 155, 157, 158, 162

Namibia 233
Nanjing 180
Nanterre 216, 226
Napoleon Bonaparte 10, 42, 54,
  56, 61, 67, 69, 145
Natal 308
National Assembly (France) 46,
  51, 52, 68
National Assembly (Germany) 70,
  77, 83, 84
National Assembly (Vietnam) 167
National Democratic Revolution
  (South Africa) 304
National Directorate (Nicaragua)
  269, 270, 272
National Liberation Front
  (Vietnam) 177
National Organization for Women
  225
National Party (NP), South Africa
  305, 309–13, 317
National Revolutionary
  Movement (Cuba) 194
National Revolutionary Party
  (Mexico) 117
National Salvation Front
  (Romania) 296
Native Americans 37
NATO 299, 301, 331
NDP (National Democratic Party),
  Egypt 334, 335, 342
Nehru, Jawaharlal 153, 156–65
New State (Portugal) see Estado
  Novo
Nicaragua 264–79, pl.19
Nicholas II, Tsar 12, 137, 149, 150
Nixon, Richard 173, 218, 226
Niyazi Bey, Ahmed 101, 106
NKVD (secret police, USSR) 143

non-aligned movement 163, 208, 270
North Vietnam 170–2, 175, 177, 240
Northern Ireland 127, 131

O'Higgins, Terence 128
Obama, Barack 38, 201, 212
Obrador, Andrés Manuel López 119
Obregón, Álvaro 113–17, 120–2
Occupy Wall Street 327
October Revolution 11, 12, 105, 136–51, 171, **pl.9**
Okubo Toshimichi 93
Okumu, Washington 313
Operation Rolling Thunder 215, 225
Operation Vula 308
Opium Wars 87, 89, 179, 191
Orange Revolution 23, 319–23

Orozco, José Clemente 118, **pl.8**
Orozco, Pascual 112, 113, 121
Ortega, Daniel 265, 273–9
Ortega, Rosario Murillo 275
Ottoman Empire 96–109, **pl.7**
Our Ukraine (political party) 329

PAC (Pan-Africanist Congress) 306
Pahlavi dynasty 105, 252, 254
Paine, Thomas 10
País, Frank and Josué 195
Pakistan 151, 158, 165
Palacký, František 75
Palermo 71, 76, 83
Palestine 152, 268
Paris Commune 79
Paris May Days 214, 217, 226, 323
parlement 43, 52
Parliament 15–19, 22–7, 30, 40
Parnell, Charles 124
Partido Revolucionario Institucional (Mexico) 11
Partition of India 158, 162
pass laws 306, 316
Patriots, American 31, 32
PCP (Portuguese Communist Party) 231, 232, 233
Peace Moratorium 226
People's Republic of China (PRC) 171, 179, 182, 189, 192
People's Republic of Kampuchea (PRK) 243, 249, 250
perestroika 291
Perry, Matthew 89, 94
Persia 98
Pestalozzi, Johann Heinrich 74
Peter the Great (Russia) 142
Pétion, Alexandre 62
Phillips, Walter Alison 128
Phnom Penh 238, 240, 250, **pl.16**

PIDE (secret police, Portugal) 229
Piedmont-Sardinia 76, 82, 83
Pinheiro de Azevedo, José 234
PiS (Law and Justice Party), Poland 288
Pol Pot 239–44, 249, 251
Poland 78, 280–90, 291, 294, 295, 302, **pl.20**
Poroshenko, Petro 328
Portugal 17, 227–39
Potemkin mutiny 149
Prague Spring 214, 218, 219, 222, 226, 301
PRD (Party of the Mexican Revolution) 118
Pretoria Minute 308
PRI (Institutional Revolutionary Party), Mexico 117, 118
Provisional Government (Russia) 138
Prussia 84
PSP (Partido Socialista Popular), Cuba 196
purges, Stalinist 139, 143
Putin, Vladimir 12, 139, 144, 145, 146, 320, 324, 327

Qing dynasty 90, 91, 99, 178, 180, 191
Quinn-Judge, Paul 321
Quit India movement 155, 162, 164

Radom 281, 282, 284
Rafsanjani, Akbar Hashemi 258
Ramaphosa, Cyril 310
Ramírez, Sergio 273
Ranariddh, Norodom 244, 245, 250
Reagan, Ronald 264, 270, 271, 272, 286
Rectification of Errors (Cuba) 200, 202, 211
Red Army (China) 171, 178, 181, 191
Red Army (Soviet) 148
Red Guards 185
Redmond, John 125
Resistance, French 49
Resurgence Party (Iran) 256
Revolución 203, 204
Revolutionary Guard (Iran) 260
Revolutionary Offensive (Cuba) 198
Reza Khan, Shah 254
Rhodesia 229, 233
Rieger, František Ladislav 72
Rivera, Diego 118
Rivonia trial 316
Robespierre, Maximilien 10, 47, 48, 51, 53, 54
Rochambeau, Donatien 61
Rochefoucauld, Duc de La 7, 8

Rodríguez, Carlos Rafael 198
Roman Republic 82, 84
Romania 73, 75, 291, 294, 295, 297, 298, 303
Roosevelt, Franklin D. 266
Rose Chamber Edict 107
Rose Revolution 319
Roth, Stefan Ludwig 74
Rouhani, Hassan 259
Round Table Talks (Poland) 287, 288, 289, 290, 302
Royal Irish Constabulary 129
Rubin, Jerry 218, 224
Rukh 326, 330
Rulewski, Jan 286
Rushdie, Salman 262
Russia 98
Russian Federation 291, 320
Russian Revolution 11, 136–51, 167, **pl.9**
Russo-Japanese War 95

Sá Carneiro, Francisco de 231, 235, 237
SACP *see* Communist Party (South Africa)
Saddam Hussein 257
SADF (South African Defence Force) 306
Said, Khaled 336, 342
Saigo Takamori 86, 93
Saint-Domingue 55, 60, 61, 67, 68
Saint-Just, Louis-Antoine de 47–9, 53
Salazar, António 227, 228, 234, 237
Salt March 154, 162, 164
Sánchez, Celia 204
Sandinista Popular Army 270, 272, 276
Sandinistas 264–79, **pl.19**
Sandino, Augusto César 267, 278
Santamaría, Haydée 204
Santo Domingo 61, 67, 68
Saraiva de Carvalho, Otelo 232
Sartre, Jean-Paul 49
Satsuma Rebellion 6, 93, 95
satyagraha 153, 162
Saudi Arabia 260, 342
SAVAK (secret police, Iran) 255
Savio, Mario 222
SCAF (Supreme Council of the Armed Forces), Egypt 338, 339
Second World War 131, 145, 151, 164, 166, 168, 177, 227, 240, 282, 395, 324
Securitate (secret police, Romania) 296
Self-Strengthening Movement 90
Seven Years War 30
Sèvres, Treaty of 108
Shafik, Ahmed 337, 338

Sharpeville Massacre 306, 316, 317
Shevardnadze, Eduard 293
Sierra Maestra 195, 210
Sihanouk, Norodom 240, 242, 245, 248–50
Singh, Bhagat 159
Sinn Féin 124, 126–35
Sino-Japanese War 95
Sisi, Abdel Fattah el- 339, 340, 342
Sisulu, Walter 317
slavery 34, 53–5, 58, 60, 67–9, 159
Slovakia 297, 301
Slovenia 303
Slovo, Joe 311, 314, 316
Smith, Tommy 218
Soares, Mário 231, 236
Social Revolutionaries (Russia) 140, 150
Solidarity (Solidarność) 280, 281, 284–90, 294, 302
Solidarity Citizens' Committee 287, 288
Somoza, Anastasio Jr. 268, 275
Somoza Debayle, Tachito 268
Somoza García, Anastasio 266, 278
Soulouque, Faustin 57
South Africa 11, 229, 233, 304–18, pl.21
South Vietnam 170, 171, 175, 177
Soviet Union 11, 137, 138, 139, 141, 150, 173, 182, 194, 197, 198, 200, 211, 233, 264, 268, 272, 280, 286, 291, 294, 303, 319, 320, 324–7
Spanish Succession, War of 23
Special Period in Times of Peace (Cuba) 200, 202, 206
Spínola, António 229, 230
Stalin, Joseph 136, 138, 141, 142, 145, 146, 148, 150, 168, 169, 241, 330
Stamp Act 40
Stasi (secret police, GDR) 298
Stolypin, Pyotr 149
Students for a Democratic Society 225
Suleiman, Omar 337
Summer of Love 225
Syria 253, 333, 334, 338
Szczecin 283, 290

Tahrir Square 333, 334, 342
Taino 59, 202
Taiping Rebellion 178–80, 191
Taksim Square 327
Tambo, Oliver 316, 317
Tantawi, Mohamed Hussein 338
Tanzimat era 103, 107
Tatlin, Vladimir 10
Ten Years War (Cuba) 210
Tennis Court Oath 46, 52

Terror (French) 8, 43, 47, 48, 51, 53
Terror (Soviet) 137, 142, 143
Tet Offensive 172, 173, 214, 226
Thatcher, Margaret 286
Third Estate 42, 43, 44, 46
Thomas, Mary 59
Tiananmen Square, Beijing 186, 187, 190, 302
Tlatelolco plaza, Mexico City 216, 226
Tocqueville, Alexis de 72
Tokugawa shogunate 86, 89
Tokugawa Yoshinobu 94
Tokyo 93, 94
Tongzhi Restoration 90
Tories 17, 19, 23, 30, 32
trade union 280, 281, 286, 288
Transylvania 73, 74
Treaty of Paris (1783) 40
Treitschke, Heinrich von 77
Trenton, Battle of 40
Trotsky, Leon 146, 148, 275
Troubles (Northern Ireland) 124
Trump, Donald 36, 38, 259
Truong Chinh 167, 169, 170, 172, 173, 176
Truth and Reconciliation Commission (South Africa) 318
Tuileries, storming of 53
Tulip revolution 319
Tunisia 333, 337, 338, 342
Turkey, Republic of 102, 108
Turkish War of Liberation 102
Tymoshenko, Yulia 324, 328, 329

Ukraine 145, 319–23, pl.23
Ukrainian Insurgent Army 330
Ukrainian SSR 321, 325, 330
Ulster 16, 124, 125
Ulyanov, Vladimir Ilyich see Lenin
Umkhonto we Sizwe 304, 306, 316
Union of Soviet Socialist Republics (USSR) see Soviet Union
United Nations 65, 244, 259, 310, 317
Universal Declaration of Human Rights 49
University of California, Berkeley 215
Urbina, Tomás 114
Urrutia, Manuel 196
US Marines 266
UVF (Ulster Volunteer Force) 124, 125, 134

Valley Forge 40
Valmy, Battle of 53
Vance, Cyrus 310
Velvet Revolution 294, 295, 303
Venetia 76

Venezuela 269
Verdi, Giuseppe 76
Vertières, Battle of 61, 67, 69
Victoria, Queen 79
Vienna 83
Viet Cong 214, 248
Viet Minh 168, 171, 175, 177
Vietnam War 172, 227
Vietnamese Revolution 166–77, pl.12
Viljoen, Constand 306, 312
Villa, Pancho 112, 113–16, 120, 121
Vodou 58, 60, 63

Walentynowicz, Anna 283
Wałęsa, Lech 283–90, 303, pl.20
Warsaw Pact 219, 224, 226, 290, 293, 301, 303
Washington, George 2, 33, 36, 39, 40
Webster, Noah 32
Whigs, Whig history 16, 17, 19, 20, 23, 24, 30, 32
White Revolution (Iran) 255, 262
Whole Earth Catalog 220
William III (William of Orange) 7, 15, 16, 17, 19–23, 25–8, pl.1
Wilson, Woodrow 113
Wojtyła, Karol see John Paul II
Women's Liberation 219
Woodstock festival 226
World Values Survey 323

Xi Jinping 188
Xinhai Revolution 99, 104, 178

Yakovlev, Aleksandr 293
Yanukovych, Viktor 320, 321, 324, 327, 328, 329, 331
Yeltsin, Boris 144, 324
Yemen 199, 333, 334, 338, 342
Yippies 224
Yorktown, Siege of 31, 40
Young Italy 82
Young Turk Revolution 96–109, pl.7
Yuan Shikai 191
Yugoslavia 291, 297
Yushchenko, Viktor 23, 320, 324, 328–32

Zapata, Emiliano 112, 115, 116, 121, 122
Zelensky, Volodymyr 328
Zhang Chunqiao 186
Zhang Xueliang 182
Zhao Ziyang 187
Zhivkov, Todor 302
Zhou Enlai 13
Zhu De 181
Zuma, Jacob 314